CULTURE**SHOCK**!

A Survival Guide to Customs and Etiquette

CUBA

Mark Cramer
Marcus Cramer

Marshall Cavendish
Editions

This edition published in 2007 by:
Marshall Cavendish Corporation
99 White Plains Road
Tarrytown, NY 10591-9001
www.marshallcavendish.us

Other Marshall Cavendish Offices:
Marshall Cavendish International (Asia) Private Limited. 1 New Industrial
Road, Singapore 536196 ▪ Marshall Cavendish Ltd. 119 Wardour Street, London
W1F 0UW, UK ▪ Marshall Cavendish International (Thailand) Co Ltd. 253 Asoke,
12th Flr, Sukhumvit 21 Road, Klongtoey Nua, Wattana, Bangkok 10110, Thailand
▪ Marshall Cavendish (Malaysia) Sdn Bhd, Times Subang, Lot 46, Subang Hi-Tech
Industrial Park, Batu Tiga, 40000 Shah Alam, Selangor Darul Ehsan, Malaysia

Marshall Cavendish is a trademark of Times Publishing Limited

ISBN 10: 0-7614-5405-5
ISBN 13: 978-0-7614-5405-2

Please contact the publisher for the Library of Congress catalogue number

Printed in China by Everbest Printing Co Ltd

ABOUT THE SERIES

Culture shock is a state of disorientation that can come over anyone who has been thrust into unknown surroundings, away from one's comfort zone. *CultureShock!* is a series of trusted and reputed guides which has, for decades, been helping expatriates and long-term visitors to cushion the impact of culture shock whenever they move to a new country.

Written by people who have lived in the country and experienced culture shock themselves, the authors share all the information necessary for anyone to cope with these feelings of disorientation more effectively. The guides are written in a style that is easy to read and covers a range of topics that will arm readers with enough advice, hints and tips to make their lives as normal as possible again.

Each book is structured in the same manner. It begins with the first impressions that visitors will have of that city or country. To understand a culture, one must first understand the people—where they came from, who they are, the values and traditions they live by, as well as their customs and etiquette. This is covered in the first half of the book

Then on with the practical aspects—how to settle in with the greatest of ease. Authors walk readers through how to find accommodation, get the utilities and telecommunications up and running, enrol the children in school and keep in the pink of health. But that's not all. Once the essentials are out of the way, venture out and try the food, enjoy more of the culture and travel to other areas. Then be immersed in the language of the country before discovering more about the business side of things.

To round off, snippets of basic information are offered before readers are 'tested' on customs and etiquette of the country. Useful words and phrases, a comprehensive resource guide and list of books for further research are also included for easy reference.

CONTENTS

FOREWORD

It is the year 3007. Things have changed during the past 1,000 years.

By the year 2100, human beings finally discovered that organic agriculture was possible from a scientific perspective and thus, they eliminated chemical pesticides, herbicides and fertilisers.

During the same period, the human culture also came to the conclusion that fossil fuels were going to destroy the world, that is, if the world did not first destroy itself fighting for the remaining fossil fuels. As a result, the bicycle and newer human-powered vehicles became a primary mode of commuter transport. Gradually, the epidemic of inactivity-related diseases subsided. Architectural preservation became a fundamental value of civilisation, with glass-box skyscrapers and impersonal highrises being relegated to the status emblems of human error. Newer structures were built on a human scale, often acquiring an admirably aesthetic appearance by renewing indigenous, medieval, and colonial designs.

In summary, from perspectives of health, environment and aesthetics, quality of life gradually improved in the years following 2100.

One important headline from this year 3007 has been labelled the Great Archeological Discovery. Evidently, during the end of the twentieth and the beginning of the twenty-first centuries, one modest culture had already instituted organic agriculture on a national level. During the same period of this island culture, there were no signs of the massive highrise building fad that had plagued the rest of the world in the second half of the twentieth century and beyond. Instead, they found considerable relics of colonial architecture, suggesting that the entire capital city had skipped the beat of modernism. Also unearthed were an enormous number of bicycles and bici-taxis, in a proportion that made this island one of the few civilisations whose streets were unclogged by carbon-burping vehicles.

Archeologists were dumbfounded that they were unable to unearth any statues of the apparently theocratic leader of the period.

This dig was completed on the largest island of the Caribbean Sea, and the culture was labelled 'Cuban', though another culture, quite different, centred in the south of the Florida peninsula, was also known as Cuban.

During the first decade of the twenty-first century, there had been a great influx of visitors from other cultures, presumably to witness the Cuban lifestyle that was so curious compared to their own gas-guzzling, couch-potato, urban-renewal cultures. Archeolinguists have interpreted some of the documents of these travellers and it appears as if most viewed Cuba as a curiosity piece and an anachronism. Few of these travellers' chronicles noted the possibility that so many of the Cuban customs, then considered quirky and anachronistic, would be later adopted by the end of the twenty-first century.

In much of this travel literature, the diggers found a murky political theme, but in fact, it appears that most of the Cuban innovations, except for the admirable development of medicine, culture and education, were a question of mere circumstance rather than political imposition. An economic blockade by the great northern neighbour and the withdrawal of support from a crumbling eastern empire evidently obligated Cuban leaders to adapt certain draconian measures, including the massive conversion to organic agriculture. This transition period was not without considerable deprivations among the local inhabitants.

By the year 2007, observers had already appreciated the agricultural achievements and architectural authenticity of Cuba, as well as the unclogged arteries that were mostly free for commuting cyclists and children playing stickball and soccer.

A new breed of traveller rushed to the island, hoping to view this culture before it became engulfed in pesticides, rush hour traffic and highrise fundamentalism. They wanted to observe a place unburdened by the fatal seduction of unsustainable consumerism which characterised much of the world during this period. Little did these travellers know that they were playing a role on the island in this fatal seduction.

A small minority of these travellers, branded naive and gullible, believed that such a civilisation could survive, that even during the period of an unbridled global economy, this one little country could move forward on a different track from all the rest. Judging from travel diaries of the time, it was a period of more questions than answers, except for the ideologues on the two polarised extremes, each thinking they had all the answers. Once you got past those extremes, Cuba became a most exciting place to visit, much more complex than any arriving traveller would have imagined.

A Cuban lady holding a figurine of an *orisha*

ACKNOWLEDGEMENTS

My thanks to hundreds of Cubans who made me feel at home and shared their ideas to help me with this book, including Arnulfo, Caridad, Colorado, Dolly, Eduardo, Everardo, Giselle, Ibis, Jesús, Ivan, Jorge Luis, Julio, Lourdes, Michel, René, Rogelio, Romelia, Rosita, Tomás and William. And thanks for interviews from dozens of seasoned travellers who experienced Cuba as their second country, including Bethany, Erik, Guy, Gina Margillo, Pablo, María Elena, John Kavulich, Jon Torgerson, Jorge Crisosto, Serge Kasimoff, and the Vidals. Thanks to the editorial team at Marshall Cavendish International (Asia) Pte Ltd. And to Trigg for capturing what it's all about.

To Gabriela, Monty, Siomara and Marcus, who give me the distinction of having four children who have travelled to Cuba on their own, each in a different period, plus my fifth, Vivian, who married a Cuban.

MAP OF CUBA

FLORIDA

• MIAMI

THE BAHAMAS

ATLANTIC OCEAN

• **HAVANA**

CUBA

GUANTANAMO

CAYMAN ISLANDS

HAITI

JAMAICA

"Only in Cuba have history and circumstance combined to enable a whole society to preserve the cars and turn them into a national treasure. Of the sixty thousand vintage cars, about half are from the 1950s, another 25 per cent from the 1940s and a similar number from the 1930s. How these cars survived is like, How did they build the pyramids? They're just magicians and wizards, pure and simple."
—Rick Shnitzler, urban planning consultant, as told to Mireya Navarro, "Cuban Wizardry Keeps Tail Fins From Drooping," *New York Times*, 5 June 2002

CUBA IS A COUNTRY

...where people at a bus stop, milling around in no perceivable order, suddenly know exactly who is ahead of whom when the bus finally arrives;

...where you can buy an orange in one place for the equivalent of a dollar and in another place, usually a farmer's market, for the equivalent of a penny (in the dual currency economy);

...where the chambermaid in your hotel may recommend a more moderately priced room with a family two blocks away;

...where 2 per cent of the population of Latin America represents 11 per cent of its scientists, and where a scientist earns less than a policeman;

...where urban neglect enabled the capital city to preserve its stunning architectural patrimony at a time when development was destroying the architectural integrity of the other Latin American capitals;

...where 1940s and 1950s Chevys and Fords regularly cruise the streets, where the horse and buggy acts as public transport in some smaller cities, and where the bicycle is the main form of private transport;

...where an accomplished musician can be 'discovered' at the age of 88 and then go on to a highly successful international career;

...where citizens enjoy a life expectancy equal to that of the developed western world;

...where education, health care and culture are more easily accessible than breakfast, lunch and dinner;

...where a trade embargo intended to topple a president actually helped keep that president in power for more than four decades;

...where that president invited people like the Pope and Jimmy Carter to go on national TV to criticise him;

...where overt control of the press has inadvertently done much more to foment critical thinking than CNN or *USA Today*;

...where some ancient African musical forms have remained vibrant and then been reintroduced into Africa;

...where some ancient European religions, such as Catholicism, have been reintroduced, and where some citizens know more about Elegguá and Yemayá than about Jesus Christ;

...where during the decades when private enterprise was prohibited and religion frowned upon, the only private business allowed to continue was the kosher butcher;

...where it is virtually impossible to remain outside the ideological fray, but where these reporters will attempt to present a balanced account.

Before you've downed your first *mojito*, minutes after leaving the José Martí International Airport, intoxication seeps in. At first it's the sweetness in the air, the whiff of sugar cane and organic urban agriculture, then the unrivalled charm from the contagious smiles of black, brown and white Cubans, often in a crowd that's hung out together since childhood. The backdrop is vintage colonial architecture, some of it well-preserved thanks to a massive restoration project but much of it still threatening to crumble.

These friendly Cubans beckon you and you are seduced. Here lies the drama for those intrepid few who actually desire to pass through the borders of tourism apartheid and actually integrate with Cubans.

The people you encounter, the ones who proudly refer to your favourite football squad or your number one classical violinist may be (a) looking to build international bridges in communication or (b) seeking a quick hustle in which you will be the participant in the redistribution of wealth.

There is, of course, a third group (c), more numerous but touchier to define. These are the ones who are networking: nothing so different from New Yorkers at a cocktail party or would-be actors in West Hollywood but without a set of social guidelines that will define for the beckoned a clear posture. They seek authentic friendship but they also hope that their foreign friend can be of help to them in one way or another. Given the unfathomable gap in currencies between the CUC (Cuban Convertible Peso), pegged to the tourist dollar, and the subsistence Cuban peso, how could they feel any other way? The foreigner, an engineer perhaps, may have purchased his plane ticket with a month's salary. For the Cuban engineer to travel abroad (and he is allowed to for sure), he'd need to accumulate ten years' salary. For travel abroad, Cubans need an invitation and a sponsor abroad, so if we put ourselves in their position and we wanted to travel, we'd be waiting at the tourist hotel to be the first to welcome and befriend foreign arrivals.

Cubans are caught in the perverse dynamics of an entirely unbalanced dual currency system. Until the calamitous "Special Period" in the early 1990s following the demise of Cuba's Soviet bloc support, there was a single currency: the Cuban peso. There was not much you could buy, but every salaried Cuban received a similar salary, with the same rights to rationed food and other necessities. During some periods it was even possible to have money left over at the end of the month, for few Cubans had to pay more than 10 per cent of their salary in rent. If their salary was equivalent to US$ 10, they paid a dollar in rent.

But with the fall of the Soviet bloc and the subsequent loss of oil and food subsidies, Cuba was on the verge of collapse. Even against the wishes of Fidel Castro himself, the nation was obligated to get hard currency, lots of it, in dollars. Cubans were told to be patient, and that the tourism industry was part of a formula that would save the day, along with organic agriculture and the pharmaceutical industry.

With the tourism industry, came the dual currencies. Possession of dollars was legalised. Some Cubans, those who worked within tourism or those who received care packages from relatives abroad, had access to dollars.

A waiter in a hotel restaurant could make thirty or forty times as much in tips as a doctor's salary. Others, many of them in the Communist Party (who had to follow the rules), many of them black (who had no relatives abroad), had no access to dollars.

The dual currency system created the beginnings of a class system. Hungry Cubans were told that the infusion of tourism would stop the crisis and resolve (*resolver*), and little by little, it did, but not exactly the way the government had planned it. Along the way, some women realised that going dancing with a tourist and then maybe sleeping with him might bring in US$ 20, which was more than two months salary. That would be equivalent to a US$ 5,000 gig for a Sunset Boulevard streetwalker. They could do the same thing with a Cuban boyfriend, but the food might not be as good and the objective result would be entirely different.

Many people developed a primitive but clever informal economy whose primary purpose was to bring tourist dollars into the pockets of those Cubans who had no access to them. At best, a tourist could buy fine Cohiba cigars smuggled from a factory or damaged rejects (almost impossible to tell the difference) for an attractive price. At worst, some of the most creative swindlers in history found ways to remove dollars from a tourist and maybe the visitor would not even realise until hours after his or her 'friendly' Cubans vanished into the poorly lit Havana streets.

It's not like the streets of Calcutta or east of Main Street in downtown L.A. Poor Cubans look healthy, seem well educated, dress well, and flash a cool smile. You can advise every visitor to be careful but so many first-time arrivers, even knowing the advice, are still seduced.

For your first impression in Cuba, you have a choice. You could take an entirely guided trip through an agency and not really meet a single Cuban. (A 2006 law, in fact, does not allow tourism workers to make contact with visitors but such laws come and go or are benignly neglected.)

If this is what you want, this book is not for you. *CultureShock! Cuba* is for travellers who wish to integrate with the people of the land they are visiting or going to reside in. That would leave you with two options. The first, recommended by the authors, is the advice of our friend José, "Don't let Cubans approach you. You approach them." This book will show you numerous ways to do this.

The second option, not recommended, is to take the beckoners on, engage, and do your best to filter out the swindlers and establish friendships with the authentic ones. This is the option that the authors took, for it was our job to get to know everything about Cuban ways of life, and that meant knowing how the sometimes exotic, sometimes nefarious informal economy functions. Should you choose this precarious route, we'll show you many survival skills.

Since its 1959 revolution, Cuba has been one of the most controversial countries in the world. Our father-and-son task (Mark and Marcus) was to dodge the arguments as best we could and write a non-political narrative that would help the reader integrate within Cuban culture. Our approach was simple: get intensely involved in the daily life of Cubans and take in a compendium of perceptions and opinions of local inhabitants, foreign residents, non-partial diplomats, and written sources.

This non-partisan approach will inevitably be considered political by both extremes: the United States foreign policy establishment with its Cuban exile lobbyists, and Cuban officialdom. Dominant sectors of the U.S. State Department, the Cuban exile community, and the Cuban government have one thing in common: either you're with them or against them. These two extremes monopolise media coverage of Cuba but represent only a small portion of richly textured Cuban public opinion. Once beyond the extremes, you rarely hear the expected platitudes.

There is a dilemma in transmitting one's daily experiences with Cubans. On the one hand, there is a continuity of culture that would exist regardless of the political system. But overlapping the cultural continuity are profound social transformations stemming from the Cuban Revolution.

Whatever happens in Cuba's political future, many of these transformations have become so deeply rooted that they will remain in the Cuban spirit. A sense of the dynamics between centuries-old customs and post-1959 cultural transformations requires a lengthier historical introduction than customary in *CultureShock!* books.

One prime example is worth introducing at this point. Prior to the revolution, Cuban society was marked by conspicuous class and race distinctions. The revolution changed alot of that. No longer does one hear the type of linguistic terminologies of social humility still prevalent in much of the rest of Latin America when humble people address their superiors. Even though tourism and the introduction of the dual currency are creating incipient economic and class divisions, Cubans are unlikely to revert to past customs of addressing others as their social superiors.

As Cuba's national poet, Nicolás Guillén wrote in his classic poem *Tengo* (I Have):

I have the joy of going
to a bank and talking to the administrator,
not in English,
not in sir,
but simply in compañero, *as they say in Spanish*

I have, let's see,
that being a black man
no one will halt me
at the door of a dance hall or a bar

Independent of whatever political or economic system may emerge in the future, Cubans now have a deeply engrained need for social equality. But life is tough on this island where a debilitating U.S. trade embargo and a communist regime that cleverly deflects economic sabotage from abroad engage in a *danse macabre*. As with most poor countries, many people wish to leave and find fortune elsewhere. But in Cuba it's different from Mexico, Sri Lanka, Morocco or Mali. Some Cubans leave in order to escape what they perceive as Stalinist control. Other Cubans leave to escape what they perceive as the incursion of capitalism which has damaged their chances for social equality.

THE SPECIAL PERIOD

The dramatic scenario of one of the world's best educated populations struggling to survive under an awkward mix of socialism and capitalism after the 1991 implosion of the socialist bloc was bound to create an unprecedented test of will for the nation. Drama is an understatement. No visitor can remain unmoved and many are moved to bitter-sweet tears that blend sublime joy with overwhelming pathos.

This has been the undeclared extension of the "Special Period". A "Special Period in a time of peace" was Fidel Castro's name for an austerity program, initiated since the loss of Soviet subsidies around 1990 and the subsequent escalation of the U.S. trade embargo. Under the special period, Cuban people have been asked to bear with severe shortages in food, fuel and medicines, until Cuban agronomists can expand and diversify food production and the tourism industry can bring in needed foreign currency. Children and the elderly receive extra rations but everyone else is expected to make ends meet creatively, planting urban gardens, raising chickens, bartering, using oxen to plow fields and riding bicycles (given out virtually for free) because there is little gasoline for public transportation.

But one way to make ends meet, unplanned by Fidel, was *jineterismo*. A *jinetero* is someone who looks for tourists in the hope of getting money out of them. They often work in networks, and sometimes, are linked with prostitution. A *jinetera* often refers to a prostitute.

Olga Gasaya, vice-chair of the Department of Psychology at the University of Havana has said that the "resurgence of prostitution is connected to the economic crisis. Although the crisis affects most women to the same degree, all women look for different ways to solve it and only a small percentage of them resort to prostitution."

The visitor who does not want to remain cloistered in a hotel room or marooned on a tourist beach has no choice but to take this ride of contradicting emotions. Cubans are quick to bare their feelings and they expect you to respond to probing questions as if you'd known them their whole lives. Given the hardships, the stories they share with you are apt to be poignantly dramatic, almost always with a sly sense of humour in that uniquely Cuban nasal chant of Spanish.

In Human Development Indicators 2005, Cuba was ranked 52 among all nations, under the category of High Human Development countries, as opposed to Medium Human Development and Low Human Development, with life expectancy at birth being 77.2 years (compared to 77.3 in the USA). Some of the other indicators include infant mortality (6 per 1,000 live births) and average literacy (96.9%).

Hardships have been gradually but unevenly diminishing. Though the "blockade" and the aftershocks of the Special Period continue, Cuba maintains a respectable ranking in United Nations indicators.

GETTING TO KNOW CUBANS

Cuban pastimes include music and dance, baseball, sports in general, and increasingly soccer, an afternoon on the beach, and a good old-fashioned party. Multi-dimensioned Cubans embrace apparently opposite diversions such as scientific research and eroticism.

But if there is one form of entertainment that most characterises the Cuban culture, it is hanging out with friends, neighbours and family (and sometimes strangers, too), usually at outdoor public gathering places; this is the social support system that health specialists so admire. When Colombian novelist Gabriel García Márquez asked Fidel Castro in what place he would like to be, Castro responded, "hanging out on some street corner."

For the foreigner, the Cuban way of life can be remarkably accessible, if he or she takes the necessary precautions. This book will explain the social context that can affect interaction between Cubans and foreigners.

Even without the benefit of foreign travel, a significant number of Cubans have been schooled to communicate effectively in English. Rarely in other countries in this hemisphere, except bilingual Canada, do high school language courses so effectively teach students to communicate. But

In Acapulco, Mexico, daredevil divers are a tourist attraction. But here at the Malecón seawall, Havana's outdoor living room, these after-school divers are just part of a great neighbourhood.

Cuba remains a predominantly Spanish-speaking country, and a rudimentary knowledge of Spanish will get you a long way in the realm of human relations. Cubans are remarkably patient in dealing with the broken Spanish of a well-meaning visitor.

Cuba is a country of neighbourhoods, and the best method for foreigners to become part of the scene is to choose a neighbourhood that fits their affinities, and use it as a home base. By all means branch out and take trips. But establish your turf.

If you do not plan to live in Cuba, you may find, that the friends you make on your first visit will draw you back. Most of the people I encounter who have been to Cuba once are lured back for repeat visits.

Should you choose to remain in tourist compounds like Varadero, you'll have a good time for sure, but you'll miss the profound joy of becoming part of a real community. "A person who has come to Varadero has not seen Cuba," declared Cuban architect Miguel Coyula.

HISTORY, GEOGRAPHY AND POLITICS

CHAPTER 2

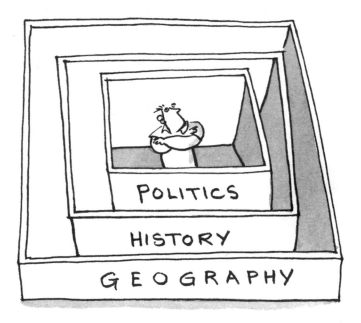

"Brilliant as [Fidel] is, spirited and resourceful as his people are, his endless rule seemed like some powerful vine wrapping its roots around the country and while defending it from the elements choking its natural growth."
—Arthur Miller, from "A Visit with Castro,"
The Nation, 12/19 January 2004

ECONOMICS: A HISTORY OF DEPENDENCE

With the fall of the Soviet Union in 1991, most political analysts predicted a speedy end to Cuba's socialist experiment. They failed to consider national pride, a cultural trait that transcends the avowed Marxism-Leninism of Fidel Castro. Ever since Spain's first settlements on the island in 1512 and the subsequent defeat of Hatuey, the Taíno Indian *cacique* (chief) a year later, Cuba's relationship to the rest of the world has been constrained by a traditional colonial model: provider of a monocultural raw material (sugar, minerals) to the coloniser and consumer of manufactured materials from abroad.

U.S. Control and the Platt Amendment

Until its belated "independence" in 1902, this dependence was maintained under the gun of the Spanish crown. Between 1898 and 1902, following the Spanish-American War, Cuba was controlled by the United States military. Although nominal independence was achieved in 1902, it was granted by the United States only after Cuba had signed the 1901 Platt Amendment, which allowed for U.S. intervention in Cuba to protect American interests. The naval base at Guantánamo, established in 1903, was the first tangible result of the Platt Amendment, and today remains attached to Cuba like a tick to a deer, off-limits to Cubans.

Economic dependency precludes value-added products, those that receive industrial or intellectual elaboration prior to export. Only value-added products can create new local jobs and stimulate an export economy. But most of Cuba's raw materials went straight from the farm or mine to the docks.

Two decades after the Platt Amendment and following various U.S. interventions, U.S. companies owned a majority portion of Cuba's farmland and mines, and the Amendment, no longer needed, was abrogated in 1934.

Into the Soviet Circle

Whether the revolution of 1959 was communist from the outset or simply nationalist in the tradition of Cuban patriot José Martí is still argued among historians today. Whether Cuba drifted into the Soviet orbit by design or necessity, the result was three more decades of dependency on a foreign power. Economically benevolent as the Soviets may have been, they maintained Cuba as a monocultural supplier of sugar. Instead of allowing the economy to attain a certain degree of self-sufficiency, the Soviets seduced Cuba into receiving cheap products, including vital oil, in exchange for sugar, for which the Soviet bloc paid a premium price. Cuba's dependent agricultural technology was based on a classic, unsustainable model used by both the Soviets and North Americans.

Cuban agricultural scientists "express resentment toward Soviet and other socialist bloc advisers who were responsible for technology transfer to Cuba, and they were self-critical for having had a 'colonised mentality'," according to agrarian experts Peter Rosset and Medea Benjamin.

THE SPECIAL PERIOD

In effect, Cuba did not become truly independent until 1991, and by that time, a powerful globalised economy made it virtually impossible for any one small country to create its own local form of survival, although audacious Cuba has strived against all odds to do just that. With the collapse of Soviet support, the then three-decade U.S. economic embargo against Cuba was intensified, in expectation of the imminent fall of the Fidel Castro government.

The post-Soviet hardships suffered by Cubans are now legendary. But Cuba's health care and education systems, the best in all of Latin America, have remained functional, although reeling from the crisis.

This is the so-called "Special Period in a time of peace," where Cuba was in the midst of reconstructing her economy in the absence of Soviet aid, while the United States tightens the embargo. The people have been asked to tolerate huge shortages of food, medicines and fuel. During this period of 'independence', Cuba has turned to tourism, 'a necessary evil', and to courageous but risky experiments in organic agriculture to lift herself out of the Special Period. In the meantime, the 1992 Torricelli Act in the United States prohibited foreign subsidiaries of U.S. corporations from trading with Cuba and placed a six-month ban on ships that have docked at Cuban ports.

The 1996 Helms-Burton law allows U.S. investors to take legal action in U.S. courts against any foreign company that utilises property in Cuba confiscated during the revolution. Post 11 September 2001 clamp-downs on travel and cultural exchanges with the island have had some effect in damaging Cuba's wobbly recovery.

National Pride

Throughout her history as a colony and neo-colony, Cuba was forced into the severe constraints of economic dependence on major world powers. Nationalist sentiment arising as a countercurrent to this dependency may explain why Cuba did not follow in the footsteps of Eastern European countries and accept the terms of the Western financial establishment. If there were ever a chance for Cuba to find her own wobbly path, it was in the 1990s, since she was now a satellite without a planet to revolve around.

National pride alone could not shield the spirit of most Cubans from the hardships of the mid-1990s and the after effects in the early years of the 21st century.

Guantanamera

During the height of the Special Period, one of Cuba's greatest filmmakers, Tomás Gutiérrez Alea (1928–1996), directed his final film, *Guantanamera*. As in his internationally-acclaimed *Fresa y Chocolate* (1994), in *Guantanamera*, Gutiérrez Alea and his co-director Juan Carlos Tabio deflect a potential tragedy by using the Cuban talent of mixing pathos with humour. The film is a poetic portrayal of Cuba's most difficult post-1959 historical period, scripted by the great Cuban writer Eliseo Diego. The film's title and lyrical chorus is derived from the classic *guajira* (country folk song), a traditional medium for mixing tragedy with improvised comedy.

Guantanamera is required viewing for anyone who wishes to see how Cubans cope, survive, and eventually emerge with a victory of the heart. Like *Fresa y Chocolate*, a poignant critique of a formal policy that ostracised homosexuals, *Guantanamera* is sharply critical of Cuban bureaucrats, in a most comical way. All the main characters of the Special Period make their appearance, especially the creative hustlers who sneak contraband bananas in a hearse and receive a commission for bringing travellers to a clandestine restaurant. There is a brief cameo for the *jineteras*, and sex and eroticism are presented as the primary escape from hardship. The issue of the double currency is highlighted when the government funeral bureaucrat, lacking dollars, is denied service in several public establishments.

The Black market

One of the contradictions of Cuba from the 1990s to the 2000s is a thriving black market. Foreigners will be approached by young men who will try to make money with any combination of seductive products, legendary charm or crafty deception. Relationships with Cubans are vulnerable to being tainted by the juxtaposition of two incompatible economies. Deeper human relationships are achieved when the visitor breaks out from the tourist mold and lets it be known that he or she has come to Cuba to live the daily life, though official restrictions make such relationships difficult to achieve.

Responses

Today's youth of Cuba did not experience the pre-1959 Batista period and were too young during the pre-1991 Soviet period to recall the days of full employment and more comprehensive social protection. At the same time, they are too old to qualify for the subsidies enjoyed by children under eight years of age. Cuban youth are the most likely sector of the population to harbour cynical attitudes towards the Cuban socialist experiment during a time of hardship.

Committed revolutionaries are also vulnerable to the cynicism of the times. "Those less dedicated to the revolution have risen to a superior economic status through black market activities," says Dr. Jorge Crisosto, a Chilean doctor who does volunteer work in Cuba through Catholic Relief Services. "But the more militant revolutionaries, those who truly believe in socialism, neither receive currency from abroad nor find it comfortable to participate in the underground economy, so it is they who suffer the most during the Special Period."

During times of hardship, some Cubans find solace in the fact that there was once a much greater gap between people of privilege and the majority. Most black Cubans cannot forget that before the 1959 revolution they were the victims of overt racism, and that today's Cuba, with all its faults, has earnestly attempted to give citizens of African origin the same chances as whites, as even the hypercritical Oppenheimer admits in *Castro's Final Hour*, his premature "obituary" on Cuban socialism.

While receiving some privileges, even the Communist Party insiders are not protected from the tribulations of the people. Ricardo, a Bolivian journalist friend, investigated the much-commented-on food lines and found the wife of the Minister of Culture waiting in line like the rest of the people. According to anti-Castro journalist Andrés Oppenheimer, Politburo member Carlos Lage's mother was often seen standing in line for hours at her neighbourhood bakery.

But 95 per cent of all Cuban exiles are white. With white Cubans more likely to receive dollars from abroad, there may be a racial component embedded in emerging social divisions.

Colonialism

At the outset of the Spanish colonial period in the early 1500s, native Americans who did not die in revolts were put to work on *encomiendas*, Spain's term for a landholding in which Indians received religious instruction in exchange for their labour. *Repartimientos*, another legal ploy to obtain free Indian labour, were permits granted by the crown to gather temporary labour forces for specific projects in mines, plantations or public works. Those Indians who did not perish from overwork would succumb to imported diseases like smallpox. Whether a few descendents of these native Cubans survive today is an unresolved polemic.

In their place, African slaves were brought in. By the 1840s, there were nearly half a million Africans on the island, the major portion being of Yoruba descent.

During the first century and a half of colonial rule, Cuba was besieged by pirates. Forts of stone masonry in Havana and other bays around the island were built to repel enemy attacks. Virtually abandoned by the mother country after gold reserves were exhausted, Cuba became a haven for smugglers and low-lifes. Tobacco production eluded colonial control until the establishment of a Spanish trade monopoly. But British occupation between 1862–1863 opened the country to free trade.

Colonial society was dominated by a white planter class. New class divisions emerged when peninsular Spaniards gained privileges at the expense of resentful *criollos* (Spaniards born in the Americas). Beneath the creoles were the free blacks, with black slaves holding up the system from the bottom.

SLAVERY

Colonialism and slavery in Cuba lasted nearly four decades longer than in other Latin American countries. Some reformers, including Father Félix Varela, were advocating independence and the abolition of slavery since the early 1800s. But the 1823 U.S. Monroe Doctrine defended the rights of Spanish dominion over Cuba, since the United States was hardly interested in seeing a Cuban slave rebellion that might spread to its own doorstep.

The triumph of former slaves in Haiti and brutally crushed Cuban slave rebellions in the 1830s and 1840s generated abolitionist sentiment and the planter class feared that the last chapter of its dominion was unfolding. To preserve their status, many planters flirted with having Cuba annexed by the slaveholding South of the United States. In 1850, former Spanish general Narciso López led an insurgency in the name of annexation by the United States.

A defeated López became the first famous Cuban exile in Miami. He later returned with a new outfit of soldiers and was defeated once again and executed. With the British hindering Spanish slave trade and the Spaniards vowing to phase out slavery, Mexican Indians and Chinese workers were imported to cut sugar cane.

Although Carlos Manuel de Céspedes freed his own slaves, he avoided abolitionist pronouncements in order to secure the support of the landed aristocracy.

THE FIRST WAR OF INDEPENDENCE

In 1868, landowner Carlos Manuel de Céspedes launched an independence revolt. Like the later Cuban Revolution, this military movement surged forth from the Oriente, the eastern region of the island of Cuba. By 1869, the insurgents had produced a constitutional document declaring the slaves free, although they were to continue to work on the plantations for a salary. The Spanish colonial armies were backed by the United States.

When Céspedes lost his influence and later his life in an ambush by the Spaniards, Máximo Gómez, a black exile from Santo Domingo, and Antonio Maceo, a Cuban mulatto, continued the ill-fated movement. Most insurgents yielded in 1879 in exchange for amnesty.

Cuban hero General Antonio Maceo rejected the amnesty. Maceo had to deal with racial resentment and intrigues from white underlings. (I found an eloquent letter written by Maceo to the president of the independence movement in which he called for racial equality and threatened to go abroad if his protest was not heard.) By the third quarter of the 19th century many landowners found it cheaper to pay their workers and let them otherwise fend for themselves. Slavery was phased out and ultimately abolished by the Spaniards.

But a caste system had evolved in which most preferred government jobs were granted to the creoles, with Afro-Cubans restricted to agricultural employment. Another ill-fated independence insurrection began in 1879 and was repressed after a year. With slavery abolished in 1880, a system of indentured servitude called *el patronato* continued for another six years until an 1886 royal decree declared it illegal.

The evolving sugar, mining, cattle, and tobacco industries in Cuba increasingly sought United States investment as the Spanish Crown remained intransigent with respect to any autonomous Cuban development.

José Martí

Cuba's most venerated national hero, José Martí, was the central figure in the escalating anti-colonial struggle. Martí spent his childhood in Spain. Upon his return to Cuba, he was shocked by the inhumane treatment of black slaves. During the ill-fated first independence insurrection in 1869,

Martí published the newspaper *La Patria Libre*. He was jailed with hard labour and then exiled for anti-Spanish political activity.

After the first war of independence had been squelched in 1878, Martí returned to Cuba with a law degree from Spain. In 1879, he was arrested again and deported as a subversive, ending up in New York after passing through Europe. In New York, he helped organise an educational centre for black Cuban exiles.

In 1895, Martí, the Dominican Máximo Gómez and Antonio Maceo parlayed their efforts into a second war of independence. The objectives of Martí's Cuban Revolutionary Party were freedom from political and economic domination by any foreign power, be it Spain or the United States, equality among Cubans regardless of class or colour, and establishment of democratic processes. Martí did not live to see the short-lived victory as he was killed in battle. He was an advocate of racial equality, and had he remained alive, some of the anti-racist measures that had to wait until the 1959 revolution would have been enacted earlier. Martí is also remembered as a poet and essayist.

Gómez and Maceo asked the Cubans to suspend all economic activity that might be advantageous to the royalists, in what resembled the Special Period of the 1990s. Maceo was killed in Pinar del Río, and Gómez's troops were isolated in the eastern region. Riots broke out in Havana, and the U.S. battleship Maine was apparently sent to protect American citizens.

SPANISH–AMERICAN WAR

The pretext for U.S. intervention in Cuba in 1898 was the explosion of the battleship Maine, in which 266 U.S. sailors died. The Spaniards called the explosion an accident, triggered by the ship's ammunition supplies, but the U.S. called it an act of war. Some Cuban historians hypothesize that some zealous Americans themselves might have blown up the Maine as a pretext to intervene.

A weakened Spain would have preferred to capitulate with honour but was obligated to enter a hopeless war. On

San Juan Hill, near Santiago, the Spanish soldiers, outnumbered by seven to one, held off a horde of Teddy Roosevelt's rough riders. The day-long battle resulted in heavy casualties on both sides, with the Spaniards retreating. Spain eventually achieved its goal of surrender while minimising casualties. Victory was quick for the United States, helped mainly by the fact that Cuban independence insurgents had already debilitated the Spanish royal army.

INDEPENDENCE

With Spanish surrender, the U.S. army should have handed Cuba over to victorious rebel leader General Calixto García. But García and most of his troops were black, so the U.S. decided to leave Spanish municipal governments intact. General García continued his war against the Spaniards.

The Cubans were not invited to the 1898 Paris peace treaty ceremony between the U.S. and Spain. Cuba was placed under U.S. occupation, and the U.S. army disbanded the largely black rebels. White Spaniards remained in positions of authority.

General Leonard Wood, a medical doctor, injected a measure of idealism into the U.S. intervention by helping to eradicate yellow fever. But with the 1901 Platt Amendment limiting Cuban self-determination, Cuban independence was constrained and the country fell under the reins of corrupt intermediaries with discriminatory policies until 1959. The United States intervened with force to put down an anti-racist rebellion of former slaves in 1912 in the western province of Pinar del Río, in the wake of massive anti-discrimination protests at the other end of the country that were squelched by government repression.

The U.S. stock market crash of 1929 catalysed an economic depression in Cuba, calling attention to the negative effects of a dependent economy. The crisis was mitigated during the U.S. 'prohibition' period in the early 1930s, when Cuba became a haven for rum-drinking tourists, with prostitution and gambling emporiums burgeoning.

In 1930, the great African-American poet Langston Hughes visited Cuba in search of the roots of Afro-Cuban music. He met his counterpart, Cuban poet Nicolás Guillén. The two poets would later translate each other's work, and Hughes encouraged Guillén to highlight the rhythms of Afro-Cuban music in his poetry. Guillén became the stimulus of a revolutionary cultural awakening.

Political revolutions of the times were less inspiring. Street fighting erupted between the government led by Gerardo Machado and a throttled Cuban opposition calling for an independent economy. The revolution of 1933 forced Machado to flee from the island.

Batista

A sergeant in the Cuban army by the name of Fulgencio Batista piggy-backed onto the rebellion, which also included Ramón Grau San Martín, a socialist and anti-imperialist. Grau became revolutionary provisional president and immediately enacted labour reforms. Grau denounced the Platt Amendment and the United States denied recognition to his government.

In control of military factions, Batista, instigated by U.S. ambassador Sumner Welles, forced Grau out of office in 1934. The United States immediately recognised a government headed by a Batista appointee. A subsequent Treaty of Reciprocity gave preferential treatment to United States exports in Cuba. Batista crushed a labour rebellion in 1935.

After a period of interim regimes, Batista faced Grau in a 1940 presidential election. The Cuban Communist Party (PCC) chose to support Batista over the more progressive Grau. (The PCC's later failure to support the Castro revolution was not an isolated ideological quirk.). Grau later won back the presidency, only to allow his regime to decay in corruption.

Never Fails to Fail
Cuban election politics were typical of many Latin American countries, long on idealistic proclamations and short on honesty.

Dizzy Gillespie and Afro-Cuban Music.

A depressing political scenario failed to inhibit Cuban culture. Like Langston Hughes, the great bebop trumpeter Dizzy Gillespie was enchanted by Cuba's rich cultural textures. Jazz legend Gillespie became enthralled with Cuban music during the late 1940s and collaborated with Cuban *bongo* and *conga* drummer Luciano (Chano) Pozo in a symbiotic relationship that would influence both Cuban and U.S. music, by way of Cuba's West African heritage.

Chano, associated with a Nigerian sect, spoke no English but Gillespie got him to teach his bassist Al McKibbon and drummer Max Roach complex Cuban "layered" rhythms. The immediate result was a music called Cubop. Contemporary Latin jazz is still influenced by the Dizzy-Chano synergy.

Cuba's liberating cultural scene often contrasts with dictatorial politics. On 10 March 1952, three months before an election that Batista had no chance of winning, he took power in a bloodless coup. Working-class Cubans and peasants were excluded from economic prosperity during the Batista dictatorship and protestors faced unprecedented repression.

Fidel Castro

An opposition figure during the Batista dictatorship was Fidel Castro, the son of sugar planters from eastern Cuba. Castro studied under the Jesuits and became a law student at the University of Havana. He graduated from law school in 1950, after having travelled abroad to participate in rebellious activities in Santo Domingo and Colombia. Had his pitching been a notch more effective, he might have found a career in professional baseball. As a post-coup candidate before aborted elections, Castro circulated a daring petition to depose the Batista government. Although the court ruled against the petition, one bold judge, Manuel Urrutia Lléo, did not comply with the majority. Castro would later reward him for his revolutionary stance.

American Tourists

Batista himself was too dark to be admitted to the Havana Yacht and Country Club and had to inaugurate his own country club.

The administration of Fulgencio Batista was burdened by corruption. Class and race distinctions divided the Cuban population, and illiteracy and unemployment made the island no different from other impoverished Latin American countries, except, as a playground for affluent American tourists, these contradictions were more blatant.

Wealthy and middle class Cubans were relatively well off, in stark contrast to the impoverished majority, many of them mulattos and blacks.

U.S. crime syndicate influence in the pre-1959 Cuban tourism industry is legendary.

REVOLUTION

After making no headway politically and seeing a partner tortured to death, the Cuban opposition movement, which included Fidel Castro, staged the 26 July 1953 assault on the Moncada army barracks. As usual, the insurgency had begun in the Oriente region.

Of the 119 insurgents, 55 were later tortured to death. Castro's men fled to the mountains but Fidel was captured. Strangely, he was put on trial in spite of orders to have him killed. The young lawyer's defence statement became his famous manifesto, "History Will Absolve Me." Castro was sentenced to 15 years.

In 1955, Batista interested in improving his international reputation, liberated all political prisoners. Castro fled to Mexico while the movement he left behind was co-opted by the government.

On 2 December 1956, the persistent Castro landed at the shores of Cuba with about 80 companions, among them Ernesto "Che" Guevara, the Argentine doctor-adventurer. After initial setbacks, the guerrillas scored some successes in 1957 and Fidel Castro was portrayed as an idealist by Herbert Matthews in the *New York Times*.

Later in 1957, a suicidal attack on Havana's presidential palace, whose object was to assassinate Batista, met with failure. Anyone associated with the attack and who could be captured was executed by Batista's troops.

The brash Castro would stop at nothing and characteristically made bold moves against heavy odds. He and his brother Raúl established fronts in the Sierra Maestra, *Radio Rebelde* began its broadcasts, and general strikes provided urban support. But notably absent from the escalating rebellion was the Soviet-style Cuban Communist Party.

Without communist support, Fidel's 300 rebels seemed especially vulnerable, and Batista sent in 10,000 troops to the Sierra Maestra to once and for all liquidate the revolution. The Batista attack was repelled, arms captured, and with the support of the people, Castro had now gained the upper hand. (Less than a decade later, Che Guevara would attempt a similar David versus Goliath insurgency, a strategy labelled *foquismo*, in Bolivia, but without the network of social support enjoyed by the Cuban rebels.)

Guevara and Camilo Cienfuegos set up new fronts, and the revolution retraced the path of the independence wars, pushing westward.

Honeymoon Gone Wrong

On New Year's eve, 31 December 1958, my friend Art and his wife were anchored in Havana on a honeymoon cruise, as the revolutionary forces advanced westward. After the midnight toasts, Batista made a New Year's resolution to abandon the country, along with 40 million dollars from the Cuban treasury. Fearing revolutionary violence, Art's cruise captain decided to turn away from Cuba, and to this very day, Art believes Fidel owes him a honeymoon.

Che and Camilo were the first to enter Havana on 2 January, with the support of a general strike called for by Fidel Castro. Castro arrived in Havana six days later.

TURNING TOWARD THE SOVIETS

Ever since the arrival of the Spaniards, Cuba had been manipulated by foreign powers. Some historians believe that a bizarre, self-fulfilling prophesy, originating in the U.S. White House, pushed Fidel into the arms of the Soviets. Others say that Fidel had always been a Marxist, as he himself later declared.

Questions about Cuban history, following the 1959 overthrow of Batista, revolve around two issues. First are Cuba's experiments with utopian social reforms, some of them successful, others failed. Second is the conflict between Cuba and the United States, with historians divided as to who pushed who first.

Cuba vs the U.S.—Who Pushed Who?

Supporters of the Cuban 'process' of social change say that the U.S. began the conflict. They dig back into a history of U.S. interventions epitomised by the Platt Amendment. They also argue that when Castro attempted to visit U.S. President Dwight D. Eisenhower, the American military hero purposely scheduled one of his famous golfing excursions in order to elude the bearded warrior. Vice-president Nixon, who was in the process of accusing everyone to the left of John Wayne of being a communist, made accusations to the effect that history would not absolve Castro, following a meeting with the Cuban leader at the White House.

Anti-Castro historians allege that Cuba pushed first, by enacting the first agrarian reform on 17 May 1959, expropriating U.S.-owned property, and failing to resolve the issue of indemnisation.

As several interim presidents presided over Cuban agrarian reforms, with confiscations of companies like United Fruit, the C.I.A. and former Batista mafia cronies attempted to spur uprisings against Castro. The regime of John F. Kennedy and the C.I.A. attempted on numerous occasions to assassinate Castro by using mafia hit men, according to investigator and historian Seymour Hersh, but the would-be exploding cigars never went off in Castro's face. The Kennedy regime flirted with plans for a full-scale invasion of the island.

The besieged Comandante responded to U.S.-backed military threats by creating popular militia and purging the opposition. A mass exodus of Cuban technical experts and professionals to the United States exacerbated the expected economic upheavals that always come with revolutions. News of summary trials and executions of 500 former Batista collaborators and those attempting to overthrow the revolution left many foreign observers trying to decide if Fidel was an idealist, a Stalinist, or some combination of the two. Che Guevara justified the executions with an "us or them" morality.

Marxism had preached that a deposed ruling class will never peacefully allow a revolution to exist and this axiom was behind the executions. (When Chile's elected socialist president Salvador Allende was overthrown in a violent 1973 coup, defenders of the executions would say "I told you so," but revolutionary humanists argued that "you could have locked them up without killing them.")

In June of 1960, the U.S. State Department urged U.S.-owned refineries to refuse to refine Soviet crude oil. Cuba responded by nationalising the refineries.

In July of 1960, the United States suspended the Cuban sugar quota, effectively cutting off 80 per cent of Cuban exports to the United States. Was this policy a reaction against increased Soviet influence or did it accomplish the opposite of its intention, obligating Cuba to look for a new 'sugar daddy'? It looked much like a self-fulfilling prophesy when the Soviets stepped in to buy the sugar that was refused by the United States.

The suspension of the U.S. sugar quota was followed by Cuba's August 1960 nationalisation of U.S. private investments. Were these nationalisations in the cards or had a cause-and-effect phenomenon kicked in?

In less than a month, the United States responded with the now internationally unpopular economic embargo, and the Cuban government responded with more nationalisations.

While this was all happening, the Comités para la Defensa de la Revolución (CDRs) were organised. Depending on your political philosophy, these committees were an example of participatory democracy with grass roots support for neighbourhood health care and universal culture and education, or they were the eyes and ears of Big Brother, or both.

By early 1961, the United States had broken diplomatic relations with Cuba, soon followed by the C.I.A.-backed Bay of Pigs invasion at Playa Girón, which was defeated within 72 hours by the Cubans.

One planner of the Bay of Pigs invasion was E. Howard Hunt, who would later gain infamy by botching the Watergate burglary of Democratic Party headquarters that led to the downfall of president Richard Nixon. Nixon had opened commercial channels with the two greatest communist threats, the Soviet Union and China, but maintained the embargo against tiny Cuba.

SOCIAL REFORMS

During the heady early years of the revolution, Cuba was able to lift the status of blacks and women. Prostitution became an unnecessary profession as movies like *Lucía* taught women's dignity and literacy campaigns wiped out illiteracy. Although many Cuban doctors had left the country, a nationwide effort to establish universal health care led eventually to Cuba's position as the Latin American country with the most equitable health care system.

Unlike other Latin American budgets, Cuban financial resources went directly to the needs of its people, and this was reflected statistically with great achievements in culture, sports, and medicine. On the other hand, Cuba's increasing dependency on the Soviet Union created a scenario ripe for future economic crises.

Across the Gulf, in Mexico, the dominant Institutional Revolutionary Party (PRI) was maintaining itself in power for seven decades with a party dictatorship. But by holding heavily-manipulated elections every six years, Mexico continued to qualify for trade with the United States.

From the beginning of the revolutionary experiment, the Cubans attempted to maintain a certain degree of independence from their Soviet benefactors. In September of 1961, for example, Cuba was the only Latin American country at the founding conference of the movement of non-aligned nations. Could Cuba be a part of the non-aligned camp and yet still function within the Soviet umbrella, or was there a split personality within the Cuban body politic?

By late 1961, Castro had declared that "I am a Marxist-Leninist, and I shall be one to the end of my life." Some historians believe that Fidel was simply a Cuban nationalist, pushed into the arms of the Soviets by U.S. Cold War politics. Others insist that he had always been a Marxist-Leninist. In the nationalist tradition of José Martí and Antonio Maceo, Fidel Castro may have drifted into the Soviet camp as the only perceived means to stand up to the giant to the north. His domineering, macho personality, more paternalistic than the typical Latin American *cacique*, gave him the audacity to pull it off.

In early 1962, the Organization of American States (OAS), dominated by the United States, launched the ill-fated Alliance for Progress as an alternative to socialism and suspended Cuba's membership. Cuba responded with calls for all Latin American people to "rise up against imperialism."

In October of 1962, the "Cuban missile crisis" was resolved when the Soviets, without consulting the Cubans, agreed to withdraw the missiles from Cuban soil in exchange for a U.S. pledge to not invade Cuba.

The United States then resorted to diplomatic methods in an attempt to engulf the island. In July of 1964, the Organization of American States adopted mandatory sanctions against Cuba and required all members to sever diplomatic and trade relations with the Castro government. Although such measures tended to push Cuba ever closer to the Soviet bloc, Castro would later criticise the Soviets for their relations with Latin American oligarchies. One of those oligarchies defeated Che Guevara's 1967 military incursion in Bolivia. After being captured, Guevara was summarily executed by the Bolivian military.

LATIN AMERICAN SUPPORT

Support for Cuba eventually came from within Latin America. Mexico had immediately refused to comply with the OAS sanctions and the Latin American arts and letters community continued to back the Cuban reforms, which included the 1968 nationalisation of 55,000 small businesses.

In late 1969, the first of many volunteer contingents of what was called the Venceremos Brigade arrived from the United States to help with the sugar harvest. The story of the culture shock of idealistic middle-class Americans cutting sugar cane and their adjustment to rural Cuba is told in Sandra Levinson's 1971 *Venceremos Brigade* (Simon & Schuster).

Many Latin American writers withdrew their support for the Cuban revolution when their Cuban colleague, poet Heberto Padilla, was arrested for activities against state security in 1971. Padilla was imprisoned for 39 days, ostracised, and later obligated to make a humiliating confession. He later went to Spain, criticising the Castro regime for "a basic suspicion of all intellectuals". For Padilla's account of the episode, see his *La Mala Memoria* (Bad Memoires), published by Plaza and Janes in Spain in 1989.

The defection of foreign intellectuals following the Padilla incident did not include a cadre of supportive writers led by Nobel Prize winning Gabriel García Márquez, who has remained faithful to the Cuban revolution to this very day, standing beside Fidel during the 1998 visit of the Pope.

García Márquez is well aware that in 1997, on a scale of 1 to 10, Cuba ranked 0.9, beneath all Latin American countries in the categories of access to information and free pluralistic exercise of freedom of expression, according to the Third Ibero-American Forum on Communications. But it's not hard to understand why García Márquez would prefer a flawed Cuban system to the drug violence, political corruption, and ruthless human rights abuses in his native Colombia.

Curiously, many Latin American intellectuals, such as Pablo Ramos, former chancellor of Bolivia's national university in La Paz, who battle for freedom of expression in their own countries, continue to support the Cuban revolution. "To be poor in Cuba is to share the problem with everybody," Ramos told this reporter. "Nobody dies from lack of medical attention. To be poor in the rest of Latin America is to live with uncertainty, without access to medical care or quality education."

Ramos blames the United States trade embargo for many of Cuba's problems and defending Cuba is his way of standing up against "an imposed economic doctrine from the north that has only brought suffering to our country."

More recently, the rise of democratically elected left-wing govornments in Latin America put in question the effectiveness of the United States' anti-Cuba policy in the continent. President Hugo Chávez of Venezuela provided cheap oil to Cuba in exchange for Cuban medical assistance for poor Venezeulens. Another ally was Evo Morales from Bolivia, who with Venezuela and Cuba, joined the ALBA, Bolivarian Alternative for the Americas, a social, political and economic treaty meant as an alternative to the Free

Trade Area of the Americas proposed by the United States. Mexico, however, became more distant with Cuba since the election of U.S. supported and ideologically conservative presidents in 2000 and 2006.

U.S.–CUBA CONFLICT

A billboard in Havana within view of the U.S. Interests offices, depicts a soldier shouting across the Carribean to a threatening Uncle Sam: "Hey imperialists, we are absolutely not afraid of you."

For U.S. administrations, the existence of prisoners of conscience in Cuba is one of the excuses for maintaining the trade embargo and rejecting diplomatic relations. But even Latin American intellectuals not so friendly to the Castro regime as Ramos, often question the moral standards of U.S. policy, citing the fact that far more repressive regimes in their own countries have received U.S. blessing and support.

Anti-Castro extremists in the U.S. have been tolerated by the FBI. In October of 1976, a bomb was planted on a Cuban airliner, killing 73 people. Luis Posada Carriles, a Cuban exile and former C.I.A. employee, was arrested in Venezuela and charged with the bombing. Cuba responded by suspending its 1973 anti-hijacking accord with the United States. Posada eventually escaped from Venezeula but ended up being convicted in Panama for a plot to kill Castro in that country in 2000. He was later pardoned and left that country, only to end up being arrested in the United States in 2005 for illegal entry. Both Cuba and Venezeula asked the United States to extradite him to Venezeula, a request the United States has refused. This situation has created a dilemma for the United States, since collaborating with the rival countries of Cuba and Venezeula would be a show of weakness, while refusing to extradite a known terrorist would be in contradiction to their declared intention of fighting terrorism. A certain number of anti-Castro extremists have attempted to rationalise such deliberate attacks against civilians in Cuba. After a rash of 1997 bombings of hotels and restaurants in Cuba, an obvious attempt to disrupt the tourist industry, Cuban exile leader Francisco Hernández declared: "we don't consider these actions terrorism, because people fighting for liberty cannot be limited by a system that is itself terrorist."

Geopolitical analysts explain that Cold War politics were behind the U.S. embargo of Cuba, since Cuba was in the Soviet camp. But in 1991, after a total divorce between Cuba and the Russians (Aeroflot doesn't even fly to Cuba anymore), the United States stiffened its trade restrictions against Cuba's economy. The 1996 Helms-Burton law was signed by a reluctant President Clinton after Cuba shot down two planes piloted by Hermanos al Rescate, an organisation of Miami exiles. Whether or not the planes were illegally buzzing Cuban air space is a political rather than geographical opinion.

Helms-Burton allows U.S. investors to take legal action in U.S. courts against foreign companies utilising their confiscated property in Cuba. It also prevents the lifting of the trade embargo until the Castro government no longer presides over Cuba and requires U.S. representatives to international financial organisations to oppose loans to Cuba. During the Bush administration, restrictions on dealing with Cuba were tightened.

There is an ultimate cultural irony to the U.S.–Cuba conflict. Most Soviets who lived and worked in Cuba hardly integrated with the Cuban population, rarely learning Spanish and confining themselves to educational and social enclaves. The Soviets never overcame culture shock in Cuba, and generally failed to partake in the joyful Caribbean culture. People from the United States, on the other hand, have many cultural affinities with Cuba, from Hemingway to baseball to Latin jazz.

> From a cultural standpoint, Cuba's relationship with the Russians was a total flop, and her estrangement with the United States has been a tragic divorce between neighbours who would have gotten along fabulously.

INTERNAL MEASURES

During the revolutionary ferment of the 1960s, the concept of banking, a dominant aspect in most cultures, was considered of less moral virtue than cinema or sports. How could Che Guevara, an adventurer, a doctor, and a motorcyclist, be named the president of Cuba's National Bank?

A typical turn-of-the-century exchange with a disgruntled Cuban: "It's time for Fidel to step down. What we need is another Che." Che Guevara attempted to forge an economy based on moral rather than material incentives. He called this cultural transformation *El Hombre Nuevo* (The New Man). He did not live long enough, however, to follow through on his programme.

Guevara expected his bank employees to increase productivity through moral rather than monetary incentives. Cuba's economic system was supposed to function through a cultural transformation. Guevara wanted to create *el hombre nuevo*, a new human being guided by moral values rather than materialism. He and his cohorts assumed that an idealist culture would generate productive forces better than one based on greed.

The banning of self-employment and the nationalisation of small businesses in the late 1960s presumed that small enterprises fomented the same cultural maladies of exploitation and greed as larger enterprises and corporations. This unsuccessful policy was reversed 30 years later, and although heavily restricted, the small business is today an important tax-paying sector of the economy.

In the late 1990s, rigid state controls were established to prevent a wealthy commercial class from rising above the rest, as Cuba gropes for methods to expand its economy evenly, without causing gaps in social and economic class. The monocultural dependency through sugar production and the near exclusivity of trade with the Soviet bloc was less an error and more an obligation of circumstances. This policy severely distorted Cuba's productive forces. Several attempts were made to diversify the economy, only to be abandoned in the throes of crisis situations that demanded escalation of sugar production.

These are but a few of the errors now openly recognised by most Cubans, including members of the governing party. But in spite of these errors, the quality of life at the bottom end of Cuban society was notably better than that of poor people in the rest of Latin America, in the realms of health, education and culture.

"In fact," writes skeptic Oppenheimer, "some of the government's claims were legitimate, even if exaggerated. That was why many Cubans were still finding positive aspects in a revolution that was otherwise marked by economic failure."

"It was true that in the Cuba of the late 1980s you didn't find the pockets of misery you stumbled on in virtually any other Latin American country," wrote Oppenheimer, whose book against Castro was banned in Cuba but widely read anyway. "There were no beggars on the streets—at least no full-time ones ... Cuba had eliminated misery at the cost of imposing a general poverty."

Will Cuban utopian attempts to forge a new, non-materialist culture eventually succumb to what critics call human nature?

Stevenson, along with runner Alberto Juantorena and javelinist María Colón represented Cuba's first generation of Olympic champions. In Montreal in 1976, Juantorena broke the record for the 800 m and then went on to win the 400 m, the first man to take both events in the Olympics. Also in Montreal, María Colón became the first third-world athlete to win a gold medal in women's athletics, at the same time that back in Cuba, women's literacy was equalling that of men, also an unprecedented achievement for a third-world country.

Teófilo Stevenson

The more politicised Cuban ideologues seemed demagogic in their sloganeering, as if they were posturing to satisfy their Soviet backers. But Cuba's greatest all-time heavyweight boxer, Teófilo Stevenson expressed the ideas of the *hombre nuevo* by his actions.

Heavyweight boxer Teófilo Stevenson would face his greatest decision out of the ring. In 1972 in Munich, they called Stevenson "the most impressive Olympic boxer since Cassius Clay." The United States' Duane Bobick had defeated Stevenson in the previous Pan American Games. But Stevenson went home to work on his right hand to accompany his stinging left jab. Bobick went into the rematch unconcerned. But the improving Stevenson battered the American and the fight was stopped in the third round. Germany's Peter Hussing was also knocked out by Stevenson. "I have never been hit so hard in all my 212 bouts," said the seasoned Hussing.

After Stevenson's first gold medal, fight promoters were after him. They wanted him to fight Mohammed Ali for the heavyweight championship. Stevenson responded that he was more interested in his studies and in the revolution than in making a million dollars. So they offered him two million.

"Professional boxing treats a fighter like a commodity to be bought and sold and discarded when he is no longer of use," responded Stevenson. "Mohammed Ali makes millions, but he's exploited nonetheless."

In the 1976 Olympics, Teófilo Stevenson knocked out his first three opponents in a record 7 minutes and 22 seconds. His last opponent was the Romanian Mircea Simon, who dodged Stevenson completely for the first two rounds. When Stevenson finally hit his opponent in the third round, Simon's seconds immediately threw in the towel.

Simon defected to the United States. Stevenson went back to Cuba.

In 1980, in Moscow, a slower Stevenson became the first boxer to win three Olympic gold medals in the same division.

Liván Hernández

A classic case of a star athlete offered millions to defect is baseball pitcher Liván Hernández. Cuba has no celebrity industry, and an athlete who excels like Liván is going to end up teaching Physical Education with only a few extra perks like the use of a house, a car and travel expenses abroad. But Hernández's skills were worth millions of dollars in the global economy. Hernández became the four-million-dollar man and led his Miami team to a world series baseball championship in 1997.

In Cuba, Hernández's name was banned from all media. His half brother, Orlando "El Duque" Hernández, older and perhaps even better than Liván, fell under uncorroborated suspicion that he had helped Liván escape. El Duque, a national hero, was banned from Cuban baseball.

The irony was that El Duque Hernández, a committed communist in the tradition of Teófilo Stevenson, had been subjected to repeated aggressive recruiting whenever playing abroad and had always refused millions to defect. Once ostracised, El Duque depended on Livàn's gifts from abroad to supplement his income as a physical therapist. But a further irony is that El Duque rarely received economic help from his wealthy brother abroad.

In ruining El Duque's career at home, the Cuban bureaucracy scored points in either incompetence, paranoid behaviour, or both. It was not the first time that a zealous bureaucrat had given a bad name to the very system he was supposedly defending. A committed socialist and ideal sports ambassador for the Cuban system, El Duque himself was obligated to flee, and in his case, he did not do it for the money.

"Surely you must understand the motives of guys like Livàn Hernández," I argued to a faithful Cuban party member. "Not every star should be expected to resist like Teófilo."

Off the record, he went beyond the official discourse:

"We understand what Livàn did," he said. "But what we don't understand is the way he did. He could have arranged to go there and send back half his salary to contribute to

the education of his countrymen, like other Cubans who go abroad do. Liván has a contract for four and a half million! Does any human being need that much?"

Given the enormous financial incentives, it is amazing that so many Cuban baseball heroes have refused to defect. When star infielder Omar Linares was under intense pressure during the 1996 Atlanta Olympics to remain in the United States and play for the New York Yankees, he responded: "I'd rather play for 11 million Cubans than 11 million dollars."

FREEDOM OF MOVEMENT

The history of emigration from Cuba since 1959 involves numerous examples of apparent limitations on freedom. The most contemporary phenomenon is the so-called "Palestinians," rural Cubans who emigrate to the city. When shantytowns of "Palestinians" began appearing in pockets of Havana, the government clamped down and prohibited migration from rural areas to the capital.

I asked a Cuban diplomat why it was that so many Cubans leave their country. Typical of Cuban officials, even when presenting ideas that are obviously in accord with government policy, he asked that his name be withheld. "There are more Bolivians outside of Bolivia," he responded, "than Cubans who've left Cuba. The whole Cuban population that has left the country is equivalent to the number of Mexicans who leave Mexico in one month."

"The problem is economic," he continued. "In fact, more than any other national group, Cubans are lured to the United States because they receive a special welcome there, with social benefits."

A chronology of Cuban emigration since the revolution begins in the years between 1959 and 1962, when any Cubans who wanted to leave could simply hop on a daily flight to Miami, with the condition that they leave behind everything they owned. In the second half of the 1960s, the U.S. government automatically declared all Cuban immigrants to be eligible for residency, a dream always denied to Mexican neighbours. A quarter of a million Cubans took advantage of the offer.

In 1980, a totally different wave of emigrants, the *marielitos*, of humbler origins, were allowed to leave Cuba. A crafty Fidel used the crisis to dump convicted prisoners and the mentally ill on the United States. The crisis began when 7,000 Cubans were allowed to seek asylum in the Peruvian embassy in Havana. By 1984, the ever-creative Castro found a new tactic. Former political prisoners and their families were allowed to flee the island, thus ridding the system of its most vociferous dissenters. The 1996 Amnesty International report expresses concern over Cuba's recurring to exile as a form of ridding herself of internal opposition.

In the early 1990s, in the wake of a youth riot, Castro allowed the *balseros* (emigrants in make-shift rafts) the right to navigate to Florida, with President Clinton opening the doors at the other side. Immediately following the Soviet collapse, Cubans had been subjected to intense hardships, and many felt they had nothing to lose. Many never made it through the shark-infested waters. Clinton eventually rescinded the invitation and the *balseros* were picked up at sea and taken to Guantánamo Naval Base. Most of them ended up in the United States anyway.

Although anti-Castro activists say such migrations have been political, most Cuban emigration seems mainly economic in origin. The *balseros* rightfully received the sympathy of many people in the United States, although ironically, the U.S. blockade was at least partially responsible for the economic asphyxiation that led to their flight.

In a larger context, illegal immigrants from Mexico and Central America, whose economic situation has been even more desperate than that of the *balseros*, since they enjoy no social protection, choose to risk death by dehydration and set out to cross the Arizona and California deserts or suffocate in truck trailers while trying to make it to Los Angeles. Those who arrive are not welcomed like Cubans, and are considered an alien enemy by media-driven public opinion within the United States.

Constraints on freedom of movement for Cubans also come from the American side. While restrictions had already existed, the United States, under the fiercely ideological Bush administration, closed loopholes in the law that allowed Americans, including Cuban exiles, to travel to Cuba and spend money there. This angered many Cuban-Americans, since it limits their possibilities for visiting their relatives in Cuba.

THE SPECIAL PERIOD IN A TIME OF PEACE

Communism collapsed, the U.S. embargo stiffened, and Cuba confronted ominous food, fuel and medical shortages. Eastern Europe caved in and hoped that primitive capitalism would solve its crisis. Grotesque social inequalities and a rise in organised crime at that time left many Eastern European countries in economic purgatory. Eastern Europeans found it easy to discard an economic system that was imposed from abroad.

But in the face of a U.S. "blockade," for Fidel Castro to give in would have been nothing less than total surrender, hardly in keeping with the tradition of José Martí. Castro decided to

Love him or hate him, you can't deny that Fidel is one of the most important and audacious figures of the twentieth century.

defend Cuba's socialist experiment. This meant an extended period of drastic penance during which many of the people who once loved Fidel would learn to hate him.

To counteract fuel shortages, Cubans were given new bicycles, and Castro, sounding like fellow authoritarian and idealist Don Quixote, said that this would be good for Cubans' health and the country's ecology. Castro pointed to Holland, where the use of automobiles is discouraged and the bicycle is lauded. Oxen replaced gas guzzling tractors and urban dwellers were encouraged to make trips to the country to resolve the food shortage by planting and harvesting, with questionable results. Many refused but many more went back to the land and in typical Cuban style, found a way to party while doing so.

Tourism has been expected to bail out the country but the clumsy relationship between the new dollar economy and the Cuban peso created new divisions in social class.

Laws permitting self-employment and small private business suddenly made many new products available. Can a flawed but egalitarian Cuba survive? At least some improvements have emerged. Power outages have greatly diminished, oil is now available thanks to a partnership with Venezuela and new foreign trade partners, notably China, are providing an escape valve.

Many Cuban insiders are not pleased with the results of the dual currency economy and resulting social inequities. Long-time-insider Ricardo Alarcón, president of the National Assembly of People's Power, was remarkably frank to the foreign press during the Pope's visit:

"While it is true that we have some things in our reality that are not to our liking—the dual economy, the circulation of dollars," he said, "that was done out of necessity. But it is something that we should try to eliminate, the sooner, the better."

In 2004, dollars were removed from circulation and the dollar-pegged CUC was expected to reduce some of the contradictions of the dual currency. Nonetheless, most Cuban workers do not have access to CUCs through their salary and must find other means for obtaining the stronger currency.

DRAMATIC TIMES

At the outset of the decade, investigators like Andrés Oppenheimer gloated over the hardships of the Special Period and predicted the imminent downfall of Fidel Castro. But by 1997, with a growing economy, Castro had outlived the dire predictions, and the January 1998 visit of the Pope injected new energy into the Cuban system. The Pope criticised the existence of political prisoners within Cuba but he also lashed out at the U.S. trade embargo.

Less certain was what would happen to the bedrock of revolutionary Cuba, the health care system, universal education, a high level of culture and what remained of social equality. Only this modicum of equality, as well as a thriving underground economy, prevented the disaffected youth from breaking out in violent acts of rebellion.

Foreign tourism entrepreneurs have been allowed to recover their initial investments before sharing their profits with the Cuban public, which means that expected benefits from tourism had not yet kicked into full force by the time of the Pope's visit in 1998. Business regulations were in constant flux. In the early years of the new century, further restrictions were placed on foreign enterprises.

Even the most cynical Cubans interviewed for this book testified that by the late 1990s, daily life had improved considerably, but most people are still reeling. "We've never fully recovered from the special period," said Sonia, a retiree from Old Havana. The image of Fidel Castro became increasingly tarnished among a large sector of youth but this does not mean that they want Miami exiles to control their fate. A new phenomenon involves socialist exiles who leave the country because of tourist-related social inequities, adding further complications to an already convoluted social scenario.

"Do the people criticise Castro?" many Americans would ask.

"Yes they do," I answered. On every street corner you could hear them. But one of the typical codas to an anti-Fidel sonata is: "We need someone like Che," hardly the response that the Miami exile elite wanted to hear. The question remains whether the government can juggle two diametrically-opposed tiers of the economy, using doses of capitalism to save socialism.

"Why not embrace full-fledged capitalism at once?" wrote Andrés Oppenheimer. "In the minds of a growing number of Cubans, cold-blooded capitalism would make more sense than well-meaning socialism with dwindling social programs."

Not so, according to Adam Kufeld, whose three trips to Cuba extended over a two-year period and ended during the most difficult phase of economic crisis. Back in 1994, he wrote: "Many are frustrated with the authoritarianism and the intolerance of political dissent," but "hardly anyone thinks capitalism is the answer" when they see the sobering reality of the market economy on neighbouring island countries of Haiti, Jamaica, the Dominican Republic and Puerto Rico."

"I think the future belongs to democracy," said Ricardo Alarcón, "but not to capitalism, because they are opposite camps. We believe the government has to intervene precisely for the benefit of those who would be deprived if you leave democracy to the market."

The future was on the minds of people around the world when Fidel Castro was hospitalised in August of 2006 and still had not recovered enough to attend the Conference of Non-Aligned Nations in September, where he would have basked in stardom. He was able to see Kofi Annan and heads of state in his hospital room.

In the meantime, Cuban culture continues to enthrall virtually everyone who dares to visit the island. The Cuban way of life, independent of economic systems and political discourse, is highly contagious, to everyone, it seems, but the Soviets who remained here in their enclaves.

FOREIGN ADVENTURES

Many Cubans are today critical of Cuba's past militant involvement in affairs on other continents. Cuba's defense of Angola against South African mercenaries, although temporarily successful, led to a loss of lives of many Cuban soldiers, the best trained in all of Latin America. This excursion in Angola against South Africa's racist regime won Cuba favour amongst the non-aligned nations, a group that represented an alternative to Soviet dominance. In 1984, Cuba agreed to withdraw from Angola in exchange for the removal of South African troops from Namibia. But when Cuba sent troops to Ethiopia, entering a sectarian squabble between two communist factions, it did so to satisfy the demands of the Soviet Union.

After the assassination of Grenadan socialist Prime Minister Maurice Bishop in October 1983, Cuba denied a request from the Grenadan coup leaders to assist the island country against an impending U.S. invasion. Three days later, 8,800 U.S. troops invaded Grenada, where 734 Cubans were on the island at the bequest of the murdered Bishop to construct an airport. Only 43 of the Cubans were military personnel. U.S. forces captured 642 Cubans, killing 24 and wounding 57.

HUMAN RIGHTS

In 2007, hundreds of people had been held for over five years. For a long time, three children between the ages of 13 and 15 were among them. For some time they were held in steel mesh cages, until they were finally moved to a facility with plumbing and ventilation. Most of these prisoners have not been charged, nor are they allowed access to any legal process. Among them was a taxi driver who was set free after nine months. According to the BBC, "He was never charged and still does not know why he was arrested." Both Amnesty International and Human Rights Watch have spoken out against the deplorable conditions of these detainees.

If you imagined this was Cuba, you were right. It's Guantánamo, in the United States military facility, and the prisoners were mainly picked up in Afghanistan, though they come from many countries around the world. They were being held by Uncle Sam.

In 1988, a delegation of U.S. human rights leaders inspected Cuban prisons, in exchange for a subsequent visit by a Cuban delegation to U.S. prisons. The U.S. group reported that "conditions in Cuban prisons were generally no worse than those in U.S. prisons and that there was no evidence of systematic abuses." The U.S. group also concluded that some prison policies in Cuban jails, such as conjugal visits, are more humane that those in the United States.

Recent reports by Amnesty International and Human Rights Watch refer to deplorable conditions in most Latin American prisons, including those of Cuba. U.S. prisons are also singled out for inhumane conditions, such as widespread incidents of rape. When one reads all these reports, it is difficult to make a case that Cuba's prison conditions are any harsher than those of comparable countries.

The presence of prisoners of conscience in Cuban prisons is hardly the right public relations for the Cuban regime. When this reporter challenged a Cuban official on political prisoners, the response was predictable. The official cited the Puerto Rican and Native American political prisoners in U.S. jails and suggested that writers like me have applied a double standard. Why do books on Cuba but not on other Latin American countries always feature sections on political prisoners?

"Where can you find a single victim of assassination, torture, or disappearance [in Cuba]," writes Cuban vice-president Carlos Lage, who affirms that "for us, human rights go beyond the fundamentals listed in the Universal Declaration and include social justice, true equality and a just distribution of wealth."

I then point out that year after year Cuba earns the lowest ranking of all Latin American nations in the openness of the press and media. One is hard-pressed to find any criticism of the government or high-ranking officials. The usual response is that the U.S. trade "blockade," terrorist attacks sponsored by the CIA and Miami Cuban exile groups, and financing of false journalists by the U.S. Special Interests Section in Havana are equivalent to subversion and a country under siege needs to take exceptional measures of protection: same argument used by the Bush administration to defend the practices of the Guantánamo prison camp and the draconian measures of the Patriot Act.

My response to the Cuban official: why smother dissent when Cubans read banned books and engage in behind-the-scenes criticism of the government anyway? The word gets down to people on the street, and their anger is already apparent. So why not let them vent this frustration in a more open journalistic environment?

Their response: in the rest of the Americas, a poor person cannot own a newspaper and less so a TV station. With the owners belonging to the privileged class and with advertisers influencing content, public opinion is very effectively manipulated.

My arms go up in frustration. It is difficult to break through the ideological barrier. Tight Cuban control of the media does nothing to make the population less critical, so why not stop the ineffective clampdown.

Prior to the Pope's January 1998 visit to Cuba, the Vatican had presented the Cuban government with a list of 270 political prisoners it wanted released. Within weeks of the Pope's departure, more than 300 prisoners were released and, for the first time, the Cuban government tacitly recognised that political prisoners existed. But in a follow-up article in *Granma*, Fidel warned that the release of prisoners should not be construed as a softening of Cuba's political position.

Amnesty International added a nuance to the freeing of political prisoners, noting that allowing dissenters to leave the country is a convenient way of ridding the system of opposition.

Since the Pope's visit, the grip of Cuban authority has been loosening and then tightening, depending on the events of the day. It loosened with Jimmy Carter's historic visit in May 2002. The most prominent American political figure to visit Cuba since 1959, Carter was given unprecendented freedom to speak to the Cuban people. He called for an end to the embargo and praised Cuba's medical assistance to poor nations but he also bluntly labelled Cuba as undemocratic and repeatedly publicised the Cuban dissident "Varela Project" campaign for democratising Cuba. Carter's strong criticism was broadcast over public television and reprinted in communist party newspapers.

TRIGG.

But a year later, the grip tightened once again.

In March 2003, some 75 dissidents, many considered independent journalists, were arrested, tried and sentenced to up to 28 years in prison, the most severe crackdown in recent history. Some had been involved in the Varela Project, named after 19th-century Cuban priest Felix Varela, an independence advocate. The Varela Project, led by Christian activist Oswaldo Paya Sardinas, was based on Article 88 of the Cuban Constitution, allowing for a referendum if an initiative had 10,000 signatures. On the eve of Carter's visit, 11,000 signatures were handed to the National Assembly, and following Carter's repeated mention of the project, another 30,000 signatures were reportedly gathered. The Cuban government alleged that the dissidents were directly funded and promoted by the increasingly aggressive U.S. Interests Section in Havana. The Varela Project called for democratic reforms including free elections.

In April 2003, eight armed Cuban hijackers took control of a ferry with some 50 passengers aboard, departing from the Havana harbour in the direction of Miami. They were captured when the ferry ran out of fuel. They were tried within a week and three days following the sentencing, on 11 April, three of them were executed by a firing squad.

The repressive measures of 2003 were too much for some of the same European countries that had regularly voted against United States resolutions critical of Cuban human rights in Cuba. Suddenly, the "Old Europe" was no more popular with Fidel than it had been with Rumsfeld.

Cuban diplomats insisted that the jailed dissidents were working directly with the United States government to undermine Cuba. Cuban officials may have considered the executions of the hijackers as a deterrent, for further hijackings would discourage the tourism that is so vital for Cuba's economic recovery. (The rationale for the 1999 crackdown on street hustlers related to the fact that harassment of tourists was considered subversive to Cuba's economy.)

The issue of human rights is a festering sore. Some of the opponents of the Cuban Revolution have more effectively defended Cuba's policies than her Stalinist friends. These critics recognise the hypocrisy of the anti-Cuba lobby, which brandishes the flag of human rights and supports a universally condemned trade embargo, and then espouses friendly trade with countries like China, Russia, Saudi Arabia, and Israel, which for very different reasons have all been criticised in the international community for abuses of human rights.

In the aftermath of the 2003 measures, I attended an event in Paris for Cuban solidarity. I expected to hear some healthy debate. Some friends of the Cuban social process raised legitimate criticism about the executions, in the context of their own opposition to the death penalty. They were hooted at by doctrinaire defenders of the Revolution and some of us suspected that Cuba's egalitarian future would be brittle indeed if its defense were left to such sectarian fundamentalists.

CUBA IN THE FUTURE

Long before Fidel Castro's grave illness in the summer of 2006, militant insiders told us that journalists were wasting their time conjecturing about Cuba after Fidel Castro, that even before Fidel's illness, many important decisions were decided collectively and that some of these decisions went against the wishes of the "Maximum Leader".

Furthermore, they said, the mechanism was in place for militias loyal to socialism to defend the Revolution against the orthodox laissez-faire system that was depriving Eastern

Europeans, Russians and Chinese of their access to health care and widening the gap between rich and poor.

This book is being revised nine months after Fidel's brother Raul Castro took over command in a very low-key way. Fidel himself was so ill that he could not even make a brief appearance at high profile international conferences in Havana, no less run his country.

At this writing, Cuba has continued without Fidel at the helm. Whether or not Fidel Castro is still alive when you read these lines, Cuba's future is not in his hands, nor does it depend on his presence.

Throughout this book, you will read a diverse array of Cuban opinion regarding the future of their country. At the moment I write these lines, an international tug of war is taking place. On the one hand, the United States government would want to install a orthodox free market model in Cuba. On the other hand, Latin American progressive governments, elected because orthodox free market models in their countries had failed, would wish to defend Cuba's right to social equality.

As long as a balance between these two poles remains, the Cubans will be able to determine their own destiny. On the streets of Havana, I am reminded of South Central Los Angeles on the eve of the riots. The dual currency society has created social inequality and more than a few people are enraged by what has happened. In intellectual circles, many Cubans believe there is still a chance to save the best parts of their system and they are willing to fight to do so.

As co-author of this revised edition, I have tried to portray all the nuances of Cuban opinion. People on most sides, for there are more than two sides, would lament if Cubans were to lose their universal access to health care, education and culture. From my own perspective, it would be an environmental shame if Cuba were to lose its truly revolutionary system of organic agriculture (see Chapter 9).And for all those people who see bicycle commuting as one of the important progressive measures against global warming, it would be catastrophic if clean Cuba would go the way of China and abandon its bicycle culture in favour of the automobile determinism that is wreaking havoc on the world.

Few Cubans would lament, however, if there were a long-awaited opening in the realm of freedom of expression. At the end of February 2007, three foreign journalists were told that their press credentials had been revoked. None of the three had been particularly offensive to the Cuban regime. It looked like the hand of the so-called "talibans", those young Cuban technocrats who prove their allegiance by being more zealous than the leaders they want to please.

On the other, during the same period one witnessed a remarkable opening up of expression. The official newspaper, *Juventud Rebelde*, published investigative reports highly critical of dysfunction in Cuban life, the work of major writers like Cabrera-Infante and Heberto Castillo, whose literature long been banned as counter-revolutionary, was resuscitated at the 2007 Feria del Libro, with Raúl Castro and other party leaders in the audience.

Some observers consider that such contradictions represent a power struggle but Cuban life has never been as monolithic as the caricature would present it.

In the end, as James Michener has written, "…the Cuban is a being apart, colourful, enterprising, and chock-full of verve … regimes may come and go in different guises, but the essential Cuban will remain the same."

CULTURE AND CLIMATE

Mainland Cuba is a tropical island in Latin America. In general, Latin Americans from lowland regions tend to be more spontaneous and exuberant than those from cooler highlands. Just how much of the Cuban spontaneity comes from her tropical heritage and how much is uniquely Cuban?

I have travelled for two decades in search of an answer to this enigma, through other lowland habitats such as Veracruz, Mexico, El Salvador, Costa Rica, Panamá, and Ecuador. My subjective impression is that frankness and spontaneity among Cubans, or between Cubans and

Valley of Viñales, famous for tobacco growing and the flat-top mountains called *mogotes*.

foreigners, is yet more prominent than in other regions of the tropics. Tropical Caribbean stereotypes are only partially applicable to Cuba.

Anthropologists still debate the effect that setting has on character. Many Cubans I've interviewed sincerely believe that their Miami brothers and sisters have lost some of the collective spark (*la chispa*) by having been subjected to a way of life that trades in community values for stressful consumerism.

Cubans on their native turf have no choice but to get along with each other, cramped as they are in the odd camel buses (*camellos*), two-humped windowed trailers hauled by diesel truck cabins. Back in Miami, Florida, air conditioning, elaborate home entertainment products, and an automobile lifestyle, leave most streets empty. In Cuba, small apartments with no air conditioning encourage people to occupy the street, the park, or the Malecón, the long seawall in Havana, which all become the neighbourhood living room.

Without discerning more precisely which aspects of setting have greater or lesser impact on the culture, let's take a glimpse at Cuba's physical setting.

GEOGRAPHY

Most of Cuba is one island 1,250 km (777 miles) long (west–east) but only 191 km (119 miles) wide (north–south) at its widest section. The island is like a misshapen fish, 160 km (100 miles) southwest of the Florida Keys and 210 km (130 miles) east of Mexico's Yucatán Peninsula.

But the Republic of Cuba is more than an island. It is 1,600 islands, islets, and keys: an archipelago. It is a haven for a yachtsman with time to explore. The second largest piece of real estate on the archipelago is Isla de la Juventud, a sparsely populated beach paradise. Cuba's 6,073 km (3,770 miles) of coastline include bays with narrow entrances that open out into great harbours, rugged cliffs, coral reef, and various marshlands.

North and east of Cuba lies the Atlantic Ocean. To her west is the Gulf of Mexico. To her south is the Caribbean Sea. Cuba is the fifteenth largest island in the world. One fourth of her surface is forested mountains. The rest is comprised of fertile plains, somewhat depleted by chemical agriculture, but now being restored with an ambitious plan for organic agriculture. Sugar cane, cattle, tobacco, rice and coffee are Cuba's most traditional crops. Citrus fruits are making a comeback after a failed experiment to convert Cuba into a dairy economy. Colonial and neocolonial powers have used Cuba's land to produce non-nutritional farm products: sugar, tobacco, coffee and rum. Cuba's land has traditionally yielded a myriad of after-dinner delights without setting aside enough of its acreage for the main course.

Mountain Ranges

The main island is not known for its mountains, but three attractive ranges, referred to as *alturas*, look down on its green plains and valleys. The Cordillera de Guaniguanico, in the western province of Pinar del Río, reaches its highest point with El Pan de Guajaibón at 692 m (2,270 feet).

Continuing from left to right, we find the second range, the Sierra de Escambray, in the southern part of Cuba's central provinces of Cienfuegos and Sancti Spíritus. The highest peak in this range is San Juan, also called La Cuca, at 1,156 m (3,793 ft).

Continuing eastward, the third and most fabled range, near the southeast coast just west of Guantánamo Bay, is the Sierra Maestra, which sheltered the revolutionary forces of Fidel Castro between 1956 and 1959. The highest peak here, climbable in six hours and with a breathtaking view, is Pico Real del Turquino, at 1,974 m (6,476 ft), high enough for a refreshing change in climate.

With most of Cuba's population density in the environs of Havana, many nooks and crannies, including pristine beaches and unexplored coves, await the meditative sojourner. For at least another few years, Cuba will remain one of the least commercialised paradises in the world, with none of the drug problems that plague other Latin American and Caribbean regions. Nature lovers can delight in fishing, hiking, scuba diving, bird watching, and cross-country bicycle trips.

Rivers

The majority of Cuba's more than 500 watercourses are short and skimpy with water, but may rise to the occasion during the rainy season. Cuba's largest rivers are found in the southeast, where the 370-km (230 mile) Río Cauto springs out of the Sierra Maestra above Santiago and travels northeast, emptying out into the Gulf of Guacanayabo.

Climate

Cuba lies in what is considered a torrid zone at the northern edge of the tropics, although one rarely feels such notorious extremes in heat of summers as in U.S. or southern European cities. Trade winds of northerly origin temper the extremes that would be found in other tropical regions at the same latitude of the Tropic of Cancer.

The annual mean temperature, for example, is only 26°C (79°F). This average dips to 23°C (73°F) in January, the coolest month, and rises to no more than 28°C (82°F) in August, the hottest month, in mid-summer vacation.

During a normal year, Cuba's high temperature is only 32°C (90°F). For comparison's sake, consider that there is never a summer in Washington D.C. that doesn't see the mercury hit at least 37°C (99°F), with equally high humidity as Cuba. (Humidity averages about 80 per cent.) The lowest possible temperature during a normal year will be 16°C (61°F).

If the weather has a say in determining your travel to Cuba, bear in mind that the heart of the rainy season extends from May through October, and the hurricane season runs from June through November, although September and October are the most likely months for a hurricane. Cuba is pleasantly mild from late-October through March.

Living Things

Ever since colonial times, Cuba has been victimised by deforestation. Her three mountain ranges have acted as fortresses against the total decimation of her forests.

As might be expected, the palm tree is Cuba's most characteristic sight, with the royal palm on the country's coat of arms. The unusual big belly palms appear as if they are pregnant. My favourite Cuban tree is the multi-trunked *jaguey*, whose shade is more refreshing than that of any other tree I've known. Although the *jaguey* is kind to human beings in this respect, it kills every plant around it, so bring a blanket if you do not wish to sit in the dirt under this tree.

Other trees are the silk-cotton tree (wide trunk, swelling at the top), and big-leaf trees like the banana tree and *yagruma*. I've spotted *agaves* in dry areas, the same century plants used in Mexico to make tequila.

Orchid lovers will be pleased by Cuba's numerous species. My favourite flower, because of its aroma, is the jasmine. The *mariposa*, or butterfly jasmine, is Cuba's national flower. More than 3,000 surviving species of plants are native to Cuba, and several thousand others have been imported to the island during different historical periods.

In order to appreciate Cuba's animal life, you'll have to get beyond her developed tourist regions. Public transportation is sparse to the offshore islands, the mountains, and the swamps of Ciénega de Zapata, so consider hiring a yacht to the islands, hiking or cycling from the nearest town to the mountains or swamps, or taking an ecotour.

The animal kingdom in Havana lacks what is so prominent in other Latin American capitals: stray dogs. Shortages in red meat and food in general or a hyperefficient public health system may partially explain the virtual absence of strays in many neighbourhoods.

There are a few notable surviving wild animals. In the Ciénega de Zapata resides a living fossil called the alligator gar (*manjuarí*), part fish and part reptile. Even more difficult to find is a nocturnal snake in the python family called *majá*, who won't dare visit your hotel room or backyard garden.

A large bat population performs its social function, going on nightly hunting forays and thereby preventing mosquitos from bothering Cuba's human population. Other rare beings include the manatee, a living sea fossil, and the *jutía*, a mammal nicknamed "tree rat" that is rarely found in populated areas. Cuba is not an ideal place for lovers of wild animals.

Melania, a gourmet cook, cringes at the thought of eating the *jutía* "because it looks like a big rat," but her husband Nufo says it tastes fine. Melania prefers the meat of the *majá* snake.

Bird watchers will have a better opportunity to observe unusual species. Start with Cuba's national bird from the quetzal family, the *tocororo*, easy to pick out with its red, white, and blue feathers that match the Cuban flag. Among Cuba's 350 bird species is the world's smallest bird, the bee hummingbird (*pájaro mosca*), but Cuba's urban development has exiled this rare bird to the Ciénega de Zapata.

My favourite Cuban bird, because of its streamlined beauty, its "social" function, and its willingness to pose for pictures, is the white cattle egret, called *garza*. It seems as if one egret has been assigned to each cow by the government bureaucracy. The egret devours evil parasitic insects called *garrapatas* from the cow's hide.

Cultural centre in town of Viñales, province of Pinar del Río. With scarce resources, Cuba went against conventional Latin American wisdom and invested heavily in rural areas, while leaving colonial city streets in disrepair.

Perhaps Cuba's greatest hero in the animal kingdom is a parasitic fly called the *Lixophaga diatraeae*, big name for a small guy who devours the deadly sugar cane borer and thereby saves Cuba's foreign exchange.

REGIONS WEST TO EAST

Regions in Cuba should be called slices. Cuba is shaped like a long sea animal with the mouth to the left (west) and the fins to the right (east). Regions are divided by north-south slices. Moving from left/west to right/east, below is an annotated list of Cuba's regions or provinces.

Pinar del Río

This province, whose capital city is of the same name, has a population of less than 150,000 and is the core of Cuba's tobacco region. Tobacco fields are presided over by the *mogotes*, flat-top limestone mountains that resemble the peculiar outcrops in Guilin in southern China. Throughout the area, around the immaculate, pinetree town of Viñales, are remarkable cave labyrinths, carved out by rivers and waterfalls.

Resorts are scattered throughout the lush green, mountainous province. Bird watching, swimming, fishing, scuba diving, ecotourism, and visits to cigar factories are a few of the activities available to visitors.

Province of Havana

The City of Havana is Cuba's main attraction, while the province of Havana remains a well-kept secret. It is often easier to find transportation to more distant regions than to places right around Havana, like San Antonio de los Baños, famous for its school of cinema and its Museum of Humor.

The City of Havana has been exempted from the contradictions of every other major city in Latin America. Architect Miguel Coyula, of the Group for the Integral Development of the City of Havana, explains why. "It is a city that hasn't been touched by the second half of the twentieth century because efforts of renovation have been focused on rural Cuba, in order to correct the tremendous imbalance between country and city so typical of Latin America."

The emphasis on rural development spared Havana from the anarchic waves of rural-to-urban immigration so typical in Latin America, and averted the spawning of a rural-rooted urban under-class that has bred social violence in cities like Caracas, Lima and Mexico City.

Since Havana originated in the east and spread west, a walker can time travel through the historical periods of the city, beginning in colonial Old Havana, with each subsequent sector representing the next historical style of architecture. Along the way are baroque, rococo, art nouveau and art deco buildings. One begins on narrow streets lined with ornate facades and balconies. Walking farther west, the streets become wider, the green areas larger, and the styles of buildings and homes more modern.

"Old Havana is the only colonial city in Latin America with a totally intact infrastructure," explains architect Coyula with glee. "That's because there was no land speculation there."

Old-Fashioned Revival

The new pediatric rehabilitation centre exemplifies the best of utopian thinking of the Cuban Revolution. Housed in a

Vedado neighbourhood of Havana. Old cars are so common that they've become a part of Cuba's psychic geography.

patiently restored 18th-century mansion, it is part of the restoration and reconstruction of the crumbling heart of Old Havana (La Habana Vieja).

Something more noble besides tourist currency is driving the restoration effort. The goal is to harmonise tourist development with the social needs of the old city's residents.

The mastermind of this unique effort is the award-winning historian and city planner Eusebio Leal Spengler. "We are creating a system that deals not only with bricks and mortar, but also with social and educational programs," he told reporter David Adams, in "Reviving Havana" (*St. Petersburg Times*, 10 September 2001).

As more and more buildings have been returned to their past splendour, Leal and his project have won international awards and generated support from Europe and the United States. Even some anti-Castro exiles in Miami have proudly lauded the project, "politics aside."

Havana was blessed with a dazzling array of colonial, arabesque and art deco architectural styles. The irony: thanks to lack of care and funds (all resources had been directed toward boosting the provinces), this outdoor wonder escaped the onslaught of modernist architecture that has pockmarked the other capitals of Latin America. In exchange for salvaging architectural integrity, the city suffered through decades of shocking neglect.

Now, the buildings are being restored to their near-original state, malfunctioning infrastructure is being repaired and Havana may lose the trendy bombed-out look that attracted iconoclast travellers. Leal has skated craftily through Cuba's often slippery bureaucracy to achieve a degree of autonomy that only Fidel and his closest advisors could have enjoyed. His successful recipe is professional integrity, legendary charm and a remarkably unassuming appearance. In talking with his colleagues, I sensed that they were his loyal congregation and he was the high priest of soulful urban revival.

Leal's position on the Cuban Communist Party's Central Committee and the Council of State gives him access to the high command. Of Catholic upbringing, he became a secular activist in the Cuban Revolution. Rescuing the city has become his personal crusade.

After most of the city's wealthiest people fled to Miami in the early '60s, the city's historic buildings were occupied by poorer residents with no means to keep up their homes. Cuba's new leaders were interested in a quick fix, new mass housing based on cheap, functional concrete-block models, in periphery zones, imported from both eastern and western Europe.

Leal warned officials that Cuba would pay a high price for neglecting Havana. Back in the 1960s, lacking funds and political backing, his work was limited to a few projects. He persisted. In 1979, with a team of four architects, he drew up the city's first restoration plan. Small, underfunded projects were initiated. They faced the awesome task of dealing with 4,000 ailing structures of historical or architectural value inhabited by 74,000 residents.

In 1982, the United Nations declared the Old City a World Heritage Site. But not until 1993 was Leal's work granted full political recognition in Cuba. At the time, the island was floundering in the Special Period.

Leal argued with exquisite precision that state investment in restoration would more than pay for itself in revenue from tourism. He was handed extraordinary land-use powers to

This old Havana street exudes a charm, untouched by the twentieth century consumer culture.

rescue the Old City through creating hotel and real estate joint ventures with foreign investors.

Today, Leal's office controls the budget and infrastructure of the city, through a complex web of companies that run a network of hotels, restaurants, bars, shops and museums. His staff now consists of nearly 4,000 architects, construction workers and hotel and restaurant employees. Salaries are about 10 CUC a month, the average wage in Cuba's state-subsidised economy. Top architects in Leal's office make 20 CUC a month. The project also runs its own school to train the carpenters, masons, painters and metalworkers needed to carry out the work.

Profits are poured back directly into local projects, with only a small percentage going to the state. In the year 2001 alone, the businesses generated 10,000 jobs and earned US$ 60 million. Running a sustainable operation that would be the envy of the international capitalist financiers, Leal has remained loyal to the social goals of Cuban socialism. About a third of the profits are directed to social education projects and restorations designed to help local residents: public schools, libraries, health clinics and public space in the form of parks and squares.

For example, the abandoned 1718 Convent of Belen was transformed into a utopian day-care centre for the elderly financed by an adjoining hotel and museum. Long life of a city is not divorced from long life for its inhabitants.

But the restoration has its social cost. Overcrowding means that some 30,000 long-time residents must move out for good. People with residential seniority in the community are on the top of the list of those allowed to remain.

While some are reluctant to leave homes to which they have grown attached, despite leaking roofs, collapsed stairwells, and rickety balconies, they are being offered new apartments in other parts of the city. Leal's writings seem acutely aware that overgentrification is not sustainable and can lead to the type of lifeless Old Town without an authentic daily life. A tall apartment building soon to house foreign tenants paying 1,200 CUC a month is in the vicinity of Cuban tenants in other buildings who pay only a few CUCs per month in subsidised rent.

I participated in a santería ceremony of tenants on the day they were moving back to their restored building. It was an exciting event, with rumba musicians, fruit offerings to the *Orishas* and dancing in rounds. The beer flowed freely. But a few doors down, where the roof had collapsed, residents faced the probability of relocation to the Alamar highrises, not far from the beach but in a neighbourhood void of charm and dynamism. The quality of housing is much improved for those who move, but many are reluctant to leave the old neighbourhood.

I visited the interiors of some of the buildings slated for restoration. There were illegal bathrooms causing infrastructural plumbing problems, and makeshift mezzanines which seemed like interior balconies, within an area that used to have high colonial ceilings. Dark stairways like labyrinths led to apartments within apartments, as if there were both outer and inner shells.

More recently, the constuction of a limited amount of new housing has been permitted. This represents a certain change of orientation for the restoration policy, since the idea, especially defended by Eusebio Leal, was to avoid new constructions. But now, under certain unavoidable conditions, it has become acceptable or tolerated that the new can coexist with the old. For example, new housing with harmonious architecture can be built in the place of a building that was beyond repair anyway.

Leal admits it's not always possible to satisfy everyone's needs. One can only hope that a large enough percentage of the old residents will remain as planned, in order to prevent Old Havana from becoming a type of Main Street Disneyland. Given that most Olde Townes end up as tourist enclaves void of authentic community life, Leal stresses the need to preserve the Old Town without the e's. Thus far, there remains a sustainable balance between cash-producing tourism and residential authenticity.

Playas del Este

These "east beaches," about 19 km (12 miles) from Havana, are reached through the Havana Bay Tunnel or by alternate roads splitting through Regla and Guanabacoa, two communities of vibrant African traditions with attractive colonial centres and industrial outskirts.

Tourist guides map out Playas del Este as a single place but in reality it splits into two enclaves. On the west segment (the side nearest Havana) are the beach resorts of El Megano and Santa María del Mar, off limits to most because of the steep price. On the east side are communities converging around Guanabo, a real Cuban town. The hotels are less touristy and *paladars* and home stays more at hand. The palm-lined beaches seem less manicured.

Matanzas

The capital, of the same name, is about the size of Pinar del Río. This province is mainly known for the resorts in Varadero and the historic Bay of Pigs, now a favoured spot for scuba divers. Many Cubans find Varadero offensive, as it is off limits

Author's daughter (centre) chooses public beach, Playas del Este, instead of the tourist enclave, and is treated to Cuba's racial harmony.

to them economically. My daughter went there anyway and found the underground beach-dune economy fascinating. But she preferred Playas del Este to the east of Havana.

From the obligatory visit in Varadero included in most tours, the traveller can get a taste of the real Cuba only 16 km (10 miles) to the southeast, in Cárdenas, the home of Elián Gonzalez, the child who was rescued from a shipwreck near Florida in which his mother died. Elián then became the centre of a custody war between his father in Cuba and the exiled family of his mother in Miami. Pandering to the militant Miami exile community and opposing his boss, in a prophetic attempt to win Florida in his projected bid for the presidency, then vice-president Al Gore called for keeping the boy in Florida. Elián's father won his child back in the courts and Gore lost the Florida Cuban vote and the presidency.

Cárdenas allows you to see the typical small city life of Elián's hometown, similar to many other unsung cities. Public transport consists of a horse and buggy ride for a peso, and the primary private transportation is the bicycle. You don't find many overweight people in Cárdenas. You wheel past well-preserved colonial residences with high ceilings and mosaic floors, a quaint art gallery, a couple of eclectic museums, a lively farmer's market, and a dancehall. Off the tourist track, one is unlikely to confront the ubiquitous hustlers who hang around more famous sites. An 1888 steam engine still transports sugar from the nearby José Smith Comas plantation.

Villa Clara and Cienfuegos

Villa Clara (north) and Cienfuegos (south) share the same slice of central Cuba. Villa Clara's capital, Santa Clara, approaching a quarter of a million inhabitants, has typical Cuban *ambiente* but without significant numbers of tourists. Songs about Che Guevara feature Santa Clara, the site of Che's historic 1958 military victory that led to the downfall of Batista. One can cool off in picturesque mountains south of the city, part of the Sierra de Escambray. Remedios, one of Cuba's more original colonial towns, with some structures dating back to the 1500s, is northeast of the city of Santa Clara.

The bay city of Cienfuegos (about the size of Pinar del Río and Matanzas), is a large industrial centre. The province of the same name is probably the least African of all Cuban regions. It shares the Escambray mountains with both Villa Clara and Sancti Spíritus.

Sancti Spíritus

The city of Sancti Spíritus is rather small for a provincial capital, with less than 100,000 inhabitants. Within the province of Sancti Spíritus is also the colonial city of Trinidad with 50,000 inhabitants, declared a World Heritage Site by UNESCO. If you had to choose one baroque place to visit during a trip to Cuba, this might be it. It's about 450 km (280 miles) from Havana, a six-hour ride. Also in Sancti Spíritus is the highest mountain of the Escambray range, Pico San Juan (La Cuca).

Ciego de Ávila and Camagüey

This province, whose capital of the same name has less than 100,000 inhabitants, is one of the flattest regions of Cuba, saved from oblivion by fishing and water sports in its keys to the north and south.

Father and son in neighbourhood bar, Santiago de Cuba.

Like Ciego de Ávila, Camagüey is all flatland, and once more, the sea to the north and south of the province is of major interest. The City of Camagüey, with more than 300,000 inhabitants, features both a spirited *ambiente* and a colonial setting, and is yet to be besieged by tourists.

Las Tunas

Even fewer tourists stay in the Province of Las Tunas, whose capital city has a population of above 100,000. But don't be fooled. The people are as friendly as can be and the untouched beaches are reserved for romantics or lovers of solitude.

Holguín and Granma

The Provinces of Holguín to the north (birthplace of Fidel Castro) and Granma to the south, occupy the same north-south slice of the island, and mark the beginning of Cuba's 'fin.' These two provinces also share a rugged mountainous area that includes the Sierra Maestra and other lesser ranges. The Sierra Maestra's hideaways were a perfect refuge for Castro's guerrilla army.

Both provinces are embellished with modern resorts and superb scenery. The city of Holguín has a quarter of a million people, while Granma's capital, Bayamo, is more typical in size of Cuba's provincial capitals, with less than 150,000. Bayamo is a good place to get away from the tourist subculture, while taking in the history of the country's first independence insurgent, Carlos Manuel de Céspedes, in Parque Céspedes.

The most adventurous feature of the Province of Granma, shared with the panhandle of the Province of Santiago, is the Gran Parque Nacional Sierra Maestra, whose entrance is at Alto de Naranjo. Hikers will enjoy wooded trails with spectacular views, historic sites from the Cuban Revolution, and highland rain forest scenery. It takes three days of hiking from Alto de Naranjo to the coast at Las Cuevas in the Province of Santiago, and those who plan to do the whole trip should hire a guide.

Santiago

The Province of Santiago shares the end of Cuba's 'fin' with Guantánamo. If you fancy what is old, African, musical, and mountainous, Santiago is the perfect place. With nearly a half million inhabitants, Santiago de Cuba is the country's second city.

Most of Cuba's revolutions began in Santiago, the site of the Moncada Barracks attacked by Fidel Castro's guerrillas. Pico Turquino and Gran Piedra are challenging hikes taking you up to cooler climates.

Guantánamo

The mountainous province of Guantánamo is the setting for the famous song *La Guantanamera* as well as the United States naval base (the only place on the island where you can buy a Big Mac). There is no access from the Cuban mainland to Guantánamo Naval Base.

The dry south coast, laden with cactus, looks out of place in Cuba, and contrasts with the lush north coast of the same province and its hauntingly beautiful colonial town of Baracoa. The south coast city of Guantánamo has more than 200,000 inhabitants, but the scenery of the north coast countryside is more attractive to most visitors.

Isla de la Juventud

Although Isla de la Juventud (Isle of Youth) is too sparsely populated to be labelled a province, it is the second largest island of the Cuban archipelago, an unspoiled spot on the earth for scuba diving or just plain meditation, with Indian cave paintings at Punta del Este, and Galápagos-type wildlife of turtles, lizards and sea birds on the surrounding coral keys. Both José Martí and Fidel Castro were imprisoned here.

These brush-stroke descriptions of Cuba's provinces are intended as a convenient overview, so that readers may choose which settings (according to their persuasions) merit further investigation. (If you like mountains, for example, you will prefer Santiago over Camagüey.) Encyclopedic lists of churches, museums and resorts rarely help to capture the essence of a place. Cuba's network of tourist services, from the specialty agency in your home country to on-the-spot tourism offices, provides all the needed pamphlets; regional guide booklets are available in all hotels and airports.

LA HABANA

PLACES OF INTEREST

1. Castillo del Morro (El Morro)
2. Castillo de la Punta (El Punta)
3. Estación Central (railroad terminal)
4. Hotel Nacional de Cuba
5. Coppelia ice cream palace
6. Universidad de La Habana
7. Terminal de Omnibus Nacionales (bus terminal)
8. Jose Martí monument
9. Plaza de la Revolución
10. Estadio Latinoamericano
11. Cementerio de Colón
12. Teatro Karl Marx
13. Consulatoría Jurídica Internacional
14. Maqueta de la Ciudad
15. Cira Garcia International Clinic

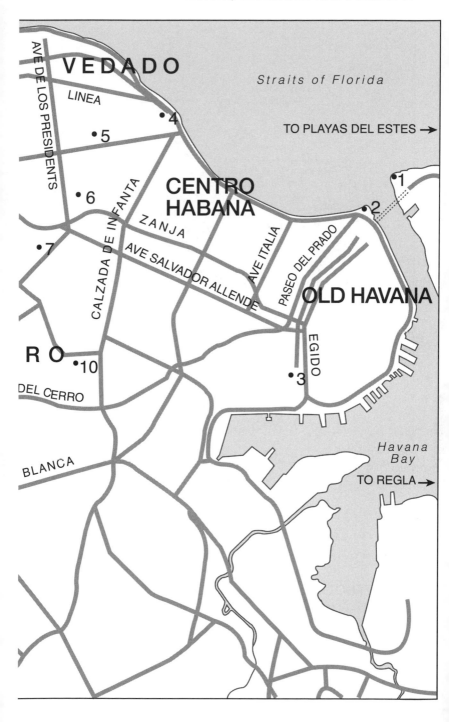

VEDADO

Straits of Florida

AVE DE LOS PRESIDENTS

LINEA

•4

•5

TO PLAYAS DEL ESTES →

•6

CENTRO
HABANA

CALZADA DE INFANTA

ZANJA

•7

AVE SALVADOR ALLENDE

AVE ITALIA

PASEO DEL PRADO

•1

•2

OLD HAVANA

R O

•10

EGIDO

•3

DEL CERRO

*Havana
Bay*

BLANCA

TO REGLA →

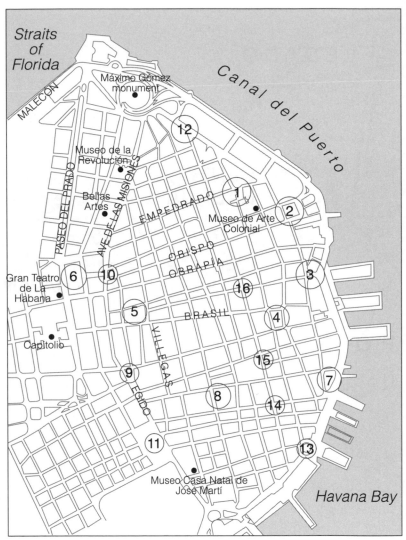

Straits of Florida

MALECÓN

Máximo Gómez monument

Canal del Puerto

12

Museo de la Revolución

PASEO DEL PRADO

AVE DE LAS MISIONES

Bellas Artes

EMPEDRADO

1

Museo de Arte Colonial

2

OBISPO

OBRAPÍA

Gran Teatro de La Habana

6

10

3

16

5

BRASIL

4

Capitolio

VILLEGAS

15

9

EGIDO

8

14

7

11

13

Museo Casa Natal de José Martí

Havana Bay

Compliments of the Office of the Historian of the City of Havana, Master Plan.

OUTDOOR GATHERING PLACES IN OLD HAVANA

1. Plaza de la Catedral
2. Plaza de Armas
3. Plaza de San Francisco
4. Plaza Vieja
5. Plaza del Cristo
6. Parque Central
7. Plazuela de la Luz
8. Plazoleta de Belen

9. Plazoleta de las Ursulinas
10. Plazoleta de Albear
11. Estación Central (railroad terminal)
12. Maestranza
13. Plazuela de Paula
14. Plazoleta del Espiritu Santo
15. Plazuela de Santa Clara
16. Plazuela de san Fco. el Nuevo

CUBANS

CHAPTER 3

"My friends in Cuba, sometimes I envy them,
hanging out and playing football."
BBC World Service, interview, 2006
—Carlos Acosta, world famous dancer, first
black dancer in London's Royal Ballet

THE OLD NEIGHBOURHOOD

Cuba is a country of neighbourhoods. Political forums and elections thrive at the neighbourhood level. The health care system is based on the neighbourhood family doctor who must live on the street where he works, often in the same building of the local clinic. Even a big metropolis like Havana is comprised of many smaller "towns," with all the advantages of belonging to a social network and all the disadvantages of everyone knowing what you're doing.

Forget Privacy

There's a saying in Spanish: *Pueblo chico infierno grande* (small town, big hell). If you come from a culture that values solitude and privacy, you'll have to adjust to Cuba's incessant social interaction.

"It can get pretty intense," says Serge, a former Spanish student of mine and accomplished classical and jazz musician, who now specialises in Cuban music. "Morning and night you're always talking to people. My Spanish is good but sometimes I don't understand everything that's being said. What happens is that you give the impression you've understood more than you have, and this adds to the intensity."

Serge is a very communicative person, socially active, and exuberant in exchanging ideas. When he was in my Spanish class and had just become interested in Cuba, I rated him most-likely to adapt to Cuban culture. I bumped into him by chance a decade later when I went to a restaurant in Los Angeles to hear a group called Makina Loca play Afro-Cuban music. To my surprise, there was Serge at the piano. He'd already been to Cuba three times, with more trips planned.

"I suppose you had no trouble adjusting," I said.

"I'm used to living alone," he replied. "Sometimes it can get too intense, with clinging relationships, and no time to collect your thoughts. But at the same time, that's my attraction to Cuba, where there's a sense of people helping people."

Hugo, an acquaintance of mine, recently left Cuba, disenchanted with economic hardships and in disagreement with how the government was dealing with the crisis. But he has experienced culture in the United States, and glowingly contrasts the Cuban spirit of neighbourhood with his depersonalised suburban setting in California.

"On days off, we left our doors open. Neighbours would stroll in to chat. If someone in the neighbourhood was in need, we would all make sure that he was taken care of."

In order to integrate within Cuban life, visitors who may not be accustomed to a such a people-oriented existence should give up illusions of privacy and get used to having an intense and sometimes overwhelming social existence.

The Prado

My choice of turf was in Centro Habana, a few blocks from the *Punta* (the Point) on the Malecón, just outside of what used to be the rampart that surrounded Old Havana. The Prado was the first avenue to be built when Havana spilled outside of the rampart. Today it is one of the city's many outdoor living rooms. Its wide promenade resembles La Rambla in Barcelona. On either side of the promenade are two lanes for automobiles. Outside the vehicle lanes are sidewalks covered by pillared arcades.

Both the outer sidewalks and the inner *paseo* have built-in stone benches or steps to encourage social interaction.

Typical Cuban architecture. The buildings in Cuba may be old but the dynamism of the environment more than makes up for it.

Live oaks provide plenty of shade from the tropical sun, and big light globes hang from wrought iron lamp posts. The Prado is a tangible metaphor for a section of the traditional Cuban dance, the *danzón*, called the *paseo*, in which the dancing stops and the participants stroll around and get to know each other.

An Informal Economy

The Prado is one of Havana's core scenes for the informal economy. On the surface, it appears as if not much commerce exists, prompting observers from neon cultures to note a drabness in the scene. The absence of electric signs and colourful billboards takes much of the exterior glitz out of business, but every imaginable type of thriving commerce exists at a human scale.

In a used book store, you deal with the owner when asking about a book. At an outdoor beauty parlour (a table and chair on the sidewalk), you receive your manicure from a beautician who takes a direct interest in your satisfaction because she is the owner. If one feels too ill to go to a medical clinic, the doctor, who knows everybody personally within the urban quadrant he's responsible for, will pay you a visit. In fact, if he hasn't seen you in a long time, he'll

probably find the time to knock on your door just to see if you're doing okay.

There are restaurants galore, but few have signs. Some are designated as *paladares* (places of taste) to differentiate them from traditional restaurants. By word of mouth, you find out which apartment buildings have a *paladar*, and you will be attended to by the owner and the cook, who are probably the same person. A full-course dinner can run anywhere from 2 CUCs to 15 CUCs. An alternative is a home-cooked meal in the underground economy beginning for roughly the equivalent of a dollar in Cuban pesos to several times as much.

One makes haphazard distinctions between the formal and the informal economy since formal businesses "look" informal in a homespun way. The characters involved in the thriving informal economy constitute a subculture that is enthralling for anyone who places a value on creative hustling. The names have been changed to protect the characters but the essence of this informal economy is the same. Carlitos, for example, has appropriated one street corner where he is available to meet your every need. In particular, he excels at securing discount taxis. A ride with an "independent" taxi will cost about 30 per cent less than the official government taxi service. If Carlitos gets to know you, he'll want to chat with you about potential business ideas.

Then there is Celia, a university literature teacher who finds an occasional "date" as a *jinetera* to balance her household budget and add a few calories to her slim figure.

More than a few young men, many of them with "friends" in tobacco or rum factories, are out selling cigars and bottles of rum. It's not all business with these disgruntled citizens; if the foreigner they've approached is not interested in any of their products, a few will still want to sit down and chat, mainly asking questions about his or her country and explaining how tough it is to make ends meet.

Julio and Manuel are young men who get "commissions" from local restaurants by finding clients, and then play basketball at the local gym every night.

Amelia is one of the many women who cook creole dishes, out of the sight of inspectors, in their homes for "whatever you'd like to pay." Amelia's dinners are quite special, with a choice of chicken or pork (cooked in bitter orange and garlic), yuca (a tuber cooked with garlic), *congris* (rice with beans), and a varied salad featuring cucumber and delicious Cuban avocados. She'll also rent you her bedroom and move down a rickety spiral staircase to sleep on her living room couch.

You'll pass by street level windows, from which pizza, fruit punch, ice cream or coffee are sold. Most of these places are part of the above-ground economy and pay taxes. But the money changer who takes a small commission per CUC or Euro exchanged does not work with official approval. Once you get to know him, if exact change cannot be made, he'll spot you the difference and trust that you'll come by later with the balance. But better not even try to do business this guy, unless you thrive on risk taking and are willing to pay consequences beyond the commission.

Then there are the roving musicians who play for tips. They play and sing either romantic *boleros* or *guajira* country music. These trios are usually composed of a guitar, a bongo player, and a lead singer, also a guitarist, with all three joining in to harmonise in the chorus. The tapes they sell, for about five CUCs, are not recorded under ideal studio conditions.

Faced with private competition, government-run commerce is improving. A few interesting neighbourhood lunch spots and bars have opened up, catering to the Cuban peso crowd. A Mayabe Beer runs for a fraction of what it costs in the hotels.

You'll also be accosted by a man with a briefcase full of documentation on Cuban government abuses. He's an itinerant Jehovah's Witness, but everyone refers to him as *El Loco*.

Other features adding spice to the old neighbourhood are the bicycle-taxi carriages, the monstrous two-humped camel buses pulled by truck cabins, the vintage automobiles, including an occasional Edsel, the ubiquitous bicycles, which mellow the sound setting compared to the auto-congested neighbourhoods in other Latin American capitals, and the Malecón happening, with hustlers, kids diving off the sea wall into the slurping ocean, and the fishermen, some of whom come up with prized catches that provide a few days of dinner.

Across the strait from the Malecón is El Morro, the fortress that protected Havana against pirates during the colonial period, as seen in this illustration of a 1762 map. On the illustrated map La Punta (on the map labelled "Puntal") is seen at the end of the Prado. As Havana began to expand, the Prado was built roughly parallel to the rampart.

Today, one may transport a bicycle through a tunnel under the bay via the *ciclobus*, a bus with a specially-equipped bicycle ramp. Once on the other side, ride up to El Morro, or pedal along the coast against the pungent sea breeze all the way to Playas del Este, the favourite beach recreational spot for Havana's throngs.

It was on the Malecón where I met Felipe. On his days off, Felipe, an X-ray technician, will be looking for tourists to guide around the city with his impeccable English. Like the youthful cigar vendors, Felipe had lots of bad things to say about the Maximum Leader, but at the same time, he

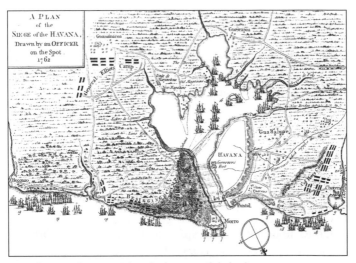

Map of Havana from 1762 (south above, north below)

and the other gripers had nothing but praise for Che Guevara and the original intentions of the Cuban revolution. After you've heard the conversation once, you might as well make carbon copies:

"It's time for Fidel to step down," said Felipe, within earshot of a policeman. "It's a shame that we lost El Che. Cuba would have been different today if El Che had stayed with us."

Whatever the inevitable changes in Cuba, the reality of a typical urban Cuban neighbourhood is not about to change. The strong sense of community, a Cuban custom long before the revolution but nurtured by post-1959 neighbourhood institutions, will remain. The informal economy, a necessity under any economic system, continues to operate in post-Fidel Cuba, mutating to fit within whatever becomes the dominant economic current.

The formal economy will continue to function as well, at a more human level than in more corporate nations. Even detractors of the Cuban system who come from countries dominated by corporate enterprise reserve a few good words for this aspect of the neighbourhood scene.

"Part of Cuba's current charm," writes a sharply-critical Raymond Schroth in *National Catholic Reporter,* "is that it lacks the junk—McDonald's architecture and fast-food plastic and styrofoam in the gutters, waste, the consumption ethic, the relentless assault of advertising."

Substituting for corporate advertising is what Cuban exile Tony Mendoza refers to as *la búsqueda* (the search), which is how people survive in the informal economy by seeking clients for cigars, rum, impromptu tours, informal home-made lunches, outdoor beauty salons and sex.

"Everyone has to *resolver* (to solve, or make ends meet)," writes Mendoza, who was bitterly critical of the Cuba of 1997, after he visited for the first time after 37 years of exile.

In the *Chronicle of Higher Education,* Mendoza urges Cuba to open itself up to modern, capitalistic growth. "People rode bicycles everywhere, reminding me of old newsreels of Asian countries. My cabdriver drove me past 1940s and 1950s models of cars; I felt as if I were in a time warp."

Old Cuban neighbourhoods are indeed a time warp. Old Havana, protected by the revolution's laws against property speculation, remained intact long enough to be labelled by the United Nations as a patrimony of humanity.

But if Cubans suddenly struck gold and were able to exchange their bicycles for automobiles, we would all choke to death in the narrow streets of Old Havana. And if fast-food outlets were to replace family-owned *paladares,* where would we again find home-made cooking with personal service? If the automobile culture were to take over Cuba as it has in much of the world, would people still hang out in their old neighbourhoods? Or would Havana metamorphose into a typical Latin American capital, pockmarked with glass box skyscrapers and plagued by crime, corruption and pollution?

Jineterismo

Jineterismo is the most bizarre aberration of the informal economy. Author Remy R. Leroux Monet's definition of *jineteros* (masculine) or *jineteras* (feminine) is, "those who engage in all sorts of traffic with tourists, even as far as offering their bodies, with the goal of obtaining *divisa* (CUCs): literally horse riders, those who ride on the backs of tourists." They may go as far as to grab the attention of foreigners (called *yumas* in Cuba) by offering to show them around, often seducing them by claiming that they will present them with the "real" Cuba, as opposed to superficial tourist attractions. They may pretend to be interested in your country. You will be suprised at how much a Cuban can know about your country, and *jineteros* will use this to their advantage in conversation. *Jineteros* often work in networks and will try to get you to meet some of their accomplices. At some point, they may introduce you to some "friends", or take you to a place where people will initiate a conversation. And this is where it is set in motion. Your new "friends" will start trying to convince you to accept deals, to fall for a swindle or to be seduced by a prostitute.

Many a Cuban resents these *jineteros*. He works hard for basic necessities while they are often voluntarily jobless, making money by dishonest means. José explains that "things didn't used to be this way", but with the Special Period and the development of the tourist industry, everything changed. "People started becoming cynical. The economic crisis of the nineties has done more than cause the degradation of people's living conditions. It has also eaten away at the moral integrity of many Cubans," José added.

Sense of Community

Mendoza's time warp culture shock is ironic; in his own adopted country, the United States, many citizens are in the process of reconsidering social policy and turning back the clock to the days when personal contact and sense of community were more prevalent, and are opposing knee-jerk municipal decisions to knock down buildings of character and replace them with windowless boxes and parking structures.

Mendoza took 80 rolls of black and white photographs. In Cuban neighbourhoods like mine, even colour photos of groups of people come out in black and white. Had he toted his camera in urban neighbourhoods in Midwest cities like Chicago, St. Louis and Detroit, some of his photos of the people would have come out in all black and the others in all white. The buildings and automobiles in Cuba may look like

Hanging out with friends, practicing the art of conversation: this is Cuba's greatest form of entertainment.

a time warp but the integration between black and white is a contemporary phenomenon that Mendoza chose to ignore.

Without the personal and domestic comforts Mendoza was accustomed to in Cuba before he left at the age of 18 and now in the United States as well, what do Cuban people do? They hang out on the Prado or the street corner or the Malecón with each other. They attend neighbourhood forums and street festivals. Corner bars and parks become public gathering places. This is the old-fashioned sense of community that seduces people from more modernised cultural settings to visit a place like Cuba.

Serge perfers to bypass political polemics. "My whole experience in Cuba was a musical experience. Just hanging out. Not necessarily attending performances. The whole vibe, the hang, it's a soulful place."

"One of my culture contrasts was returning to Miami, to the Cuban neighbourhood there," Serge added. "You just don't feel the soul, that *ambiente*. It's almost shocking!"

AFRICAN HERITAGE

More than a third of all Cubans are considered black, and most other Cubans, many of whom are mulattos, carry the African heritage within their spirit.

West Africa, in particular Nigeria, the Congo, Senegal, the Gambia and Guinea, was the source of slaves brought in by the Spaniards. Most of these West Africans brought with them the Yoruba culture, whose Santería customs (see the section Religion in this chapter) survived the colonial period. Yoruba gods were hidden behind the faces of Catholic saints. Other Afro-Cubans migrated from Haiti and the Bahamas.

Curiously, Afro-Cuban music now returns to the contemporary African music scene. Serge plays keyboard in a California-based Afro-Cuban group called Makina Loca, whose Congo-born band leader and singer , Ricardo Lemvo is of Angolan origins. He is part of the Afro-Latin diaspora which connects back to mother Africa via the Cuban *clave* rhythm.

Even though Afro-Cubans played a major role in history, as exemplified by independence leader Antonio Maceo, Batista, a mulatto, was not permitted to join the Havana Yacht Club. All forms of segregation were abolished by the revolution, and the country is now officially considered Afro-Cuban.

The Callejón de Hamel, in the eastern part of Centro Habana, is a street that has been transformed by the artist Salvador Gonzáles into an unofficial epicentre of Afro-Cuban culture and religion, with public art such as murals and sculptures, and Sunday concerts of the various genres of Cuban music from African heritage.

FRANKNESS

Let the anecdotes and compiled experiences in this book from both Cubans and foreign visitors be entered in evidence that frankness is a fundamental characteristic among most Cubans.

Having lived among New Yorkers, who have made an art form of bluntness, I sense that the Cuban penchant for calling things as they are is less brash and more naive than the New York brand, more stylised, often tinged with sly humour, and sometimes distorted by the human contradictions of the dual currency economy.

MACHISMO

For three decades, Cuban film makers have been producing movies that encouraged women to become independent. Thanks to food rationing and free health care, women have found less of a need to be dependent on men.

With basic necessities assured and equal access to professions, a Cuban woman is much less likely to remain in a bad marriage out of economic necessity, as many of her unfortunate counterparts in other Latin countries do.

Lucía was the first post-1959 film to ridicule the institution of machismo (male dominance). In the third of the film's three related stories, a man risks being ostracised by the whole neighbourhood when he balks at allowing his wife Lucía to participate in evening theatre activities. Enjoying the support of her neighbours, Lucía defies her husband. Decades before Mr. Mom, Lucía's husband was obligated to deal with domestic and child-raising duties traditionally reserved for women.

"But machismo still exists," says Melania, a young woman from the colonial city of Trinidad. "A Cuban woman will split as soon as she finds out her man is not supportive or faithful. All Cuban men chase after women," she adds, smiling and pointing at her husband Nufo.

"That's not true, and you know it!" responds Nufo.

Is Nufo faithful? It's hard to tell because it's not socially acceptable among men to admit that they don't play around on the side. But at least Nufo is not embarrassed to change a diaper.

Many Cuban women think preventively, preferring to live with a man without formal vows, at least until their partner's loyalty is proven.

To what extent does machismo, the Latin form of male dominance, still exist in Cuba? I've asked this question several times in groups of Cubans. My inquiry always provokes a lively debate. The consensus has been "yes, it still exists, but not nearly as much as it used to."

In most of Latin America, male literacy statistics are superior to women's, by more than a few percentage points. In Cuba, male and female literacy are virtually the

same. There are as many women doctors as there are men. Machismo may still exist, but the Cuban woman has been given the educational and economic tools to find her own fulfillment, independent of traditional domestic obligations, should she choose that route.

PERSONAL HYGIENE
In tropical Cuba, informal dress is the rule, but don't let that mislead you. Cubans are extremely fastidious about cleanliness and manage to look well-dressed even with the simplest of clothing.

Writing about post-Soviet hardships, Oppenheimer noted that food scarcity "was not what seemed to bother Cubans the most. What people seemed most irked about was the shortage of soap, deodorant, shampoo, toothpaste, shaving cream and perfume."

PUBLIC GOOD VERSUS INDIVIDUAL RIGHTS
The one custom most apt to cause a case of culture shock among visitors from Western countries is Cuba's stance

regarding the public good. In issues where public good enters in conflict with individual rights, Cubans opt for public good. There is no constitutional right in Cuba, for example, for citizens to own firearms. Individual ownership of guns is against the law. Cubans point to statistics on high murder rates by armed aggressors in the United States as an example of how certain individual rights can harm the public good.

One telling illustration is Cuba's policy for deterring the spread of AIDS. In the United States, gay and civil liberties activists did everything they could to prevent the stigma

> Cuba's first known case of AIDS in 1985 came with a heterosexual soldier returning from Mozambique. The disease later spread to homosexuals.

of AIDS from leading to job dismissals and housing discrimination. The fear of insurance companies dropping coverage for HIV-positive clients was another civil rights issue that influenced public policy on AIDS. These were real fears, as anti-gay sentiment was on the rise.

Fears of infringements on civil liberties caused public health officials in the United States to refrain from applying standard public health disease-containment measures of routine testing of at-risk individuals, even though such individuals would have the right to refuse testing. Also prevented was full-scale confidential reporting; an aggressive attempt to get notification of sexual partners of HIV-positive patients to health authorities was hampered by the individual rights issue.

According to reporter Chandler Burr, "the gay community decided that the disease hurt homosexuals vulnerable to a hostile society at least as much by pitilessly outing them as it did by killing them."

Some organisations defending the individual rights of HIV and AIDS victims warned policy makers that the government could use the virus as an excuse to conduct a new holocaust. The dangerous example they highlighted was Cuba. Cuba was vulnerable to such criticism because of her former policy of social and professional ostracism of homosexuals, a theme explored critically in the prize-winning film *Fresa y Chocolate*.

"Cuba has been notorious for its draconian treatment of people infected with the virus that causes AIDS," wrote Juanita Darling in the *Los Angeles Times* (24 July 1997). "The government has rounded up everyone infected with the human immunodeficiency virus and locked them up in sanitoriums until they developed AIDS and died."

Instead of such draconian measures, many Western countries resorted to sex education, condoms, teaching people how to act with care.

Stories of concentration camps in Cuba for HIV-positive citizens were bandied about without much documentation. In order to set things straight, Cuba sponsored a public conference on its AIDS policy on 7 August 1997. Jorge Pérez, director of Cuba's Pedro Kouri Institute of Tropical Medicine and most responsible for "the most hated AIDS program in the world," was the main speaker.

The statistics Dr. Pérez gave to the audience were confirmed independently by the World Health Organization. Per capita there were 35 times more deaths from AIDS in the United States than in Cuba. The most recent figures from 1993 showed that there were 276 new cases of AIDS per million in the United States. Cuba had only 7 per million. Puerto Rico, a Caribbean territory under the U.S. public health system but culturally similar to Cuba, had 654 new cases per million. But had human rights been trampled to attain these impressive statistics? Was this the classic case of Mussolini getting the trains to run on time?

Delegates to the conference were taken to Cuba's largest sanatorium, Santiago de las Vegas. It was discovered that people with AIDS could choose to stay in or leave the sanatorium. Most choose to stay, since the medical care is superb and they receive 3,500 calories a day in food, much more than the rest of the population was receiving during the Special Period.

Cuba's public health statistics in other realms are equally impressive as its AIDS record, and this comes without economic incentives for its leading professionals. Cuba's chief epidemiologist at the Department of Public Health earned US$ 23 per month at the time of the conference.

Dr. Pérez asked the delegates for more cooperation from outside Cuba. "I want to make people understand," he said, "how damaging the blockade is to our ability to control the AIDS epidemic, to our getting publications, data, research and medicines."

In controlling the spread of AIDS better than any other country in the world, Cuba has used traditional methods of thorough testing, reporting and notification to an extent that may be considered intrusive by civil libertarians, with a sanatorium system that causes advocates of freedom in Western democracies to recoil with culture shock.

"What's different in Cuba," writes author and former AIDS reporter Elinor Burkett, "is that people don't think about individual rights. Most Americans think that when we're balancing social good and individual rights, we err toward the latter. Cubans are trained in the opposite mentality, so my friends in the sanitoriums believe there's a social good coming out of it."

SENSE OF HUMOUR

The Cuban sense of humour has many language-based nuances that might not be immediately understood by foreigners, and much of it is improvised according to the human relationships at hand. The most successful verbal caricatures tend to favour understatement rather than overstatement. But the more satire-oriented Cuban humour, which pokes fun of social realities, is easily understood.

Cuban films from *Lucía* in the sixties to *Guantanamera* in the nineties delight in extracting humour from the most dismal and tragic events. The caricatures of Aristide in *Granma Internacional* (available at Cuban consulates or on the Internet) are examples of a sophisticated form of slapstick. (Uncle Sam, dressed as 'The Blockade', swings a bat against Cuba but ends up knocking down American capitalists who want to invest in the island.) Cartoons that poke fun at Cuban reality and life in general in a non-political way are found on the back page of the magazine *Bohemia*.

The Museo del Humor (Museum of Humor) is located in San Antonio de los Baños outside of Havana, and offers a panoramic history of Cuban graphic humour from 1848 to the present.

WOMEN

Also at stake during the transition period is the independence of Cuban women. Olga Gasaya, vice-chair of the Department of Psychology at the University of Havana has discovered, through comprehensive research, that "in spite of their high level of social and professional achievement and public status, most women still perceive their fundamental role as wife or housewife.

Younger Cuban women who have not felt what it is like to live in more male-dominated societies of other Latin American countries, take the gains in status of women for granted, but remain fiercely independent.

"But the higher achieving they were, the greater the sense of guilt at not being able to fulfill a role in the home. And others who chose to stay at home felt guilt for not participating in professional life."

Given the high level of self-esteem among Cuban women, I wondered how there could be a resurgence of prostitution.

"I haven't done formal research on prostitution," said Gasaya in a radio interview. "But I believe it's connected to the economic crisis. But this crisis affects most women to the same degree. All women look for ways to solve the crisis, but only a small percentage of them resort to prostitution. I think that within this small percentage, many suffer from problems of self-esteem, since there are other methods of self-employment with which women can make good money.

"These are not the type of prostitutes that exist in other Latin American countries," she added, "where it's done for survival. It's very sad and painful for this country, which has made so many strides in the advancement of women."

It is precisely for this reason that the re-emergence of prostitution in Cuba has received such widespread press coverage. No one writes feature articles about widespread prostitution in Mexico and Central America. But for better or for worse, Cuba has been held to a higher standard. If increasing economic growth can be spread evenly throughout Cuban society, the new wave of prostitution should subside once again.

The visit of the Pope in January of 1998 and his call for more traditional roles for women does not seem to have encouraged Cuban women to drop their use of birth control devices and abortion, nor to convince them to marry a man before first living with him and becoming convinced that he will be trustworthy and faithful.

Lots of excitement in front of the Cathedral of Havana

Unlike other third world countries, Cuba has maintained a low birth rate, comparable to developed nations, and Cuban women's groups do not want a return to the unbridled population growth that plagues other Latin American countries.

Cuba's foremost defender of woman's rights is Vilma Espin, head of the Cuban women's federation. Espin has recently called for severe punishment for pimps as well as prosecution of rental apartment owners who allow prostitutes to enter their buildings.

RELIGION

Cuba is the least Catholic of all the Latin American countries, and this does not seem to have changed in the years following the January 1998 visit of the Pope. Why Catholicism is less evident in Cuba is open to speculation. Even before Castro closed all private schools, including those run by churches, and instituted a total separation of church and state, only about ten per cent of Cubans attended church regularly. By 1997, according to Jesuit visitor Raymond A. Schroth, that figure was less than two per cent.

Father José Felix, a Cuban church leader, said: "I have young people coming to my parish who are curious about Catholicism. But they don't even know who Jesus Christ is."

As the most oppressed sector of Cuban colonial society, blacks could be expected to identify with the underdog. In religion, the underdog was Santería, the Afro-Cuban faith with origins in the Yoruba culture of west Africa, as well as other west African creeds.

"Because Christian slave owners in the New World forbade the practice of pagan religions," according to historian Mark Kurlansky, "followers disguised the *orishas* [African Gods and Goddesses] as Christian saints."

Historically, the Catholic Church was part of the Spanish colonial regime. In Cuba, colonialism lasted four decades longer than in most other Latin American countries, and with the Catholic Church as an integral part of the colonial system, some Cubans still associate the Church with abuses of the past.

In nearby Mexico, village priests led the independence movement. But in Cuba, independence insurgents were mostly secular.

"Santería insiders calculated that there were as many as four thousand *babalaos* (Santería priests, also *babalawos*) in Cuba," wrote Oppenheimer. "In comparison, there were only two hundred fifty Roman Catholic priests in Cuba," this in the early 1990s.

Although religious belief was always tolerated during the revolutionary period, organised religion was frowned upon, and regular church goers might find it more difficult to get ahead in their professions. But the *babalawos*, who practice out of their homes, were less restricted than Catholic priests.

In November 1991, the Cuban Communist Party repealed the ban on organised religion and invited religious believers to join the party. In 1992, the Marxist-Leninist definition of the Cuban state was removed from the constitution (later replaced with "socialist" to define the state), further opening the doors to religion.

Even before the Pope's visit, Catholicism was undergoing a renewal of sorts. The Church became an accepted conduit for charitable donations from abroad during the post-Soviet period, and international Catholic organisations such as Catholic Relief Services escalated their aid programs.

"Baptisms increased from seven thousand in 1971 to more than thirty-three thousand in 1991," according to Latin Americanist Ilene Goldman.

Judaism is also making a comeback in Cuba. Recent documentaries on the Cuban Jewish community point out that "Jews suffer along with the rest of the Cuban people." While Cuban-born Jews have maintained their religious traditions to a certain extent, they have tended to assimilate. The Jewish community has no rabbi, but during religious holy days, rabbis visit from Mexico or Canada.

Interviews in these documentaries emphasize Jewish perceptions of an absence of xenophobia and anti-semitism in Cuba. Historian Robert Levine comments that Cuba gave refuge to more Eastern European Jews during World War II than any other Latin American country.

"Even during the revolutionary government's anti-religious campaign," wrote Levine, "Castro bent over backwards not to persecute Jews." He points out that the only private enterprises not nationalised by the revolution were Jewish butchers, in order to allow Jews to keep kosher.

"Hava Nagila: the Jews in Cuba," a documentary, points out that the minority of Jews who decided to remain in Cuba after 1959 were committed to the revolution's social values.

Most Cubans who spoke with this author were not believers in any organised religion but, as one man put it, "that doesn't mean we don't believe in God. But we believe that religion is a personal thing. When it gets organised, abuses occur."

By far, my greatest cultural revelation in the realm of religion was to witness how many white Cubans were followers of Cuba's African religions, especially Santería.

Chano Pozo, the conga player who introduced Dizzy Gillespie to the layered African rhythms of Cuban music, was a follower of Abakuá, a secret African religious society with its own jargon that still exists today in Havana. Abakuá is also a form of rumba performed by the group Los Muñequitos de Matanzas.

Sitting in my neighbour William's living room in Old Havana, surrounded by statuettes and dolls of Santería gods and goddesses, each with little offerings before them, is for me a lasting image of the pervasive existence of Africa in Cuba.

In the Who's Who of Santería figures, the Cuban patron saint is Nuestra Señora de Caridad (Our Lady of Charity), a mulatto virgin. Many Cuban women are named Caridad.

There is Oggún, the war god, who prefers dogs as a favourite offering.

Among the many other *orishas* are: Yemanyá, goddess of the seas, dressed in blue, who during colonial times wore the outer dress of the Blessed Virgin Mary, often referred to in the lyrics of rumba music; Changó, god of fire, wearing red and controlling lightning from the top of palm trees; Obatalá, dressed in white and associated with Christ.

"*Babalawos*," according to Kurlansky, "are trained to always ask questions that can be answered with no or yes—a zero or a one;" "a logical mathematical system," said one *babalawo*, which looks a lot like our binary computer systems.

In stores called *botánicas* in Cuban communities outside of Cuba, statuettes, candles and herbs needed to practice Santería are sold.

Religious beliefs may eventually make a comeback in Cuba. But after having travelled extensively through twelve different Latin American countries, nowhere have I seen a more secular society than in Cuba. From an inspection of Cuba's festival calendar it is apparent that fewer Cuban special events are derived from religious dates than in any other Latin American country.

STEREOTYPES

Two opposite stereotypes coincide. The first says that all Cubans are friendly and generous. The second one would have us believe that all Cubans are out to get our money. Each of these stereotypes originate from anecdotal evidence. For some visitors everything goes perfectly and for others it's a nightmare. Most of us will find something in between.

A second stereotype is that all Cubans are fun-loving hedonists, when in fact, the same Cubans who sway so elegantly on the dance floor may be found with their heads buried in good literature or scientific research.

A final stereotype is political. We are led to believe that Cubans are either for or against their political system. In reality, a whole rainbow of nuances can be seen on the political landscape.

VALUES

Liberty (individual), fraternity and equality. There is a profound sense of community, from one's neighbourhood to one's identity as Cuban. However, at the same time, live and let live prevails, so that a community is not monolithic and idiosyncasies are an accepted part of the community fabric. Each street has its quirky character who is tolerated as an added hue on the colourful palette.

The extreme hardships of the 1990s created an increasing cynicism that could eventually lead to a distortion of Cuban values. As the tourist industry creates class divisions, you are more likely to find some people taking advantage of others, and some loyal communists have left the island because of a perceived breakdown in values of equality.

SOCIALISING IN CUBA

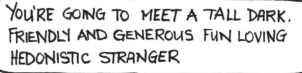

CHAPTER 4

"There is no obstacle to socialising in Cuba, other
than the dual currency that divides some
Cubans from others and converts even the most
proletarian foreigners into privileged elites."
—Author's journal.

STRANGERS IN PARADISE

I arrived late one afternoon in Los Angeles with two children and no place to stay. I'd been hired by a university to teach Latin American literature and had been told that a good place to live was Culver City.

I parked my Ford on a street in Culver City near a public phone and began checking out apartment-for-rent ads from the local throw-away newspaper. The sun was setting and time was running out before I'd have to hole up in a hotel, a difficult proposition with two young kids who needed a place with a kitchen and home-cooked food.

A lady in the neighbourhood, chubby and middle-aged, with a rasping voice and a bright smile, a granddaughter tugging at her apron, noticed we were ambling around. She asked where we were from, in a Spanish accent. I responded in Spanish, and after a few minutes of animated small talk, in which my apartment search was the primary theme, she volunteered a solution.

"Why don't you stay with us for the night, so you'll be able to look for apartments without so much pressure?"

Essentially, she had offered a total stranger a room in her house, just like that. Celia was from Cuba. I wondered if all Cuban people were so trusting of strangers.

She told me how she hated Fidel and how she was so happy to have fled from Cuba. But when the issue of schools for my children came up, she mentioned the disturbing social problems in her daughter's nearby high school. "What we need here is a Fidel!" she said.

Some years later, remarried and in Bolivia, I went with my wife to eat in a Cuban restaurant, owned by a recent arrival from Cuba. I was preparing for my first trip to Havana and was immersing myself in Cuban culture. The restaurant was closed due to an illness in the family. Arnulfo, the owner, was on the premises, and apologised for not being able to serve us.

"But let me invite the two of you to a *mojito*" (a typical rum-based minty Cuban drink). Although we had not known Arnulfo before, he told us about his sister's health problems and how an incorrect diagnosis in Washington had prompted her to come to Bolivia. Soon, Arnulfo was sharing his personal devastation over his sister's brain tumor, the terrible side effects of the medication prescribed in Washington, and the latest diagnosis in Bolivia by a Cuban doctor that there was no such tumor and that the medication itself was the cause of her fainting spells.

These were things that close friends or family members talk about. Arnulfo was telling all to strangers.

CONVERSATIONS

Upon my arrival in Cuba, I soon realised that my encounters with Celia and Arnulfo were typical of the Cuban custom of immediate and beyond-the-surface communication with strangers. In school in the United States, my children had been taught about Stranger Danger, but it seems as if Cubans are brought up to consider strangers as friends until the evidence indicates the contrary.

Blessing In Disguise

One American tourist driving through the Escambray mountains was beset by car trouble and was stranded at the side of the road. Thanks to the mishap, he explained, "I ended up with a personal guide for the rest of my vacation and was guest of honour at a local wedding."

In a country that strives to eliminate the fundamental uncertainties in life, the chance factor is embraced in the realm of human relationships.

Seika, a young Japanese woman studying Spanish and art in Cuba, was "shocked" by "how people immediately talk with you. If one has something to say he'll immediately join the conversation. There is no hesitation. This thing impressed me much in my early days in Cuba. Why do people talk to others so easily? They often say *compañero* to each other. I think this sense of companionship gives them more friendships among strangers.

"They ask anything they want to know and give their own suggestions whether you like it or not. It goes like this: 'You've had your hair cut short, but I prefer it longer. You must not have it cut next time.'

"I would like to say 'That's none of your business,' but anyhow, they mean no harm. Although their insensitiveness sometimes makes me irritated, I've given up because they care about others in any way and any means. They seldom leave me alone. It's difficult to be wholly lonely here."

Gina Margillo, a health educator from San Francisco, California, has the same impression.

"I'd never been to the Caribbean before. The openness of the people, the intense heat, there's an incredible kinetic energy.

"It's the Cubans' frankness. It is so surprising as to seem blunt. I didn't know what to expect, being from the United States. That didn't matter. They were eager to talk with me."

I had planned to spend some time meditating at the sea wall in Havana. If that is one of your objectives, you'd better find an empty beach. If there are people around, they will inevitably approach and begin a conversation.

In many parts of the United States, if you begin talking to strangers they think you're nuts. There is a suspicion about the unknown, about the 'other,' as if all outsiders must be considered as Stranger Danger until proven otherwise.

I quickly learned in Havana that if I was in a hurry for an appointment, I'd better read my map and know my streets, for if I stopped to ask directions, a conversation might ensue and I'd never get there on time.

I also learned to start out for a destination with plenty of time to spare. The people you may meet along the way are going to be more interesting than any planned activity.

The trick is to differentiate between the hustlers who need *divisa* and want to sell you something, cigars, rum, freelance tours, sex and those who simply want to talk and get to know new people from different cultures. The best technique is to be the one who starts the conversation with them rather than the other way around. If you are not used to taking the initiative in meeting people, then that will have to change. And Cuba is the perfect place to start, where you will find many people more than willing to have a conversation. Of course, that will not guarantee that the person you meet is not a hustler. I was having difficulty making the distinction when I first met Soledad. By now, at least, I had learned to counter-interrogate (something entirely acceptable), in order to assure transparency.

SOLEDAD

The sound of salsa music drew me away from my planned route and in the direction of an outdoor restaurant at a plaza in Old Havana. As I stood listening to Afro-Cuban layered rhythms, the chorus echoing the solo singer, and the jazzy bass guitar, a young, sweet voice asked in English if I was enjoying the salsa.

With so many people on the street out to sell you something, I shied away.

"*No tengas miedo*," the young black woman said, switching to Spanish. "It's our nature to talk to people."

I had heard the dangerous phrase "*no tengas miedo*" before, an all-purpose Cuban term that let foreigners know it is normal for Cubans to talk to strangers, used by hustlers and honest people alike.

"Sorry," I said, truly embarrassed. I had arrived for the last song of the outdoor jam session. The people who had been milling around outside the restaurant either went in or strolled away.

"Have you seen the new art exposition?" she asked. I hadn't, and was interested in Cuban art. She led me in toward a gallery, while asking me predictable questions like, where was I from, and looked a little surprised when I told her I was a *gringo*.

Inside the exposition, we both passed on the offer of wine and hors d'oeuvres. Here the hors d'oeuvres were simple white bread sandwiches, and there was a choice of white wine or Cuban cola. The men wore embroidered *guayabera* shirts, untucked, and the women loose cotton dresses. Some of the paintings were totally abstract, others representational. Soledad was most impressed by the ones that mixed the abstract with the pictorial.

Back outside, on the narrow streets, beneath balconies with clothing drying on the iron railings, the afternoon heat and humidity awakened my thirst. I asked Soledad where I could buy some *refrescos* and she showed me a window of a building from which fresh fruit drinks were served in plastic cups. It was one of my first introductions to the Cuban peso economy and I was elated to see that something better than Coca Cola was available to fit the Cuban budget, for just one Cuban peso. We took our drinks to a park across the street, about a block from the Malecón.

Soledad was a university student. She looked in her late teens but told me she was twenty-two. Along with a brother, she lived with her grandmother. Her mother, an ophthalmologist, had remarried, and I got the impression that within the extended family, the children had moved in with grandma a few blocks away, to give their honeymooning mother a little privacy. The mother was making up for what she'd lost. Her former husband had left for the United States in the 1980s, written a few letters, and then disappeared after having remarried.

It had taken Soledad a while to get from the "where are you from?" to the "what are you doing in Cuba?" I told her that I was a specialist in Latin American Studies and I was writing a book.

Suddenly her ebullient ebony face lost its radiance and elongated, like a melancholic Modigliani. She spoke of American writers who had come to Cuba as friends and then had written vitriolic articles that denigrated *el proceso* in Cuba. Curiously, I felt comfort in her suspicion of me, for it had the ring of honesty.

Soledad explained that she was afraid that what she said to me might be turned around into something that would harm her country.

This time it was my turn to say *"No tengas miedo"*, that I just wanted to write about reality, and that I wouldn't be in Cuba if I didn't have a profound love for Cuban culture.

She apologised for her reticence, but had I heard about the terrorists attacks against Cuban planes, hotels and restaurants? They were covert attempts by the United States, she said, to disrupt the Cuban economy.

"You'll have to just look at me, listen to what I have to say, and judge for yourself," I said. "Do I look like a terrorist?"

We remained on the park bench, exchanging ideas about everything under the Havana sun. I learned from this encounter that she was not the type of uncritical supporter of "the process" that I'd expected to meet. When I asked her why Cuba had suffered through a food shortage, she criticised the dependency on the Soviets and the lack of diversification in the economy.

"But now we are producing more food. I know because I volunteer for the student brigades that go to the country to harvest. It's not sugar anymore. We harvest things that you can eat. I enjoy the brigades. There's a great spirit and we have parties every night."

A peanut vendor came by with Cuban peanuts, the ones they sell on the street in paper cones, are roasted crisp, and have a flavour unknown in countries that receive imported nuts. Soledad bought the peanuts and I ran across the street for some Cuban canned sodas.

The peanut lady, looking to be in her sixties, white, with sharp cheek bones on a thin face, said her name was Amelia, and that she cooked for people in her home. In spite of her age, Amelia walked off with the sprightliness of a youngster. I recalled how an old factory foreman for whom I'd worked judged the potential success of job applicants by how they walked. If Amelia cooked like she walked, then her *criollo* cooking was going to be exquisite.

"You won't be disappointed," she said on her second tour of the park. "You'll recognise my apartment building by the small food stand downstairs. That's my stand, but there I only sell snacks."

The conversation with Soledad had been so intense that I hadn't realised it was now dark. I didn't want her to be stranded without transportation and offered to walk her to her bus, which left from the Prado, a few blocks from my residence. She told me not to worry, that there were buses for at least another hour or two. We agreed to meet the next day to continue our conversation. "Why don't we go to Amelia's," I suggested.

Soledad's face turned long and somber again.

"Am I wrong about Amelia?" I asked. "She seems for real."

"It's not that," she explained. "I'm not sure it's right to patronise places like that. It's money that could have gone to a government restaurant that should go directly to the needs of the people."

This new polemic extended our conversation for another half hour. If Amelia had her stand on the street, then she was a tax payer, I asserted. Soledad admitted Cuban business was taxed steeply so that a new commercial class would not emerge to dominate others. In a way, I suggested, when we patronise a tax-paying business, the money goes directly to Cubans. "That sounds better than eating in a government sanctioned, foreign-owned hotel, where a chunk of the dividends would leave the country."

As we walked to her bus stop, I considered asking Soledad to help me with my research. I needed to do at least two hundred interviews. But I wanted them to be as diversified as possible. My idea was to employ university students to do interviews for me. Soledad seemed like an ideal candidate.

"I can't pay a lot," I said, explaining my project, "but I'd pay *en divisa*" (in U.S. dollars).

"I'm not sure about it," she said. "What I do might be used in a way that could disparage Cuba."

I was shocked. Many Cubans I'd met on the street were jumping at the chance to earn dollars, but Soledad balked at the opportunity, even though her family was among the 48 per cent that had no access to dollars. "Soledad," I said. "The questions I need to ask are cultural. I'm not getting into politics."

"Between the lines of any and everything there is a message. We can talk about your idea tomorrow if you wish but I'm afraid I might do harm, unintentionally."

Soledad's concept of solidarity transcended the party line. I could tell by the pride with which she told of her mother's disobedience to authority. A Peruvian man had come to Cuba for an operation on his eyes. Somehow he'd run out of money before the operation. Soledad's mother was supposed to perform the surgery, but she was told by her supervisor that without payment, there could be no operation.

"She disobeyed her boss and operated on the patient anyway," Soledad said. "I'm proud of her for that.".

She looked up and smiled, her dark skin merging with the unlit Havana night, her large, deep-set eyes shining under the street lamp. "Tomorrow we can talk about many things."

We shook hands and I kissed her on the cheek.

"In Bolivia, when we say good-bye, we kiss the woman on the cheek. Is that the custom in Cuba, too?"

"Yes, that's our custom."

I left her on an orderly line to her bus. It was the first stop on the bus route, so when she got on, there was a seat waiting for her.

JESÚS AND MICHEL

My friendship with Soledad was an encouraging sign. Cuba's economy was wounded and stumbling, and most people were operating in survival mode, which meant getting a hold of dollars (now CUCs) in any way they could, short of violence. But there was still hope if idealists like Soledad could turn down a chance for easy dollars on the basis of principle.

She had corroborated Assata Shakur's assertions about Cuba's racial harmony, based on the daily imagery of friendships between blacks, whites, and mulattos. As a black woman, Soledad had said, "I wouldn't think of leaving Cuba. I've heard about the racism in the United States and Spain."

With the idealism of Soledad in my mind, I strolled out to the Malecón one late afternoon to watch the sea and take in the social scene. I stood by the stone wall and watched the waveless sea caress the rocks at the outer base below.

Two young men sat on the sea wall, chatting, a new portrait in black and white, another image of racial harmony, and my spirits were once more lifted.

"Where are you from?" the white man asked.

Both Jesús (the lanky black man) and Michel (a shorter white man with blue-green eyes and curly brown hair) were thrilled to have the chance to talk with an "American."

They seemed in their early twenties.

"Are you in a hurry?" Michel asked. "Why don't you sit down so we can talk?"

After a few stanzas in English, we drifted back into Spanish as the substance of our discussion got heavier. Sooner or later, the subject of economic hardships came up. I asked their opinion about the embargo.

"The blockade is not the cause of our problems," Michel said.

"It's our government," Jesús agreed.

Cuban conversations seem to soar when they are based on polemics, so I took issue. "Both of you guys speak excellent English," I said. "You learned the language in high school. In my country it's rare for students to learn foreign languages in high school classes. You must have good schools."

"We're not complaining about our schools," said Jesús. "We're complaining because we're not allowed to buy and sell things as we please."

Jesús, the black man, was studying at the university and had learned French as well as English. Michel claimed to work in a tobacco factory. They asked me where I usually ate. Politely, they suggested that if I wanted the same quality of dinner for a fraction of the price, they could take me to a place where they received a commission. It was a typical "arrangement" within the underground economy.

"By letting us help you, you'll be helping us."

When I found out how inexpensive the food was going to be, I realised that I could invite both of them and still get off for less than what it had cost me at my favorite *paladar*. Jesús and Michel exemplify the blurry middle ground between hustling and honest communication. A Cuban approaching a foreigner will almost always stand to gain something out of him: in this case, a commission. However, this doesn't neccssarily mean that the people in question are dishonest, and, in this case, Jesús and Michel, seemed authentically interested in having a conversation and talking about their lives.

The conversation with Jesús and Michel was the cynical antithesis of what I'd heard from Soledad, although with the same friendly exuberance. "You know there's racism in Cuba," Michel said. Righteous indignation seemed to flow out from the green in his sparkling eyes. The fact that a white man felt such indignation about racism, I thought, was a positive sign.

"When a black and a white guy are on the street, the cops stop the black guy and leave the white man alone," Michel added.

Michel and Jesús were pouring rain on my parade of enchantment. After Soledad's lofty idealism, I wanted so hard to become a believer. And now I'd met these cynics. Warm and friendly, but cynics nonetheless.

"Well," I explained, "that's a lot like South Central L.A., except back in L.A. or Washington D.C., the whole neighbourhood is black, and blacks complain that they're

constantly being harassed by the cops, just because they're black." "Just looking around here," I said, "it couldn't be as bad as you say. In my country, you don't see blacks and whites hanging together all the time. What's normal here is an exception over there."

Jesús, the black man, just looked on as his friend Michel continued the diatribe, always speaking in the first person plural.

"Believe us," he smiled. "Sooner or later you'll realise that we still have racism in Cuba."

"Let's go eat," I said, wanting a reprise from the unpleasant subject. We left our perch on the stone wall by the sea and crossed the Malecón boulevard. As we reached the other side, a policeman motioned to us with his index finger.

"He's pointing at Jesús," Michel said.

Jesús walked over to the policemen, took out his wallet, and shuffled for his identification card.

"You see!" Michel whispered. "Just what we were talking about! Why didn't he stop ME? Okay, they don't like Cubans harassing foreigners. Maybe that's why they stopped Jesús.

But why not me too? I may be white but don't I look just as Cuban as Jesús?"

"Maybe I can go over there and put in a good word," I suggested.

"Better not. Jesús will resolve."

As the policeman inspected Jesús's ID, I recalled the writings of a Cuban black woman, Lourdes Casal, a professor at Rutgers University. Before the revolution, she wrote, blacks were seriously underrepresented in banks, commerce and professions.

"In Havana, upper-class social clubs excluded blacks and mulattos systematically. In Cuban small towns and provincial capitals, segregation was rigidly enforced," although it blended in with class divisions.

After the revolution, she wrote, Fidel said, "we must prioritise more and more the battle to end racial discrimination at the workplace," and he also called for ending discrimination in recreation centers by integrating public schools.

The stern-faced policeman continued to scrutinise Jesús's ID with squinting eyes.

"Privately," wrote Casals, "many white Cubans—even solid revolutionaries—employ the old racist language. The difference is that there is a tremendous cost in expressing such prejudiced opinions publicly.

"The early redistributive measures of the Revolution improved the status of blacks in particular," added Casals. "The most far-reaching measure of equality was the elimination of private schools that had been mainly white."

"It can be unhesitatingly affirmed that racial discrimination has been solidly eradicated from Cuban society," she concluded. "This does not imply that all forms of prejudice have been banned or that the consciousness of the people has been thoroughly transformed."

Her last sentence referred directly to the policeman, who was now sending Jesús on his way. Jesús had signed some sort of paper.

He walked back to us and grinned.

"He gave me a fine," he said. "Nothing much. My documents were ragged and needed to be replaced."

"You see, Mark," insisted Michel. "Just like we said. Why didn't the cop stop me? Because I'm white!"

Had this been an uncanny coincidence? It had the feel of a staged performance, intended to prove the indignant accusations of Michel.

Mistaken Identity

I later heard an anecdote of a white Cuban that was asked to pay the entrance fee to a tourist site that is normally free for Cubans. Mistaken for being a foreigner, the museum visitor had to show his ID at the entrance to prove that he was Cuban.

Stereotyping is partly responsible for the policeman's behaviour, a type of reflex that supposes that skin colour is some kind of social indicator.

In the 1953 census prior to the revolution, 26.9 per cent of Cuba's population was either black or mulatto, which seems like an undercount, since Oppenheimer refers to the 1959 unofficial total as 45 per cent. But with the post-revolution white flight, Oppenheimer, citing the same unofficial source, now put Cuba's blacks and mulattos in the early 1990s at about 58 per cent of the total population.

At the height of the Special Period, blacks comprised the majority of those Cubans who do not receive strong currerncy from abroad. Only five per cent of the Cuban exile community is black. The new currency-based class divisions may therefore have an unsettling racial component.

Traditionally, Cuban uprisings have originated in the Oriente around Santiago, where Afro-Cubans are in a greater majority. One foreign diplomat in Havana told me that some whites privately fear a new black rebellion beginning in the Oriente.

Once again I had gone from one end to the other in Cuba's paradoxical spectrum. Soledad's idealism and her belief in Cuba's racial justice was the high point. But when the policeman stopped the lanky, good-natured Jesús on the street for apparently no reason, I was left with a queasy feeling in my wounded spirit.

WILLIAM, EDUARDO AND SANTERÍA

But the day had not ended. On the Prado that night, I met another young man, William, one of my neighbours. William gave a few distressing accounts about the hardships his family was enduring and then invited me to his house to meet his mother, sister and cousins.

As in most buildings in Old Havana, the visitor goes through a dark and asymmetrical labyrinth before getting to whichever apartment is on the agenda. The door from the dark hall entered directly into a living room. William's mother, looking in her late fifties, was happy to receive a visitor from her easy chair.

She noticed that I was peering at the strange statuettes on various tables in the living room. "Those are our saints," she said. "The African saints."

William proudly named each of the saints.

With white people believing in a black religion, it was going to be difficult for widespread racism to make a comeback, I thought. Back on the Prado on the way home, I saw that most of the groups of people sitting around and chatting, or strolling back from the Malecón, were interracial.

The Cuban santería religion comes from the Yoruba culture of West Africa. I had heard that many Cubans still practice this religion, even more than Catholicism. But here in William's apartment these were white Cubans who believed in black saints.

The emotional roller coaster was on its way up again. But at any moment it could take another plunge.

"The jury is still out on the impact of the Cuban revolution on race relations," wrote John Burdick in "The Myth of Racial Democracy," from *The Black Americas: 1492–1992*. "The revolution did eliminate the visible, legal pillars of racism, and it seems to have enjoyed the support of poor blacks and mulattos."

Two years later, by chance, I found myself climbing a dark and funky colonial staircase in Centro Habana. The door opened. The tone and warmth of Eduardo's voice suggested that he would be a finalist for the Gracious Melodious Meditative Host Award. Like William, the curly-haired Eduardo might be identified as a white Cuban, but since he'd worn the all-white garments for the obligatory year of those who convert to santería, the neighbours called him

"El mulatto." This was my new home stay, surrounded by figures, *orishas* like Changó, lord of fire, thunder and virility, dressed in red; Yemayá, in blue and white, the patron saint of the bay and the sea; Obatalá, in white, the god of peace, justice and wisdom (the *orisha* that represented Eduardo's identity); and Elegguá, lord of the crossroads who shows us the way (my own *orisha* of preference). Eduardo talks softly, with a priestly serenity, but his stereo blasts out the history of Cuban music, from pre-revolutionary balladeers and the original *soneros* to the modern *salseros* and contemporary classical composers, and his neighbours also call him "*El músico.*" In sensorial counterpoint with the colours of santería and the *boleros* of Olga Guillot are the crackling aromas of Eduardo's cooking.

Eduardo's friends file in and out, mainly university professors and bureaucrats. The discussions are eclectic and probing: the role of the Cuban exile music of Celia Cruz in continuing traditions, the crisis in the university as the percentage of registered black students diminishes, the heavy taxing of independent entrepreneurs. Eduardo, like so many other followers of santería, maintains a secular lifestyle. Santería helps solve daily dilemmas. There are no hordes of fundamentalists.

No five-star hotel can compare with the cultural wealth of a home stay in an earthy Cuban neighbourhood. Around the corner from Eduardo's house, I chanced upon a ceremony in the courtyard of an apartment building. The people, all of them black, ushered me in. They gathered behind three percussionists playing rumba rhythms. The beer flowed freely. They pulled me into a dance around a ceiba tree in the centre of the courtyard, where offerings of pineapple and other exotic fruit were placed at the foot of the tree.

They were the tenants, commemorating their return to their renovated building, a vivid testimony of Havana's ambitious restoration project. This building happened to have been the residence of Chano Pozo, the percussionist who, back in the 1950s, taught Afro-Cuban rhythms to Dizzy Gillespie drummers, ushering in the era of Cubop music. Chano Pozo had been a member of an Afro-Cuban cult called

A trio of conga players at a santería ceremony commemorating the restoration of an apartment building that was once the house of the famous Afro-Cuban percussionist, Chano Pozo.

Abakuá. Amidst the glorious contagion of rumba rhythms, a young man stood before the *ceiba* tree and chanted phrases from a Yoruban language.

GISELLE

The 'default' procedure in a book on Cuba is to feature a salsa performer. That's the prototypical image that seduces all of us salsa lovers. I decided to bypass the stereotype and instead profile a classical performer. After all, Cuba is a country of every imaginable music genre. (Lots about *son*, rumba and salsa in later pages.)

Giselle Grau Garcells was born in the provincial city of Holguín in 1979. Following in the footsteps of her grandfather on her father's side, she began studying the piano at an early age. By the age of ten, she had won the first of many prizes, this one for best interpretation of Cuban music, at a music festival in the province of Las Tunas.

When I first met Giselle Grau, at a solo concert, she was 18 years old, had already performed in Mexico, Italy and South America, and was an international prize winner. At her concert she played baroque and contemporary music with the same ease. I was seated next to a professional pianist, who was astounded by Giselle's professional serenity, effortless virtuosity and above all, her ability to evoke the epic passion of complex compositions like Ginestera's Sonata No. 1.

Following the concert, I hesitated before going up to introduce myself to the pianist. I'd spoken to numerous performers, even those with a reputation for being 'difficult,' like Thelonious Monk, and never had a problem. But Giselle was a prodigy, and the prodigies I'd met before had usually been spoiled and arrogant.

I congratulated her on the concert and asked if I could meet with her for a longer interview. She had been the star of the evening. Usually, when I approached celebrities for an interview, I'd be asked to explain my intentions, to give a short history about the newspaper where I worked, and a number of other preliminaries.

"Please come and visit," she said. She smiled the way one does on the street with neighbours, with no sign of the self-satisfaction of being the centre of attention. She jotted down her address and phone number in large, confident letters. It was a typical Cuban response, with immediate trust of the stranger neutralising even the most legitimate feelings of apprehension.

I watched her respond to other well-wishers. Her modesty came so naturally that I wondered if she would ever learn to bask in glory. Was this a young person who simply did not realise the magnitude of her accomplishments, or was she so mature in her simple but elegant dress that nothing fazed her?

In Havana, Giselle Grau lived with her uncle and aunt, where she could be near the National School of Music and study with the great classical and jazz pianist Andrés Alén. Her uncle Julio insisted on going to meet me at my residence and walking me to his house.

My first surprise was to see Giselle informally dressed as I greeted her with a handshake. Curled up on the sofa, she looked ten years younger than she had at the concert, like anyone's teenaged daughter. The second surprise was to

By age eighteen, Giselle Grau had played solo piano concerts on three continents, winning awards at home and abroad.

hear her talk. She sounded as mature as her interpretation of Schumann and Lecuona.

"In the beginning I studied very little," she said. "But it was not out of rebelliousness. I began to take it seriously when I was fourteen."

That was the year she'd won a trip to Italy. But with all her accomplishments, she'll only practice three or four hours a day, "because I intend to finish my regular studies."

"When there's a concert or contest, I'll practice seven or eight hours a day."

No matter how hard I tried, I could get no response that implied any sort of sacrifice, none of the self-aggrandizement that one usually hears from people who work very hard to earn their laurels. What made it worth the toil for Giselle seemed to have little to do with the glory. In fact, there is no celebrity industry in Cuba. Professionals and artists are expected to be like everyone else, receiving a few extra perks for remaining among the faithful.

Giselle seemed to fit in the mold. She spoke more enthusiastically about her joy of music than her personal goals. "There's no one period I favour," she said. "I can find something exciting in most composers and all periods. I'm charmed by Bach, but I also love Samuel Barber. You have to make a sacrifice to play some of his works, and it's worth it."

I looked around the living room for signs of privilege in Giselle's Old Havana residence. The street outside was in typical disrepair. Inside, the high walls needed painting. It was more spacious than other Old Havana apartments I'd visited. The living room chairs were generically old but comfortable. The paintings on the wall, representational art with a touch of abstraction, were interesting but not collector's items.

"We thought we had an original that might have been valuable," said Julio, pointing to one of the paintings, "but it turned out to be nothing special. But we like it."

The only suggestion of privilege in the whole living room was a Sharp fax machine, the same basic model I used at my home. What the family had not accumulated in material possessions was compensated for by culture. Julio had studied three careers at different points in his life: diplomacy, literature and a technical field. With a commercial elite still lacking in Cuba, a cultural elite had emerged, including scientists, artists and scholars, and Julio fit in perfectly.

"Those people you see out there hustling in the street," he said, "could have studied anything they liked, and for free. If they chose not to study, it's their decision."

Lourdes, Giselle's blond aunt, served me a cup of rich Cuban coffee.

A month before this interview, pitcher Liván Hernández had been named the most valuable player in baseball's World Series. He'd guided his Miami team to the championship. Hernández had earned about US$ 10 a month on Cuba's national baseball team until he'd defected to the United States where he's earning millions.

"We don't blame Liván," Julio said. "Sartre writes about man's liberty to choose. Liván made a philosophical decision. Over here he was an anonymous hero."

"We had the choice of leaving with my father in 1960," said Lourdes. "We could have left but the idea never occurred to us. We only expect that those who leave should send back a percentage of what they earn to help the country. It's not Liván's leaving that bothers us. It's the way he did it."

I was happy that Giselle's uncle and aunt brought up the question of leaving one's country. Giselle had the talent to earn a comfortable living abroad, and I'd wanted to ask her if she'd ever thought of the idea. What would she do if she received a generous offer on one of her trips to remain abroad.

"Giselle," said Julio. "Be honest with your answer. Remember that you have the freedom to choose your destiny. Whatever you choose in your life, you would do so with our blessings."

Giselle seemed far removed from the ideological implications of the discussion.

"I'd love to receive a scholarship to study abroad," she said. "But that would be temporary. I like it here."

Her response was too vague, so I asked her to be more specific about what she liked.

"When I've gone to perform in other countries," she said, "I was distressed to meet so many musicians who had to study other careers and play music on the side. Music was not considered a profession in their countries, and so they couldn't develop themselves professionally the way I can here."

"That shocked me," Giselle continued. "They do not call music their career. Here in Cuba, music or the arts in general is considered a career, just as legitimate as being an engineer or a doctor."

"Here the arts are accessible to everyone," added Julio. "I know in some countries, most people cannot afford to hear a symphony orchestra. Here, there are symphonic concerts every Sunday and they only cost five Cuban pesos (about US 20 cents)." "In spite of all our hardships these days," he continued, "we have not allowed culture to be sacrificed."

Without knowing it, Giselle Grau was a part of Cuba's cultural elite. Her total nonchalance about her professional achievements reflected a remarkable indifference to celebrityhood. The music itself, and not the glories it promised, was her sole ambition.

During most interviews, the star elaborates on his or her accomplishments and then hopes the interview will end so he can get back to his business or pleasure. Giselle Grau Garcells was relaxing deep in the sofa, enjoying the conversation, with no rush for it to end.

With today's globalised artistic structure, musical careers are international by definition, and no performer from any country can afford to remain at home. Eventually, Giselle went to Spain in order to pursue her career at an international level. Liván's case was really an exception. Like most Cubans who perform abroad, Giselle returns regularly to her country.

The Bohemianisation of Ramón

Like Giselle, Ramón is a talented professional but, with no source of *divisa*, he's obligated to camp out on the sofas of family members. Just before the fall of the Soviet Union, he earned a scholarship to study biology at a university in Eastern Europe. He learned English, French and German. He completed his degree at the competitive University of Havana and has published at least six scientific papers. He works for a government science agency and uses his considerable computer skills, earning the equivalent of US$ 14 a month. But, unlike Giselle, he sees no rosy future and makes no attempt to hide his bitterness. Since he's not a dancer or singer, he does not have the means to travel around the world and return to his home base.

Dilemma

What do foreigners do when we befriend a person like Ramón, a cultural elite who cannot afford to eat for two dollars in the Hanoi Restaurant? The dilemma for the visitor is how to differentiate between a majority of Cubans who ask for nothing and those who hope to gain from a relationship with a foreigner. There's a trickier grey area between the extremes, a type of friend like Ramón who asks for no handout but sees me as a person who might rescue him from his dilemma.

"My family supported me with great sacrifice so that I could earn a degree, but for the past eight years I've lived a disastrous economic situation. People who don't have five per cent of my studies live a hundred times better than I do."

Ramón has also published short stories, won scholarly awards, and could analyse Spinoza and Kant as well as the messages of Oggun and Changó.

Curiously, should Ramón, a believer in the ideals of Che Guevara, ever choose to leave Cuba, he would do so because of the inequalities of the incipient market economy.

Ramón represents the tricky dilemma of relating to Cubans. Even if the wounded subsidy system were to be miraculously fixed, Cubans were to survive on food coupons lasting two weeks, and housing contracts allowed tenants to pay only a tenth of their salary toward rent, there would still be the difference between the two currencies. For Ramón to travel abroad, he must pay his airfare in CUC. The airlines flying out of Cuba function within the global currency exchange, which means that they are affordable for a French or a Canadian scientist but not one from a dual economy country like Cuba.

As visitors to these countries, we must find a way to relate to people as social and cultural comrades, even though it's blatantly obvious that we've come from places with a stronger currency. Walking this adventurous tightrope of human relations can be stressful, enriching, tragic, and humorous.

REVISITING AMELIA

Two years after I'd first met her, Amelia still prepares fine dinners in her apartment that's buried in the dark, labyrinthian corridors of an Old Havana building. She sells seconds from the Montecristo cigar factory where her son works. A dollar each, five for four bucks. She also 'rents' her bedroom to lovers, willingly moving to her sofa.

"We could get married, you know, for business reasons," Amelia offers. She's 20 years my senior. I couldn't hide my surprise. "Don't worry," she assures. "You wouldn't have to have sex with me."

Here, Amelia gets by. In a capitalist country, Amelia might have become CEO.

THE CRACKDOWN

Amelia praised the end-of-the-century police crackdown that has become institutionalised. She'd once been mugged selling peanuts and tantalised me with the scar on her left leg. She feels secure about her black market operations, since she once paid taxes for a food stand.

Ramón disagreed with the crackdown. I was walking with him at night along a street in Centro Habana, along with his sister, and we were stopped by two policemen. Ramón was furious. He told the cops that they had no right to stop him just because he was black. His sister tried to calm things down. She told me to stay out of it. After five minutes of negotiating, Ramón had shown his ID and was free to continue our stroll.

"Those cops are making three times as much as a scientist, and they didn't even finish school," he complained.

"At least most of them don't carry firearms" I remarked. "Amelia seems to think the crackdown is good."

The conversation spiraled on, winding down with Ramón's remark that Cuba was a catastrophic place to live in, and that, "we need another Che."

At the same time, Fidel argues that street hustling was a subversive activity so hotels do not allow *jineteras* into the rooms of guests. When the Cuban revolution originally eliminated prostitution and crime, it did so by offering opportunity and pride to those who were in need. Policing was a mere backup. When policing becomes the only means available, when economic and social incentives are not at hand, the task becomes more difficult. Even the much-hyped crackdowns of Mayor Giuliani in New York were accompanied by an unprecedented economic recovery.

FIDEL BASHING

Defenders of the revolution refused to see it, but it was there, on every street corner, in many living rooms. By the mid-1990s and on into the new century, many Cubans were losing their faith in the man who had once done so much to improve their quality of life.

Fidel's defenders continued to reel off the same achievements in health care, education, and culture. But simmering Fidel-bashing had become a poorly kept secret. In the beginning it was the standard "we need another Che", but as time passed, the discontent ran deeper.

It's All Fidel's Fault
One afternoon, I was chatting with friends on a Centro Habana balcony and the topic shifted to food. Naively, I asked if anyone knew where I could get soy yoghurt. I explained that I was not fond of meat and used soy products as a healthy substitute. I was met by a chorus of laughs.

"And we thought that soy yoghurt was no good," said one of the men. "Because Fidel recommends it!"

Others were not so cynical. Some time before the ailing Fidel was replaced by his brother Raúl, a friend named Liván once reeled off a laundry list of Fidel's errors. "The ration system today is largely symbolic," he explained, "with subsidised food lasting a week and a half out of the month.

"But you saw, when my daughter was sick, how the clinic on our block took care of her, and how her food and clothing are provided for. We see all kinds of things that could be better, but when there's an election and we consider the alternatives, we vote on the side of Fidel."

Many of Fidel's potential detractors defended him on the grounds of nationalistic pride. They knew that Fidel bashing had been fomented by the United States government and Miami exiles. They knew that *Forbes Magazine* had blatantly invented a statement about "Fidel's millions", based on a hapless fabrication of probabilities. They knew that when Fidel was gone, they might end up as second-class citizens under the economic control of returning exiles. Meanwhile, both detractors and defenders of the revolution underestimated the cynical reactions of Cuba's disaffected youth, people like Renato.

RENATO, TRACKING DOWN ELPIDIO VALDÉZ

Progress, Renato believes, can only be achieved by hustling in the streets. The bright-eyed Renato approached me one dark night along a dark street of Centro Habana with a box of Cohiba cigars at a bargain price.

In another place and time, dashing Renato would have been picked up from the street and groomed as a star actor or pop singer. He is what Cubans call a mulatto, the combination

He's called "Colorado." He hangs out everyday on the Prado, helping people find whatever they need for a fee, just like Renato.

of Spanish and African. By his side was his faithful squire and apprentice Beto, a young white man flashing a perpetual smile, dazzled by his master's verbal gymnastics. I applied my hustler's test, asking for something impossible to find (in this case, two hard-to-get, vintage photos for a book).

"Give me a day," he said. "Meet me on this same corner, tomorrow at the same time."

"Five dollars per photo?" I said. "That okay?"

"Fine. What's your name?" he asked.

I jotted my name down on a piece of scrap paper.

"Ah," he said, studying my scribbles. "Like in the movie Kramer versus Kramer!"

"You got it."

Next day, the agile Renato, not a bad basketball player when he wasn't out hustling (a shrewd point guard) showed up with the smiling Beto tagging along. I came to the corner with ten dollars, prepared to throw in a T-shirt as well.

Renato swaggered over, flashing his prize-winning smile, holding up the photos in triumph.

I promised to return the photos one day. Since then, Renato and I would see each other from time to time, chatting mainly about his favourite subject: survival. During the Soviet presence, he'd been too young to appreciate the subsidised lifestyle. The abuses of the Batista era were distant abstractions. His formative years corresponded with Cuba's severe depression of the 1990s. At first he'd accepted the explanation that the U.S. blockade was responsible for his privations. But the Special Period extended, eroding his optimism. He quit his job and took to the streets, treasuring the material possessions he could purchase with the privileged CUCs he could earn from the tourists: a shiny belt, a leather wallet, a T-shirt with a foreign logo. Tourism was supposed to bring prosperity to Cuba, wasn't it?

Memento

The day I was leaving Havana, the two of us shook hands, with Renato suggesting: "How about if we swap wallets?" It was an uneven trade, totally in his favour, but I gladly accepted. No tourist souvenir could compare with Renato's wallet.

On my return to Cuba nearly two years later, I found myself in the same neighbourhood. My face was buried in a map, looking for the way to the Almendares River. Out of the corner of my eye, I glimpsed an agile figure moving like a point guard.

"Cramer!" he shouted, "as in Kramer versus Kramer."

He held up my wallet like a banner. He was beaming. I took out his photos from my shirt pocket. We strolled for a while.

"I've had to take a job with the Ministry of Health," he said. "The police are checking up on us. It was getting too hot for Beto, so he moved to another neighbourhood and got a job."

I had spent part of my day searching in vain for copies of vintage Elpidio Valdéz comic strips. Elpidio was a fictional hero from Cuba's war of independence. The used book store proprietors had warned me that older editions of Elpidio were hard to find.

"I'll try to find some," Renato said.

"Where do we meet?" I asked.

"I'll find you. Don't worry."

The next evening I was out strolling with some friends and I heard a voice call out. I saw some magazines under Renato's arm and I knew he'd tracked down Elpidio Valdéz. I presented him to my friends, we did business, and he melted away into the narrow dark streets of Centro Habana.

Renato pays about a buck fifty for his subsidised rent in an historic colonial apartment building in Old Havana. He has the right to go back to school for free and study a profession.

"Why study?" he thinks, "when I'm making more than a doctor or an economist, right here on the street."

JON AND TONY

Jon and Tony don't know each other, but both have made recent trips to Cuba that were written up in the *Chronicle of Higher Education*. Both are trained scholars, and both broke social and political barriers by travelling to Cuba. Tony Mendoza is from the Cuban exile community, where it is frowned upon by many to help Cuba with tourist dollars. He went to Cuba on a sabbatical and shot 80 rolls of film. Jon Torgerson was part of a group of 175 Americans who travelled to Cuba in order to defy the travel ban in 1993. Since then he has taken groups of college students to Cuba on an annual credit course from Drake University in Iowa.

Both Tony Mendoza and Jon Torgerson have interviewed hundreds of people in Cuba. They should have a lot in common. Yet they see Cuba with a totally distinct vision. I have travelled in many countries throughout the world and lived for extended periods of time on several continents. From my personal experience, no place has inspired such profoundly contrary points of view as Cuba.

I've taken the literary license to juxtapose quotes from Tony and John. Taking place when Fidel was still at the helm, this conversation is conjured up directly and precisely from the words and writings of these two individuals. How two thinking people can look at the same image and see two different things suggests that your trip to Cuba will be an existential one, with your own life experience colouring everything you see.

Tony: Passengers on the flight had warned me that I was going to find a ruined Havana, but what I saw still surprised me. The same old factories that had lined the airport road during the 1950s were still there. After 37 years of socialism, the buildings (Havana's architecture) seemed to be exact copies of the ruined monuments of Greece and Roma. Instant antiquity.

Jon: (With nostalgia in his voice) It reminded me a lot of what America was like in the fifties, except there were all the rainbow colours.

Tony: As long as Fidel is around, nothing will change.

Jon: Even though Fidel has been opposed to partnerships with foreign companies, the people discussed this and the Party Congress endorsed the plan.

Tony: [What about] the absence of most basic freedoms?

Jon: A just society is one which first provides social and economic conditions which are sufficient to implement civil and political equality. We in the United States generally focus on the latter. Thus, we condemn a society which denies freedom of the press with no corresponding word of praise for that same country when it increases its literacy rate from 50 to 95 per cent or makes genuine progress towards eliminating poverty. I gave a paper on human rights at the University of Havana and got no flak at all. I was critical that Cuba emphasizes social and economic rights at the cost of civil rights.

Tony: [What economic rights?] Most Cubans work for the state, which pays an average salary of US$ 8 a month. On that pay, it's not possible to eat two meals a day.

Jon: Some of my own students see a lot of poverty in Cuba. I don't. I think the people, compared to those in other Latin American countries, are doing quite well. (Aside):   At a 1987 Equal Employment Opportunities Commission hearing, presided over by the now

U.S. Supreme Court justice Clarence Thomas, Jon Torgerson declared: "I'd rather be among the worst 10 per cent in Cuba than the same bottom level in the United States because of Cuba's social support system. One way of judging a society is how it treats its least fortunate." Thomas got upset, and rifled off a letter to the National Endowment for the Humanities protesting Torgerson's part in a conference with NEH funding.

Tony: People look depressed, beaten down. They stare into the distance, as if in a trance, as they wait for buses or in endless food lines, or when they sit on the sea wall, staring intently toward the horizon, toward Miami. The liveliness, humour, wit, and energy that I have always associated with Cubans are mostly gone.

Jon: My students have many different opinions but they're really impressed with Cubans' sense of community, being able to do things without money. They're overwhelmed by the cultural wealth.

One day I will try to bring Jon and Tony together for a cup of rich Cuban coffee. After all, they do agree on one thing:

Jon: Americans should see Cuba for themselves, but their government won't let them.

Tony: The United States should eliminate travel restrictions to Cuba and let Americans go to Havana.

I hope Tony and Jon will read these pages and make a point of getting together. The discussion will be exciting.

Tony: Few people are happy with socialism, with the Revolution, with Fidel.

Jon: I think Cuba is a viable alternative model for developing countries.

COMMUNITY
Many Americans who delve deeply into the Cuban way of life are particularly surprised at the sense of community,

while Europeans from more traditional settings will be less perplexed.

U.S. political exile Assata Shakur says that "being in Cuba has allowed me to live in a society that is not at war with itself. There is a sense of community. It is a given in Cuba that if you fall down, the person next to you is going to help you get up."

Health educator Gina Margillo believes that sense of community contributes to the long life expectancy of Cubans by providing an emotional support system. Cuba may one day become a part of the "global village," but the local neighbourhood will remain the nucleus of Cuban social life. It remains to be seen whether the dual currency dynamic of haves and have-nots will make a dent into Cuba's sense of neighbourhood solidarity.

As has been noted, the most practical way of establishing roots in Cuba is to hang out in a neighbourhood of choice. Find out who your neighbourhood's "public characters" are. They could be a bartender, the operator of a beauty parlor, an enterprising youngster, a hotel concierge, a street vendor.

Immerse Yourself in Cuba

This concept of staying within a neighbourhood goes against the grain of even the best travel guides, which operate on the encyclopaedic assumption that the more places you visit in the shortest time, the more quickly you will adapt.

In Cuba, the fewer places in which you spend the most time will offer a newcomer the greatest chance to become part of a sense of place and culture.

Once these people have interacted with you more than once, they are more likely to offer helpful advice. By all means, branch out into other neighbourhoods and regions of the country, but having a base is the practical way to grow roots.

SOCIAL STATUS

Rosa Elena is a Bolivian woman, recently returned to her country after studying for nine years in Cuba, where she received a university degree, *licenciatura* (equivalent to a bachelor's degree), in chemistry. The theme of her thesis was zeolites as natural fertilisers. She had also lived and studied in Bolivia and Argentina. She makes comparisons between social status in Cuba and other Latin American societies.

"In Cuba, there is no barrier between professor and student, and teachers are more demonstrative." "There is often a type of partnership between students and teachers," she added, "and teachers have such a degree of self-confidence so as to be very disciplined and yet not be afraid to treat students as friends, whereas in Bolivia they maintain a greater professional distance.

"It's the same way in the society in general. In Cuba you don't feel you need to maintain appearances for social reasons. I can honestly say that I feel freer in Cuba than in any other country, and I've also spent time in Germany and Sweden besides the other countries in Latin America.

"What freedom is there in countries where you are obligated to maintain appearances based on social pretensions? For me, it's the freedom here to not have to show off this or that, to not be obligated to do things that will allow me to feel superior to others. There are some social differences in Cuba," she admitted, "but they are more cultural than based on class.

"It's not only that a person doesn't have to show off material possessions. In Bolivia, a person with a university degree must be called *Licenciado*: professionals, even the mediocre ones, fall in love with their degree, and use it to feel superior to others. This does not happen in Cuba."

"But couldn't this be a regional rather than a cultural thing?" I ask Rosa Elena. "You've referred to the Caribbean way of life and you've implied that people are less formal in tropical climates. So maybe this lack of social pretensions is simply a question of the climate. What about Santa Cruz, in your native Bolivia? It's tropical, and in that way similar to Cuba."

"In Santa Cruz, you still have people trying to feel better than others, showing off their new car, and things like that. In Cuba, even where cultural background is advantageous,

professionals are considered at the same level as everyone else. It's this freedom from a system of social pretensions that I like about Cuba. For this reason, if you gave me the choice of Cuba or any other country, I'd choose Cuba."

On the other hand, there seems to exist a type of ideological pretension among bureaucrats. A European diplomat, whose name I cannot mention because of his diplomatic status, confirmed the existence of ideological pretentions within government circles.

"Cubans have much human warmth and are quite communicative," the young man said. "But I must confess that my greatest cultural barrier here has been my failure to get through the official discourse. There's a prevailing rhetoric that prevents me from communicating at a more profound level with government officials."

Consumer Culture

Perhaps the greatest uncertainty during Cuba's transition relates to the worldwide consumer culture and how it may eventually effect social relationships. Many people are attracted to a place like Cuba because, in the absence of McDonald's, recreational shopping, new cars, glitzy commercial districts, throwaway plastic bottles, commercial

TV and a celebrity industry, the philosophy of "the best things in life are free" has been converted into an art form.

A day at the beach, dancing, playing or watching baseball, soccer, volleyball or basketball, street festivals, and mainly hanging out with friends and neighbours, these are all major pastimes in Cuba that don't cost a penny. You don't have to go shopping to be happy. In fact, the concept of shopping relates strictly to obtaining what one needs.

Cubans complain a lot, but even griping seems to be a pastime. Is it possible that those Cubans who, by choice or obligation, remain without a consumer culture have been just as happy as the throngs in the shopping malls of the surrounding countries?

"It would be hugely misleading to portray the lot of most ordinary Cubans—even those without access to hard currency—as a condition of grinding misery," wrote Oakland Ross ("Living in Cuba With and Without," *Toronto Star*, 25 May 2006). In fact, as they stride along the Obispo pedestrian mall in Old Havana or stroll up and down La Rampa in the Vedado section of town, denizens of the Cuban capital give precisely the opposite impression. Whatever their ages, they invariably seem well-dressed, well-fed and apparently content. A foreign visitor will search in vain for evidence of the desperate poverty, especially child poverty, that blots the human landscape of almost every other Latin American capital. Cubans may not earn much money, but most necessities in Cuba are either cheap or free."

In the first edition of this book, we urged that, "Someone should invent a happiness gauge." Well today, happiness research is an up-and-coming science. *The Happy Planet Index* (www.happyplanetindex.org) rates the happiness of nations based on a formula that adds life expectancy with life satisfaction (based on extensive interviews), then divided by the ecological footprint (per capita consumption of planetary resources). It represents "the efficiency with which countries convert the earth's finite resources into well-being experienced by their citizens." Cuba gets a flattering sixth place ranking. Before you jump on the next flight to Cuba, you should be aware that Cuba scores well precisely

The ideal Cuban way of relaxing, smoking cigars and hanging out in the neighbourhood.

because it consumes considerably fewer finite resources per capita than Miami or Minnesota. Within the research, one life-satisfaction indicator is not as flattering, suggesting that Cubans are less satisfied than their overall ranking.

Could it be that Cuba's sense of community has replaced the consumerist need for keeping ahead of the Joneses? With the opening of the economy, will a sense of commodity replace a sense of community? Thus far, businesses entering Cuba and catering to the local population operate in a mode of fulfilling needs rather than creating needs. Many foreign entrepreneurs seem socially committed to preserving Cuba's human ecology. But that seems likely to change, and consumerist psychology has been on the rise ever since the dual currency system was established by pragmatists within the government, against the wishes of Fidel Castro.

Etiquette

The most complex etiquette scenarios are determined by the dual currency dynamic and have been amply covered in previous chapters.

Most rules of social etiquette are either implicit or blatant in the anecdotes in this chapter as well as within the "Dos and Don'ts" part of the Endlims section of this book. Some things are worth repeating. Informal dress does not mean sloppiness, and Cubans are notorious for being impeccably neat and well-groomed. Cubans often shower twice in the day, morning and evening. You can be as different as you please on the inside, but neatness and cleanliness is the right policy.

Not much to learn about dining etiquette, which is in keeping with basic western cultural customs. As in Latin cultures, when two parties drink or dine, one invites. In the Cuban case, the person from the strong currency country (you) is the most apt to ask for the check. Cubans can invite when food or drink falls within the peso economy. When invited to a Cuban home, by all means take a gift. But rather than flowers or a bottle of wine, consider something practical, relating to the dinner itself. By all means, ask what food you can bring (and prepare, if you have a kitchen facility in your *casa particular*).

Once you get together, a favourite topic of conversation relates to the family. Strangely, in a country with a high percentage of recomposed marriages with second partners, or with couples that live together without marrying, family values are still alive and well, and in Cuba, that means extended-family values. With life expectancy on a par with developed countries, oldtimers play an important role in the community, and there are numerous programmes to help the elderly keep active.

In most Latin American countries, customs differ from urban to rural regions. Following the Cuban revolution, virtually all resources were used to bring rural quality of life up to a par with urban living. Furthermore, students from urban centres do social service projects in agricultural regions, and agriculture is promoted in urban centres. Therefore, the visitor does not face culture clash between urban and rural settings. That said, Cuban *guajiros* (rural dwellers) tend to be more timid or less socially free-wheeling than their urban counterparts.

Alternative sexual lifestyles are increasingly tolerated but Cuba is still a macho culture and an open display of homosexuality is not recommended. In 2006 and early 2007, Cuban TV was airing a soap opera that is intended to make citizens more tolerant of homosexuality. Cuba is not a Calvinist culture and heterosexual inhibitions would constitute strange behaviour.

In the end, the best way to relate to Cubans is to be yourself. As islanders, they have less of a chance to move across borders, but their relatively high level of education makes them genuinely interested in other ways of life.

SETTLING IN

"Seasoned international travellers will recognise certain proven methods for exchanging currency, renting housing, finding or creating employment and relating with local people which are constant and universal in most countries in the world, regardless of the culture. None of these methods are applicable in Cuba. The adventure of settling into Cuba is unparalleled."
—Author's journal

HOUSING

Housing is scarce, and in a country that prides itself on sheltering all its citizens, apartments are simply not available to foreigners, unless they are diplomats. The easiest way for a newcomer to survive financially in the realm of housing is to live in a *casa particular* (home stay), which is the only easy alternative to a hotel. Don't accept any informal offer for you to stay in someone's house, since even if the people are trustworthy, unapproved rentals are not allowed and you wouldn't want to trigger any legal problems for them. Authorities (policemen, CADECA employees, etc.) may ask you to furnish them with your legal address. Home stays are well-regulated and monitored. Owners risk losing their licence if anything happens to you or your posessions while you are there, so they will take precautions to insure your safety. Seasoned travellers to Cuba arrive with a hotel voucher for two days, which avoids complications with Cuban authorities, and gives you time to look for a *casa particular*. Writing for a reservation in a home stay is ineffective, as mail to and from Havana is slow and unreliable. However, it may be possible to make a reservation though associations that specialise in cultural exchange with Cuba. Of course, using a middleman makes this option more expensive. Home stay agents and sometimes proprietors themselves hang around hotels looking for clients. They will find you. To avoid a possible finder's fee, stroll in your favourite neighbourhood and you'll find the blue or green triangle sticker with *"arrendedor divisa"* or *"arrendedor inscripto divisa"* written on the doors of registered *casas particulares*. Expect to pay 20 to 30 CUCs per night. A home-cooked breakfast may be included. You may try to negotiate for a lower price if you are staying for a longer period of time, as low as 15 CUCs per night. Home stays are not necessarily less expensive in other areas outside Havana. Be aware that approved home stay proprietors pay a stiff business tax, even if they have vacancies for part of the month. The tax could thus end up more than the income from their residents. The price of a home stay is less than what it appears, considering that utilities are paid for by the owner.

When you agree to a home stay, you will usually receive some sort of contract. If none is offered, you may wish to ask for a simple one.

The best location of a home stay depends on your preference. Near tourist areas may be more convenient but getting out of the centre of town, even only a 20-minute walk away, will remove you from hustler territory.

Websites with Information on Home Stays

- www.casaparticular.info (free list, no commission)
- www.bicyclingcuba.com/casas.html (free, no commission)
- www.cuba-junky.com/cuba/cuba-casa-particulares.htm
- www.cubaparticular.com/ (a notch above in price scale, probably including commissions)
- www.casaparticulars.com/ (good site, but prices are higher because of commission to middleman)

There are ways to buy an apartment, but laws are constantly changing, currency is unstable and expected transitions in the economy mean that only experienced speculators should take the chance.

Hotel accommodation for the first day should be booked in advance so that you can give an arrival address to immigration officers. Once in the hotel, one of the cleaning staff may provide unsolicited information about a home stay. For budget travellers, the Islazul state hotel chain offers moderate prices with good quality.

I've known other foreigners who decide to live in a hotel. (Hotels are listed in the Resource Guide.) They are able to take their meals with a family, which is healthier and more economical than eating in restaurants on a daily basis.

Longer term rentals of aparthotels, condos and apartments is a new phenomenon which figures to develop. A company called Real Estate Cuba, www.realestatecuba.com/, offers aparthotels at the Eastern Beaches (Playas del Este) for 26 Euros (US$ 34) per day, and claims to have brand new furnished apartments available in Havana. This was the first company to have official government approval for such business. They also offer office space.

WORK

There are three ways in which a foreigner may work in Cuba. Idealists who are not worried about the next month's rent may volunteer with any of several "brigades". This is not a bad idea for those who would like to work alongside Cubans in housing construction or agriculture.

Most people who are considering lengthy stays in Cuba would prefer to support themselves. A second alternative is to establish a business. The third alternative is to find a source of currency from your home country. Since the cost of living in Cuba is relatively cheap and dollars go a long way, even a minimal salary from your native country will suffice, at least to survive. Your own creativity is required here. Virtually every profession may have something to learn from Cuba. For example, a music school in your country of origin could pay you to make recordings of Cuban music groups. Your community newspaper might offer you a modest stipend for articles on your impressions of Cuba. Your teachers' union might have funds available for you to study Cuba's education system. The possibilities are endless.

PERSONAL SAFETY

What will happen if the Cuban government does not find successful measures to bridge the gap between those

Read Between The Lines

According to an unclassified document from the U.S. State Department, "foreigners are prime targets for purse snatching, pickpocketing and thefts from hotel rooms, beaches, historic sites and other attractions." What the document does not say is more illuminating. Violent attacks and use of firearms in robberies are virtually non-existent; the streets of Havana are considerably safer than those of Washington, D.C.

who have access to CUCs and those who don't? Cuba is a relatively safe country, because most people have a role in the society and hardships are endured collectively, but also because police presence in the streets is very blatant. It is much safer to be out on the streets at night in Havana than in Caracas, Venezuela, Lima, Perú, or Mexico City.

Havana streets are dimly lit, and yet the one foreigner I know who was robbed in Cuba was pickpocketed at a brightly-lit dance in a glitzy hotel. Luckily, my friend from Holland had travel insurance that covered his loss. So don't suddenly let your guard down because things look safe.

If Cuba were suddenly to open its doors to an unbridled free market, class divisions would materialise quickly, and the personal safety situation would be likely to decay.

In the meantime, exercise the normal measures of caution. Violent crime is not a major concern for foreigners, but petty crime and scams involving belongings and a 'redistribution' of currency may be imminent if the traveller does not take the proper precautions. Don't flash expensive belongings. Don't put all your money in the same pocket or wallet. Walk on streets where there are many people (not hard to find in Cuba's cities at any hour of the day or night). Do not send money in the mail. I have received reports of mail theft. One traveller reported to me that she was the victim of credit card fraud after she had used her card to rent a car. She was eventually reimbursed by the credit card company. The dual currency has created a scenario of haves and have-nots heretofore unknown in Cuba, and a silent and non-violent army of Cubans desperate for CUCs, is engaged in petty hustling. Smiling hustlers may charm you out of your money. Almost any person who tries to start a converstion with you in the street will want something from you, no

matter how friendly and disinterested the person may seem at first, according to the more cynical Cubans. The best way to meet honest Cubans is to follow the advice of José: "Don't let Cubans approach you. You approach them". This will diminish the risk by far.

One of the major threats to foreigners is prostitution, an activity that is dealt with by the iron hand of the law. It is not so simple, however, since it is not always easy to tell the difference between a legitimate erotic encounter and one that has a financial goal. While some Cubans may delight in having an adventure with someone from another country, others may expect some form of financial benefit, be it CUCs, presents, free meals at a restaurant or some other experience they would otherwise not be able to afford. It is hard to tell if they are spending time with the foreigner only for financial reasons or primarily because they are intrested in meeting someone new.

Prostitutes (also known as *jineteras*) are not part of networks of human trafficking that you would find in Europe or Asia. Most of them will turn a trick because they are desperate for hard currency. The legal age for consentual sex is 16 among Cubans but for tourists it's 18: another legal dualism. Sex with a minor is a crime.

José explains that while certain prostitutes may "work" independently (though you will often see them in pairs), others may have pimps to whom they will hand over a percentage of what they have earned. Many will present themselves not as prostitutes, but as people looking for a good time, and may try to extract money from you along the way. They may appeal to your pity by explaining how difficult their life is, extracting money from you in the end, without your realising that it was all for the money. Others may be even more cynical, by trying to get the foreigner to actually fall in love with them, and creating a seemingly long-term relationship.

On how to meet someone for an adventure, José gives the following advice: "Don't let them be the ones to seduce you. As with anyone else in Cuba, you go to them. You start the conversation. Some people may try to to make you think that it was you that seduced them. It may start as a quick stare, to get your attention. Then you will go to them thinking that you are a Don Juan, a real conquerer. In reality it is them who are conquering you. So be careful. Make sure you see their ID and know where they live before you invite them to your room."

"Don't be fooled", explains José. "This is done with the hope that you will send her money from abroad. She may claim to be in love with you, but it is really for the money. Or maybe she will try to persuade you to help her leave the country". There are also those who will try to get to your wallet. They will seduce you to get access to your room and steal your money while you are not looking. You may spend a very sensual night only to have it retroactively expunged when you wake up in the morning to find your *compañera* vanished and your wallet mysteriously empty.

Some of them may even present themselves in the typically white dressing of practitioners of Afro-Cuban religion. What better way to gain your trust. This is called "putting up a saint act". In the case of pimps (*jineteros*), they will probably present themselves as friendly people interested in meeting you. Eventually, they will present you to a "cousin" or "sister" or "friend" who seems interested in an adventure. In reality it is all business.

Your "friend" is a *jinetero* and his "cousin" is not related to the "friend" at all.

As an extra precaution, you can keep your money safely hidden and locked in your luggage. Know also that you are not allowed to bring someone to your hotel room. If you are in a home stay (*casa particular*), make sure you ask the owner what his policy is regarding bringing guests into the room. One owner told me that any person I might invite to my room would have to first show their ID and sign in with him.

"This is for your protection," he explained "because if anything happens to you, I get in trouble with the authorities." Also know that an owner using his *casa particular* for prostitution is strongly punished by the law, so avoid that type of situation. Whatever the situation, always carry a condom.

Also know that pornography of any kind is illegal. As for drugs, don't even think about it. Cuba is draconian on drugs.

IMPORTANT DOCUMENTS

Very few photocopy establishments are available to the public, and it would be wise to carry a photocopy of all important documents, such as your passport, visa, and airline tickets. In most countries, we are accustomed to finding photocopy stores all around town. Anticipate your photocopying needs in advance, and get the job done before you arrive in Cuba. It is more reliable to leave your original documents in a safe place in your hotel or home stay.

PHOTOGRAPHY

Military installations are off limits to photographers. Museums may have special regulations, so the visitor should inquire at the front desk. I've seen people taking photos at airports and train stations, but legally, rail and airport facilities are off limits to photographers.

Between noon and 4:00 pm, light may be so strong as to alter the quality of color photographs for those who do not have the right filters.

TIPPING

Tips are not included in the bill. Tip a small amount, in the same currency as your bill. There is no fixed percentage and ten per cent is only a gauge for customers who need to have some figure in their mind. Most Cubans will offer help to visitors in need without expecting remuneration, but within the informal economy, hustlers expect a finders' fee. Musicians deserve your help as tips may be their only income.

EMOTIONAL CONTRADICTIONS

For some visitors, the most difficult aspect of adjusting to their stay in Cuba is the emotional bewilderment caused by constantly contradictory images and opinions, ranging from unfettered optimism to bitter cynicism.

The visitor to Cuba may be only minutes or seconds between sublime joy and heartrending sadness. The best defence against the emotional roller coaster is to arrive without preconceived notions and then to accept the fact that life in Cuba unfolds with no simplistic answers.

CUSTOMS (WHAT CAN I BRING?)

Visitors are permitted to bring to Cuba, duty-free, for personal and not commercial use: personal jewellery, a camera, a movie or video camera, a portable CD or tape player with ten recordings, a portable tape recorder, a portable TV, a portable typewriter or word processor, a children's stroller, a tent and hiking equipment, medicines intended to last for the period of stay, two bottles of an alcoholic beverage, a reasonable amount of personal hygiene products, athletic equipment such as a bicycle, fishing gear, canoes or kayaks less than five metres long, two tennis racquets, and other sports equipment, and any other articles that do not exceed a value of 100 Cuban pesos. No food items allowed.

You're even allowed to bring in cigars for personal use, but who'd need that in Cuba? Customs laws may suddenly change, so it would be wise to consult your nearest Cuban consulate if you are travelling with equipment.

But What Should I Bring?

If you plan on travelling to the back country, you might need mosquito repellent and anti-itch medication. There's no law that says you have to bring a camera, and many seasoned travellers feel distracted by having to take pictures. But you will inevitably find good friends in Cuba; photographs will thus acquire a personal value transcending the scenery. With your camera, you're allowed to bring five rolls of film. Film is available in Cuba, and camera shops are found in most urban neighbourhoods.

Other items you may need: an extra pair of glasses, an alarm clock, soap and detergent to save a trip to the store, tampons, standard medical needs, a plastic bag for soiled clothing, a Spanish-English dictionary, and a sweater or light jacket for the winter or even for the summer if you intend to sit in air-conditioned restaurants, where one can suddenly feel quite cold. The sun is sometimes merciless

in Cuba, so sun block is indispensable, especially for those with fair skin.

DOCUMENTS

Tourists will be issued a tourist card visa (around 22 CUCs, depending on when and where you get it) by a travel agent specialising in Cuba or by the nearest Cuban consulate, upon presentation of a passport valid for at least six months. Your passport is also a necessary document, and it is highly recommendable to carry a photocopy of the key pages of your passport in case it gets lost.

A business tourist visa card will cost approximately US$ 60 plus a processing fee (about a month's wait). An independent journalist who is unknown in Cuba might as well go as a tourist, since the Cuban bureaucracy is hypersensitive about journalists. The tourist visa card is usually ready in 24 hours. For a student visa, contact your nearest Cuban consulate, or for Americans, the Cuban Interests Section in Washington, D.C.

For long-term stays or more specific types of travel related to business or humanitarian organisations, consult your Cuban consulate.

MEDICAL CARE

Medical service for foreigners used to be free, and it still may be in case of emergency. Today, in larger cities, travellers must pay in CUCs at international clinics. In smaller towns, free emergency treatment may be available by default. Rules are open to interpretation by medical staff. If you travel through a tour agency, travel insurance is compulsory. For example, Cubalinda's clients pay US$ 3 per day, and that covers emergency medical treatment, hospitalisation, lost luggage, theft and other incidentals. (See www.cubalinda. com) This and other tour agencies work through Cuba's official foreign health insurance, Asistur. The advantage of having Cuban insurance is that you won't have to contact your agent back home. Asistur's Havana office is at Prado 254 and is open 24 hours a day.

If you have a health problem, ask for the nearest SERVIMED clinic. The U.S. embargo has caused a shortage of certain pharmaceutical products, so if you have a pre-existing condition, bring your medicine with you, including copies of prescriptions, in case customs authorities inquire about your medicines. Cuba has been able to produce some of its own medicines and medical equipment, and in some specialty areas, maintains state-of-the-art treatment that attracts "medical tourism." Cuban doctors may lack certain equipment or medicines, but they are as skilled and caring as the best doctors in the world.

No inoculations are required for travel to Cuba. The most common affliction of visitors to Cuba or any other developing country is travellers' diarrhoea. By drinking only bottled water, you greatly reduce the risk of getting diarrhoea. Using sunscreen, getting enough rest, and drinking plenty of non-caffeinated and non-alcoholic beverages are other preventive measures.

MEDICAL TOURISM

Among the many people I sought out who have gone to Cuba specifically for medical treatment, only one complained in any way, and his complaint involved being overcharged. I have no direct experience in receiving

I know of one case in which the foreign visitor ran out of money before finishing the treatment, and the doctor finished the treatment for nothing even though she had been advised to discontinue the treatment. I also know that Dr. Jorge Crisosto, the Chilean doctor who has done volunteer work in Cuba, when faced with deciding between Chile, Cuba, and the United States for sending his mother for cancer treatment, chose Cuba.

medical treatment in Cuba, so I am not in a position to make any recommendations.

In 1996, Cuba received 5,365 patients, mostly Latin Americans, but including 1,218 Europeans and 92 Americans. According to a BBC account, those statistics remained about the same in 2002.

SERVIMED is the organisation that oversees Cuba's facilities for health and medical treatment of foreigners. SERVIMED's Dr. Raúl Pría has mentioned Cuba's innovative treatments for night blindness, vitiligo and neurological disorders. Ciro de Quadros, a Brazilian physician who works for the Pan American Health Organization in Washington D.C., has said that Cuban medical care in some fields like orthopedics is better than the rest of Latin America.

Cuba's medical tourism is not without its social critics. By channelling limited resources to first-class treatments for a foreign market, Cuban nationals suffer shortages in certain medicines and health care amenities. Defenders of the system say that, without the hard currency that comes from medical tourism, health care for Cubans would lose some of its financing. But Hilda Molina, former director of Havana's International Center for Neurological Restoration denounced a situation of medical apartheid and resigned from her powerful post. Clearly she was holding her country to a higher standard, since dual health care systems exist anywhere in the world where private care is superior to public Medicaid programs.

Ironically, the capitalistic profit motive and not socialised medicine creates a scenario where sophisticated medicines are available for health tourists while some basic medicines are not available to Cubans. Depending on whom you last spoke with, such contradictions are caused by either the trade embargo or government mismanagement. More than 500 different medical products are manufactured by Cuba's pharmaceutical industry, yet production has not recovered to pre-1990s levels. State-of-the-art medical treatment, such as heart and liver transplants, are available to all Cuban citizens, yet some Cubans may not be able to find certain basic pharmaceutical products.

The main clinic for foreign medical visitors is Clínica Central "Cira García" in west Havana. Call SERVIMED for information. Some specialty clinics are listed on the next page. For information on these and other clinics and health retreats, contact SERVIMED through your nearest Cuban consulate. The best strategy before considering serious treatment is to speak with people who have gone before you. Travel agencies specialising in Cuba are a good source for finding previous patients who have received treatment in Cuba.

For Specific Information, Contact SERVIMED Through a Travel Agent that Specialises in Cuba

- Centro de Histoterapia Placentaria treats complicated skin disorders with a product derived from the human placenta. Dr. Carlos Miyares Cao is famous for his cures of skin disorders.
- Centro Internacional de Retinosis Pigmentaria "Camilo Cienfuegos" has personalised treatment for each patient to detain or reverse the process of the hereditary disease Pigmentary Retinosis.
- Hospital Clínico Quirúrgico "Hermanos Ameijeiras" has advanced techniques and a successful tradition of heart, lung, pancreas and other transplants.
- Centro de Microcirugía Oftálmica treats myopia, astigmatism, glaucoma and cataracts.
- Centro Iberoamericano de Transplante y Regeneración del Sistema Nervioso does promising research in the treatment of Parkinson's disease and other nervous system disorders.
- Centro Internacional de Restauración Neurológica (CIREN) has had promising results in treating Parkinson's and other nervous system maladies.
- Hospital Ortopédico Nacional.
- Villa "El Quinqué" specialises in the treatment of addictions.

STUDY OPPORTUNITIES

Education is a high priority for Cuba. Since all education was nationalised in 1961, there are no private schools in Cuba. It is free for all Cubans and compulsory between ages six and 16. Primary school lasts six years, followed by three years of basic secondary school. Pupils then continue their secondary education, choosing between pre-university education and technical and professional education (which both last three years). Those who complete pre-university education are awarded the *Bachillerato*. Technical training leads to two levels of qualification—skilled worker and middle-level technician. Successful completion of this cycle gives access to the technological institutes.

After secondary education comes higher education, provided by universities, higher institutes, higher pedagogical institutes, centres of higher education and higher polytechnic institutes.

Schools and Study Tours

For study opportunities in higher education, check the following:

- Mercadu, Cuba's largest association specialising in study sojourns for foreigners, offers courses in a wide variety of fields and in different parts of Cuba. Intensive Spanish classes are held at the University of Havana. Mercadu also organises many of Cuba's international conferences and symposiums. For information on tuition, room and board, dates and subjects, and annual seminars, write to: Mercadu S.A., Calle 13 No. 951, esq Avenida 8, Vedado, Havana 23, Código Postal 12300, Cuba. Phone: (7) 33-3087 / (7) 33-3273 / (7) 33-3893; fax: (7) 33-3028

- La Escuela Internacional de Cine y Televisión offers superb study programmes. This author has interviewed several students and former students, including one of Bolivia's foremost film makers, Marcos Loayza. Public transportation to the facilities near San Antonio de Los Baños outside of Havana is irregular, but students are given free bus service to and from Havana.
  Address: Escuela Internacional de Cine y Televisión, San Antonio de los Baños, Aptdo. Aéreo 40/41 La Habana, Cuba.
  Telefax: (53650) 38-22246 or 38-2368
  Website: www.eicTV.org

- Oficina de Relaciones Internacionales del Instituto Superior de Arte offers courses in rhythm instruments, dance, and other arts-related subjects. My friend Serge took courses here and speaks highly of his experience. Courses are participatory, and dialogue between students, teachers, and guest artists is the norm.
  Address: Instituto Superior de Arte (ISA), Calle 120, #1110 e/9na y 13. Cubanacán. Playa. Ciudad de la Habana. Cuba.
  Phone: (7) 2080017 / (7) 2080288 / (7) 20804;
  fax: (07) 33-6633; 24-7037
  Email: isa@isa.cult.cu

(Continued on the next page)

(*Continued from previous page*)

- EduToursToCuba is very closely oriented to students enrolled at high school and university levels, offering programmes with or without credit. Also, customised programmes for working professionals with a very eclectic menu of themes. People over 55 years old are also encouraged by this interesting new company that began operating in 2002.
  Address: VCC, 5059 Saint Denis, Montreal, Quebec, H2J 2L9, Canada
  Phone from USA/Canada: 1-888-691-0101, or (1-514) 982-3330; fax: (1-514) 982-2438
  Website: www.EduToursToCuba.com
- Cuba Education Tours offers a large menu of attractive and unusual learning experiences.
  Zunzún Education Services and Cuba Education Tours
  Address: 708 - 207 West Hastings Street, Vancouver, British Columbia, V6B 1H7 Canada
  Phone: (877) 687-3817 (Toll Free) / (604)-874-9048 Vancouver / (778) 859-1048 Cell; fax: (604) 874-9041
  Email: info@cubafriends.com
  Website: www.canadacuba.ca
- Universidad de la Habana. I have interviewed several people who were quite happy with their studies at Cuba's foremost university.
  Website: www.uh.cu
- Global Exchange, 2017 Mission St. #303, San Francisco, CA 94110 USA. Phone: (415) 255-7296; fax: (415) 255-7498.

Students planning to study at the University of Havana or other institutions of higher education need a valid high school diploma (*bachiller*), a health certificate, a student visa and must be willing to take compulsory Spanish courses. Cuban universities are free for Cubans but tuition for foreign students can be between the equivalent of US$ 4,000 to US$ 7,000, with financial aid available. Most of the above programmes will furnish step-by-step instructions, and your agent, may be able to circumvent some of the steps that independent travellers would have to do on their own.

CURRENCY

Before the Special Period, it was forbidden for Cubans to carry dollars, and many of those who did ended up in jail, even if some judges were reluctant to sentence them. But with the fall of the Soviet Union and the development of the tourist industry, the Cuban economy needed a strong currency, and the ban on the dollar was lifted. This created a situation where two currencies were used for different products, but where not all Cubans had access to the strong currency, creating inequalities that hadn't existed before. Many products could be sold in Cuban pesos, but for others, such as imported goods, it was necessary to pay in dollars.

This situation changed abruptly in 2004, when the Cuban convertible peso (CUC) was established, replacing a strongly devaluating dollar. One CUC is worth roughly 25 cuban pesos. The CUC is a national currency in addition to the Cuban peso, which means that Cuba still has a dual currency. This also means that there are still a majority of Cubans who don't have direct access to the strong currency, since, with a few exceptions, Cuban salaries are exclusively in Cuban pesos. Therefore, most Cubans will need to scrounge for CUCs.

The advent of CUCs has brought about some changes from the previous dollar scenario. For example, CUCs can be used anywhere and can be used to buy anything, which was not the case with the dollar. However, the situation can still be confusing for someone who is new to the environment (and even, apparently, to some Cubans!). Some stores will sell products in CUCs (therefore too expensive for most Cubans) and others will sell products in Cuban pesos. Some stores will have both types of products, and you will have to ask the owner what currency to pay in. In places that specialise in products sold in Cuban pesos, you can pay for them with the equivelent in CUCs. In this case though, you will recieve change in Cuban pesos at the exchange of one CUC for 24 or 23 Cuban pesos rather 25. For example, if you pay one CUC for 20 pesos worth of fruit in an outdoor market, you will receive two or three Cuban pesos as change instead of five. A few rare places will reluctantly accept the equivalent in Cuban pesos for a product that should be paid for in CUCs.

Cubans in need of CUCs will have to improvise to get them. Some have access to them thanks to relatives living in other countries who send them foreign currency (dollars, euros, etc.) that can be exchanged into CUCs. Others will negotiate with neighbours in posession of CUCs in order to get some. For example, one person will offer to clean another person's house in exchange for the strong currency. Many others will resort to hustling. The target of these hustlers will be foreigners. While some of them will try to honestly sell you something in exchange for some CUCs, others will try to take advantage of a tourist who is still not familiar with how things work.

One risk for people visiting Cuba is exchanging money. Creative and seemingly charming hustlers will find ways to persuade and convince foreigners of situations that don't correspond to reality in order to extract CUCs or foreign currency that can be exchanged into CUCs. They may lie about the exchange rate, pass Cuban pesos for CUCs, or use other more sophisticated fictions that create confusion among visitors who are already confused by both the dual currency and the baffling laws. For example, one technique that seems to be commonly used is to fool visitors into believing in the existence of a third currency reserved for Cubans. Of couse, such a currency would be at a more advantageous exchange rate, and conveniently, the Cuban telling you that lie would be the one to be able to get them for you. The hustler may try to do the exchange himself, or, to gain the trust of the tourist, may take you somewhere that he will pass off as "official".

Another tactic is to gain your pity by telling you how hard their life is, and then persuade you that if they take you to someone who will do such a convenient exchange, they will get a commission. They may also take you to a bar or a restaurant and place you within a charade of a money exchange that will make you think that you were somehow misinformed about currency in Cuba. It is important to take into account that these people more often than not work in networks. They may even take you for a drink first, expecting you to let your guard down under the effect of alcohol. In the end you will realise that you were given Cuban pesos that are worth practically nothing. Counterfeit money is not unheard of. Once you find out you have been fooled, the hustler will be long gone. Even savvy tourists have fallen into these traps.

The only place where you are to exchange money is in an official money change office, called *Casas de Cambio* (CADECA). Never accept exchanging currency anywhere else, no matter what people may tell you. CADECAs are not hard to find and easily recognisable by their logo. You may find one inside a hotel, or you can ask at a hotel desk where to find one. A CADECA will always have a guard at its entrance, and at the booth, they will ask you for your ID, and perhaps even the address where you are staying. Always make sure they give you a receipt. There, you can exchange euros, pounds or other currencies for CUCs. You can exchange dollars too, but you will get less in the exchange, as there is a ten per cent surcharge. You don't need to exchange for anything other than CUCs, since they can be used anywhere, and don't believe anyone who tells you otherwise.

The exchange rates at the beginning of 2007 were approximately:

Cuban Convertable Peso (CUC)	1.0000
Pound (GBP)	0.5473
Canadian Dollar (CAD)	1.2659
Swiss Franc (CHF)	1.3433
Japanese Yen (JPY)	130.27
US Dollar (USD)	1.0800
Mexican Peso (MXP)	11.829
Euro (EUR)	0.8329

CLOTHING

The north coast of Cuba, including Havana, is not as oppressively hot as other tropical areas of Latin America, but it can be stifling during the summer. Winters are mild but a sweater and windbreaker are advisable. Informal dress is the custom, but remember that in spite of their informality Cubans are extremely neat and well-groomed.

SHOPPING

It is shopping in Cuba that will show us the difference between having access or not to CUCs. Products purchased with CUCs will most often be of better quality than peso items. The rare shopping malls will sell products in CUCs, such as household items, clothing, sporting goods, food, toys, cleansers, electronic items (compatible to US appliances). CUCs are also required in other stores (mainly offering packaged food, drink and cigarettes) and restaurants. However, it is worth checking out commerce that receives Cuban pesos. Remember that such establishments accept CUCs, but give you change with the equivalent in pesos. You can then spend that change in the places accepting pesos. For example, it is advisable to go to the *agropecuarios*, the outdoor markets, where you will find good quality fruit and vegetables at surprisingly low prices. Bakeries offer a similar food shopping experience. Flea markets are to the peso economy what malls are to the

This *mercado agropecuario* is visual evidence of a Cuban revolution you rarely hear about: the only country ever to pull off a massive conversion to organic agriculture.

CUC mode. Once the peso economy opens up to you, happy discoveries may be made at cafeterias, snackstands, *bazares* (where you can get clothes, tools and sundry products) and book shops. The sweetest discovery in the peso economy are the ubiquitous ice cream stands.

MEDIA

There isn't much ideological diveristy in Cuba's press. The main newspapers are *Granma* and *Juventud Rebelde*, which, beyond the official discourse, offer valuable culture and sports sections. Other newspapers include *Trabajadores*, *El Hombre* or *Tribunes de la Habana*. Magazines such as *Bohemia*, *Mujeres*, *Pionero*, *Somos Jovenes* or *Tecnología* may be lacking in political diversity, but offer articles on art, science, health and general culture. Ideological limitations aside, Cuban publications are free from advertising and not constrained by the laws of consumerism.

The same can be said about television. There are four channels in Cuba, the most appreciated of them being *Cubavisión*, the channel offering the most variety, where you will find movies, soap operas, music and children's programmes. Other channels include *Telerebelde*, which emphasizes sports and includes cinema, and two education channels, *Canal Educativo* and *Canal Educativo 2*, highlighting cultural programming, movies and children's themes. Cuban television is more open than ideologues would lead us to believe. For a country that criticises American hegemony, you find a lot of movies and TV series from the United States. They are appreciated by the local population, with some Cubans complaining that movies from other countries are "too slow". Television is also used to address difficult issues. The popular soap opera, *La cara oculta de la luna* (the Dark Side of the Moon), for example, deals with the homosexuality and AIDS, with a mission to break down stereotypes and promote the use of contraception.

Internet, on the other hand, is not available to many Cubans. While you can go online in hotels or in places such as the Capitolio in Havana, it is simply overpriced for Cubans, at five to six CUCs per hour.

Cuban radio varies from the rapid-fire headline news and minute-to-minute time announcements on *Radio Reloj* to the U.S. government *Radio Martí* which bombards the island with anti-regime propaganda, with cultural programming sandwiched somewhere in between. Ironically, American TV series freely available on Cuban TV do more to penetrate the Cuban consciousness about the wonders of American consumer society than the clumsy *Radio Martí*.

Getting a letter processed through the Cuban postal service is less reliable than getting a heart transplant in the Cuban medical system. Letters do eventually arrive, even between Cuba and the United States, but never send money in an envelope. Telephone service is patchy, and calling from or to Cuba from Europe, for example, is more expensive than phone communication with any other Latin American country. Phone cards seem expensive by Cuban standards but are considerably more economical than other forms of telephone communication. Mobile phone companies are anxiously awaiting the funeral of the Cuban revolution. As of the year 2007, the global mobile phone revolution had still bypassed Cuba.

FOOD AND ENTERTAINING

CHAPTER 6

"Spread out before us was a feast: roast chicken, *arroz moro* (rice and black beans), fried plantains, *tostones* (plantains mashed and fried), *malanga* (a taro-like tuber) chips, yuca with garlic sauce and a simple salad of tomatoes, cucumbers and shredded cabbage. It was a delicious dinner, all the more remarkable because our hostess had prepared nearly all of it on two small burners."
—Jeremy Iggers, "The Flavor of Cuba,"
Star Tribune, 1 June 2000.

FOOD

Marta, from Colombia, is a film student at Cuba's prestigious film school in San Antonio de los Baños.

"My greatest culture shock was the lack of balance in the diet," Marta says. "At the school cafeteria, sometimes they give us a breakfast with no bread, and then we are served a lunch with mainly starch and yet with a whole lot of bread. That's just an example."

According to Cuban researchers Pérez and Muñoz in *Agricultura y Alimentación en Cuba*, the culturally acceptable diet is one that is both unhealthy (high-calorie, high-fat, high-cholesterol, low-fibre) and expensive to obtain, in that much of the food and the materials to produce it must be imported.

"Food surveys in Cuba," cite agricultural scientists Rosset and Benjamin from Pérez and Muñoz, show that what Cubans want for both lunch and dinner, every day, is rice, beans, a high-protein food (such as beef, poultry, pork, fish and eggs), *viandas* (which in order of preference are plantains, taro, potatoes, cassava [what we know as yuca] and sweet potato) and bread."

Cuba's colonial legacy, which was continued during the U.S. and Soviet periods, was that of importing *criollo* foods "neither well-suited to Cuban agriculture nor particularly healthy."

The long-term effects of the Special Period may actually be beneficial to Cuba's eating habits. Cuban agronomists are well-aware that beef production is far more costly and inefficient than using the same resources to grow *viandas*, fruit and vegetables.

During the 1990s, Cuba's government sustained a policy that encouraged the substitution of *viandas* and vegetables for wheat and rice, also substituting vegetable for animal fat. Can Cubans voluntarily change their eating habits?

Food preference is so much a matter of taste and culture that I can only relate the highs and lows of eating in Cuba from a perspective slanted by my personal taste.

Lows: fibreless white bread, fats used in food preparation that may sometimes be lard (the government encourages the use of vegetable oil, which was not always available), hotel food in general, lack of variety and absence of hot sauces. Lobster and other sea delights have not been fished sustainably and the supply is dwindling because of exports and overuse in tourist hotels. All of my eating has been with Cubans, so I have not had much of an opportunity to eat seafood.

Highs: avocados, cucumbers and other fruit and vegetables, as fresh and tasty as anywhere in the world thanks to the under-reported revolution of Cuba's organised transition to organic agriculture and urban farming; pork, prepared with bitter orange and garlic, or the juicy crispy *lechón* (roasted pig); the rice with bean dish *congris*, which in combination with salad and fruit is a nearly vegetarian meal if the *congris* were not cooked in animal fat; the root yuca cooked with garlic; fried bananas (I'm afraid to ask what they fry them in); the unbelievably tasty home-cooked food and personal service at the small family eating places called *paladares*, most of them in people's homes with a funky *ambiente*; the eating experience in Chinatown; the open air fruit and vegetable markets; boxed natural fruit drinks called Tropical Island.

Urban farming was insignificant prior to the fall of the Soviet Union. Cuba depended on exporting cash crops and importing food crops, a typical relationship between poorer countries and western powers. With the collapse of the Soviet Union, the era of subsidised foods and chemicals was suddenly finished. With no cash, gasoline for tractors was scarce. Calorie intake for the average Cuban plunged from 2,600 per day to between 1,000 and 1,500 per day in the peak crisis period of 1993.

Little by little, internal food production was maximised during a turbulent transition to organic agriculture which saw the elimination of pesticides, herbicides and fungicides with and expanding urban farm plots (*organopónicos*), which spawned a system of open-air organic food markets (*mercados agropecuarios*). An amazing 12 per cent of Havana is composed of *organopónicos*. (Read more about the technical/business applications of this process in the Business chapter.)

Annual calorie intake has now returned to about 2,600 a day, while the U.N. estimates that the percentage of the population considered undernourished fell from eight per cent in the crisis period to about three per cent in 2000-2002. Cuba may be one of the only countries in the world to have adopted wholesale a self-sustaining system of agriculture and the example is lauded by many agronomists.

A cane cutter. Through 1990, Cuba's monocultural export economy, based on sugar was a vestige of colonialism. Now, a self-sustained and more diversified agriculture is developing.

The rationing system allow Cubans cut-rate items for only symbolic payment. Speaking with Cubans you get varying versions as to whether the rations last for two weeks or two-thirds of the month, but all agree that they have to scramble to complete their monthly needs at *mercados agropecuarios*, in more expensive supermarkets or by bartering with neighbours. One Cuban commented that, "if the rations lasted through the whole month, you'd hear much fewer people griping about the government."

The food landscape in Cuba is contradictory, but one thing is certain: the public health system has made certain worthy dietary accomplishments against great obstacles, especially for children. Referring to Cuba the FAO noted that, "the prevalence of malnutrition among pre-school age children, was below five per cent at the national level. These remarkably low percentages of child malnutrition put Cuba at the forefront of developing countries."

Cuba's infant mortality rate is now lower than that of the U.S. and statistics show that Cubans are better nourished then most of the inhabitants of neighbouring countries in the region.

DAILY MEALS

Cuban taste for food does not seem to have changed except for improved calorie intake and with the *mercados agropecuarios* and improved balance of diet. Breakfast is of the continental variety, rather simple. Lunch tends to be simpler than dinner. Without the extended lunch periods of other Latin countries, Cuban employees get out of work earlier and take advantage of the mellow afternoons.

Cuba's National Dish

Cuba's national dish may be referred to as *ajiaco criollo* or simply pork cooked in bitter orange and garlic, the two magic ingredients. This meat staple is accompanied by a root (*vianda*) often yuca or potatoes cooked in garlic. Fried plantains may accompany or substitute for the *vianda*.

Often, fresh bananas are served with the food. Then there is the fresh green salad with the obligatory tomatoes, cucumbers and avocado, along with the typical tasty black beans with steamed rice. *Congris*, a more exotic variation of the rice and beans, is fried rice with red beans and pork skins.

A traditional favourite Cuban dish is chicken with yellow rice (*arroz con pollo*). The rice becomes yellow after being soaked in saffron. The taste comes from freshly ground black pepper, lime juice, olive oil, finely chopped onion, chopped bell pepper, minced garlic, crushed tomatoes, finely chopped pimentos, cumin, bay leaf, dry white wine and powdered saffron. The recipe for pork in bitter orange and garlic is equally nuanced. A treat reserved for more special occasions is *lechón*, pork cooked in its own fat, usually with the above accompanying dishes. *Lechón* is widespread throughout Latin America and is also a special dish in the Philippines.

Fish is not common on plates at Cuban household dinners. In restaurants, both salt-water fish and fresh-water fish are comparatively expensive. Many Cubans engage in fishing to economise and to add variety to their diets.

One French visitor has called Cuban desserts "the great emptiness". Cuba's typical fresh fruit cocktail may not melt in your mouth but it's vibrant in taste and healthy, missing the butters and creams that most French would consider a prerequisite for composing a fine dessert.

Eating etiquette does not differ from western cultures. In Cuban homes, food may be served by the host, or bowls of different dishes may be placed on the table in order for the guests to serve themselves buffet style.

SNACKS

Cubans and visitors alike often boast that there are no McDonalds or other globalised fast food chains, but Cuba is not without fast food outlets, especially fried chicken, pizza and sandwiches. Some of these fast-food stands deal in Cuban pesos and the pizza and soft drink are available for the equivalent of U.S. 33 cents In a chain restaurant called Rápido you can have enough to eat with drink included for less than 3 CUCs. Ambulant vendors sell crispy toasted peanuts in paper cones. You don't look for them, they'll find you. From ground-floor apartment windows they sell fruitades and may have peanuts as well.

I've never found bad ice cream at the ubiquitous Cuban ice cream stands. Ice cream becomes a total experience if you have it at Coppelia, at Calle 23 in Vedado, Havana, a bizarre structure of 60's architecture that fits well in the context of old American cars. Coppelia offers an opportunity to participate in a typical Cuban ritual, including the legendary waiting lines (Sunday's queues are the longest and most culturally intense), with the nostalgia of scenes from Tomás Gutiérrez Aleas classic film *Fresa y Chocolate*, fine service and low prices for extraordinarily delicious ice-cream, heaped generously in a bowl.

RESTAURANTS

If you're planning on living with and like the locals, most restaurants can be eliminated as part of tourist apartheid. However, you will find good *comida criolla* in some restaurants for as low as 2.50 CUC. Most travellers have agreed that the best of these low-budget high quality restaurants is the Hanoi, charming, friendly and unbeatable prices, at the corner of Teniente Rey and Bernaza in Old Havana. The *paladares* ("palate pleasers?") look somewhat like restaurants but are squeezed into family homes, part of the opening to free enterprise. Only four tables are allowed and the owners may not hire (exploit) employees, so it's entirely a family enterprise. That means you can enjoy the variations of home cooking probably prepared by the same person who serves you. The prices are range from 3 to 15 CUC. Prices in some *paladares* seem unfairly high, but understand that Cuba's intrepid private entrepreneurs pay stiff taxes and are tightly regulated.

I once ate at an illegal *paladar* for only 1.50 CUC because I had become friends with the proprietor. I asked her, "Amelia, don't you feel you should legalise your business? Wouldn't that be fair?"

"No way," she said. "I had my food stand for years and paid my taxes, so now they owe me this one."

SELF-CATERING AND VEGETARIANS

Sooner or later, foreigners in Cuba will want to settle down to a steadier daily life, which may mean eating healthier. Produce can be purchased at the *mercados agropecuarios*. Each district of most cities has its *mercado*. Supermarkets and bakeries are scattered around town for meats, cheeses, breads and special delicacies that are not available in the outdoor markets. Vegetarians can put things together by using beans as a protein-rich staple and fresh fruit and vegetables for more fibre and vitamins. You won't find many vegetarians among Cubans.

"We Cubans feel that if there was no meat, we have not eaten," says Ivan.

Recipe For Black Beans

Wash the beans and leave them soaking in water overnight with chopped pepper. Then simmer uncovered in the same water in which they were soaked, until the beans are soft.

Heat vegetable oil in a frying pan and then sauté onion and garlic. Add more green pepper to the mix. Then add the whole mixture to the beans.

Add salt, pepper, oregano and bay leaf and simmer. Then add vinegar and wine. Cook the whole thing on low heat. The liquid that remains becomes the sauce. If too much liquid remains, cook for longer. Serve with white rice.

MOJITO AND OTHER DRINKS

The *mojito* is one of Cuba's distinctive mixed drinks, and a favourite of many foreign visitors. Even people who don't like the hard stuff will wonder how this blend goes down so mellow. Mix a shot of rum with a half teaspoon of sugar, squeezed juice from half of a large lime, soda water, ice, and the key ingredient, *yerbabuena*, a pungent herb from the mint family with medicinal properties. *Yerbabuena* is a Latin American herb that has gained favour in international food stores around the world. Some people prefer to squeeze the *yerbabuena* as they deposit it in the glass in order to release its flavour.

The *mojito* may be more of a tourist drink than a Cuban drink. Beer flows freely, at dance clubs and funky bars, either because it is preferred or it is cheap. Mayabe, Bucanero and Cristal are three famous Cuban brands. Beer tasting foreigners accuse Cristal of being too weak (a breakfast beer). Tasters claim that some beers are better from a bottle than from a can. Mayabe passes all the tests.

The best and most underrated drink in Cuba is coffee. Hole-in-the-wall coffee bars abound, and no upscale coffee bar in Europe can match the hand-harvested arabica or canephora product, brewed and served fresh from the hills, accompanied by animated neighbourhood conversation.

CULTURE AND TRAVEL

CHAPTER 7

"The rumba has been mistreated by history. That's because
it has always been the music of the poorest people,
the most humble people, the black people, the drunks."
—Diosdado Ramos, director of the rumba group Los
Muñequitos de Matanzas, from Jon Pareles, "Rumba, the
Heartbeat of Cuban Music," *New York Times*, 11 June 2000

LITERARY BORDER CROSSINGS

The crossing of cultural borders is a recurring theme in a rich array of literary works by remarkable personalities who represent different aspects of the Cuban experience. Nicolás Guillén's poetry confronts the dilemma of the Cuban poet's dual heritage of Africa and Spain, and intersects culturally with African-American poet Langston Hughes, an admirer and translator of Guillén.

Alejo Carpentier's exile to Europe, return to Cuba, and subsequent diplomatic posts abroad allow him to view Latin American cultures from both beyond and within, and at least one of his novels, *The Lost Steps*, makes culture shock a primary theme.

Assata Shakur is not Cuban by birth, but has lived in Cuba for more than four decades as an exile from the United States. *Assata: An Autobiography* culminates with her adjustment to the Cuban way of life following her daring escape from prison in the United States.

The criterion for choosing to profile these three authors in place of so many other Cuban and foreigner literary personalities with ties to Cuba is that they feature the theme of crossing cultural boundaries. Had space allowed, other luminaries could have received equal billing.

But literary celebrities like Hemingway have been portrayed again and again in books on Cuba and are now the object of tourist schlock. Although Hemingway once shook hands with Fidel Castro and had denounced Batista, he had no involvement in the changes occurring in Cuba at the time he left. Perhaps it was a terminal illness that left this great reporter oblivious to the type of dramatic story he thrived on. He had left a very public existence in Havana in order to commit the most private of all acts. A year after his departure from Cuba, in the empty expanses of Idaho, he put a loaded rifle to his head and pulled the trigger.

Any visitor to Cuba will bump into relics of Hemingway's Havana period. But tourists come and go without engaging in the insights of the three literary figures portrayed in the following pages.

Double Deception: Nicolás Guillén & Langston Hughes

Can two people be born into two different cultures and yet grow up like doubles, carving out an identical path in life? Langston Hughes was born in the United States in 1902. Nicolás Guillén was born the same year in Cuba. Both Hughes and Guillén were of African heritage in segregated societies. Both were able to break through racial barriers and attend Ivy League universities. But both would drop out of college to pursue careers as writers and poets. Within the poetic output of both of these artists was a commitment to social justice. But as these kindred spirits reached the age of 28, they had never met.

When cruise lines Cunard, Panamá Pacific and United Fruit all refused to sell Hughes a ticket to Cuba in 1930, one of the ticket sellers told the U.S. poet that there was a ban against blacks travelling to Cuba. Hughes checked with the Cuban embassy, where he was told that no such ban existed.

Hughes wanted to travel to Cuba with his "rusty but serviceable Spanish" to obtain documentation on Cuban music for an Afro-American opera project. A trip to Cuba would also set the stage for an encounter with Nicolás Guillén. Thanks to the intervention of a white friend of Hughes, the poet was able to purchase an expensive stateroom ticket on Cunard's ship, *Caronia*. Hughes was not sure if he could mix with the passengers, until, according to biographer Arnold Rampersad, "he found relief that they [the passengers] were mostly Jewish."

In Havana, Langston Hughes was "amused to see clothes hanging out to dry on top of buildings" (and today, you'll see the same sights over the balconies in Old Havana). More shocking than the clothing draped out to dry was the criticism of Hughes's host, José Antonio Fernández de Castro, editor of *El Diario de la Marina*. Fernández spoke to Hughes about Yankee imperialism, the self-proclaimed U.S. right to intervene militarily in Cuba and absentee ownership of much of Cuban agriculture and industry by North Americans. Fernández was the first person to translate Hughes's poetry into Spanish. He walked Hughes down the Prado boulevard, where "everyone wanted to be introduced to the greatest Negro poet in the United States and the world."

Skin Deep

Hughes went to hear the Cuban *son* at the all-black Club Atenas, where he became a hit with the *sonero* musicians. Like the blues, the *son* had emerged from traditional African culture. Hughes had done much to publicise Afro-Cuban music abroad and hoped that a leading Cuban composer, Amadeo Roldán, would be his partner in the Afro-American opera project. But the light-skinned Roldán resented being referred to as black or Negro. Hughes reacted with disgust and immediately became skeptical about Cuban claims of racial harmony.

Hughes looked forward to meeting Nicolás Guillén, the mulatto poet who had written with pride of his African heritage. Without having known each other, Hughes and Guillén had uncanny poetic affinities.

Following their first meeting, Langston Hughes felt sufficient rapport with his counterpart to share specific ideas about Guillén's poetry. At their second get-together, he recommended that Guillén make the rhythms of the Afro-Cuban *son*, the authentic music of the black masses, central to his poetry, as Hughes had done with blues and jazz. Guillén's next book, *Motivos de Son*, did just that. From then on, Hughes and Guillén became friends, and their poetry seemed to emanate from a united soul.

Since Hughes was a supporter of the civil rights movement in the United States, Nicolás Guillén expected his friend to raise a voice of support against the '*vandálicos hechos*' of the Bay of Pigs invasion in 1961. Segregation in Cuba had ended with the revolution, and for the first time in his life, Guillén, as a man of African heritage, felt free, as expressed in his now classic poem *Tengo* (I Have). As the president of the Cuban Association of Writers and Artists, Guillén implored Hughes for vocal support against another potential U.S. invasion.

Langston Hughes had been in a similar situation when he'd asked for support from composer Amadeo Roldán, only to be met by Roldán's reticence to take a stand in favour of his African heritage. Now it was Hughes, one of the greatest U.S. poets of the twentieth century, who was asked to take a stand. Fearlessly, Hughes had written against racial oppression, at a time when it was not popular to do so.

Hughes rejected Guillén's request, however. One of his biographers suggests that he did so out of fear of personal reprisal. Hughes was aware that two U.S. poets had lost their jobs after travelling to Castro's Cuba.

But Langston Hughes was not one to walk away from an issue. His poetry itself was threatening to the U.S. establishment. For example, educator Jonathan Kozol was fired from his teaching job after having read a Langston Hughes poem to his black students in the Boston school system. The poem was considered inflammatory and revolutionary by the Boston school board.

In fairness to Langston Hughes, the anti-Cuba atmosphere in the United States came on the heels of McCarthyist blacklisting, and Hughes was well aware that African-Americans had always been most vulnerable to political reprisals. But it is doubtful that individual concerns were the motive for the courageous Hughes to leave his friend Nicolás Guillén in the wake. The civil rights movement in the United States, Hughes's great struggle, was being falsely criticised by white supremacists as "communist influenced." Any potential Langston Hughes declaration against U.S. intervention in Cuba would have been used as propaganda to undermine the civil rights movement.

Nicolás Guillén, who died in 1989, is today considered Cuba's national poet, and anyone considering travelling to Cuba would do well to read and enjoy his poetry.

Alejo Carpentier: *The Lost Steps*

Alejo Carpentier (1904–1980) was one of Cuba's great twentieth century novelists. After imprisonment by the Machado regime, Carpentier spent many years in exile, returning to Cuba after the revolution. He was nominated for a Nobel Prize several times and his baroque prose has a cult of devotees. Carpentier was also a journalist, radio station director, musicologist, composer, history teacher and the head of a national publishing company.

It is a custom in Latin America to hand out choice diplomatic posts to great writers as a scholarship that enables them to continue producing their art. Carpentier was offered the post of ambassador in Paris but preferred the lesser position of cultural attaché.

The Cuban novel recommended to me the most by Cuban lovers of literature is Carpentier's *The Lost Steps* (*Los Pasos*

Perdidos), written in 1956. A standard review of this truly magnificent novel would emphasize the plot line: a music composer living in an unnamed European country is given funds by a museum curator to travel to the remote jungles of an unnamed Latin American country in order to track down the most basic and original instruments: the source of music itself.

The unnamed protagonist's actress wife is too busy with her career to maintain an ongoing relationship. Mouche, an astrologist girl friend, very much like one of today's New Agers, tags along with him for the adventure. Among the many obstacles along the way is a prototypical Latin American coup d'état that traps the two lovers in their hotel.

The change of culture (the protagonist is returning to the land where he was raised) is cause for discord between the lovers. On the way from the city to the jungle, the protagonist meets an earthy local woman who is much less intellectual than his European companion but whose homespun philosophy is much more authentic.

Carpentier was a Renaissance man, and everything from his eclectic background finds its way into the novel, which becomes as dense as the rainforest explored by the protagonist. With so much there, the novel reads like the facade of a baroque church. Its intricate detail causes the reader to stop and contemplate, while its flowing story moves on relentlessly like the Orinoco River that inspires it.

Within the "culture shock" perspective, *The Lost Steps*' subplot is pivotal for anyone with a western cultural heritage who wishes to travel into the depths of Latin America, Cuba included.

Carpentier's life had one foot in Europe and the other in Cuba, and the cultural contrasts he perceives between the two continents may anticipate experiences of some travellers today. Others will take issue with Carpentier's point of view, as it is reflected by his protagonist.

The protagonist's European wife is so career-oriented that she has little time for her husband. He writes about the "hardness … of that city of perennial anonymity within the multitude, of that eternal haste, where eyes only met by chance, and a smile, when coming from a stranger, always concealed a pragmatic motive."

The protagonist becomes upset at being stereotyped by his lady friend Mouche, who "would attribute the animalness of my reactions to my early upbringing, which took place in a Latin American setting."

Mouche's difficulty in adjusting to Latin American culture results from her view of the people's customs as exotic rather than normal. "An aura of exoticism thickened around her, establishing distances between her figure and the figures of others." She suffered from a typical case of culture shock.

As the protagonist becomes more and more settled within the culture of his upbringing, his lover seems ever more foreign to him. However, the protagonist's new lady friend, Rosario, is also culturally removed from him. "When I looked

at her as a woman, I felt clumsy, inhibited, conscious of my own exoticism … there were the thousands books I'd read that she was unaware of; there were her beliefs, customs, superstitions, notions that I was unaware of and that, even so, represented reasons for living as valid as my own."

The Lost Steps, then, is also the story of a dramatic cultural tug-of-war, with the protagonist caught between two very distinct world views.

The apparent dichotomy between contemporary and traditional cultures is made out to be a mere cliché by Carpentier. Mouche may seem liberated, in the modern western sense, but she is imprisoned by the custom of analysing what should be left to nature. Rosario is a traditional woman who wants to serve; when speaking to the narrator she calls herself your woman. But when it comes to their intimate relationship, she does not let analytical inhibitions get in the way and prefers to surrender to "the joy of the body." Yet, she is fiercely independent, and does not see her reason for living as bound to her lover.

"According to her [Rosario], marriage, the legal binding, steals a woman's recourse for defending herself against men," a statement that coincidentally reflects the view of many of today's Cuban women.

Another cultural contradiction faced by the narrator concerns his own tendency to live for the future, a posture that clashes with a way of life in a remote village in which present tense survival is everything.

The narrator's actress wife and his benefactor, the curator, are both perplexed when he does not return to Europe. Believing him to be lost in the jungle, they dispatch a plane on a rescue mission. The narrator would prefer to remain in the remote village situated at the beginning of time and music, writing an elaborate musical composition that will probably never be performed.

But his cultural transformation is incomplete, bound as he is to his past, and when the plane lands and the pilot finds him, the narrator must make a decision of enormous consequences, based on his conflicting feelings about the two radically different cultures that now struggle for control of his spirit.

The Lost Steps is one of the great novels of the twentieth century, whose most exciting theme, often overlooked by the critics, is the dramatic clash between two ways of life within one human being. Anyone who travels from one culture to another will greatly benefit from a reading of this Cuban masterpiece.

An American Refugee in Havana: Assata Shakur

Most of us will not experience the same culture shock in Cuba as Assata Shakur. But few people arrive in Havana after such an intense and turbulent past.

Only the last chapter of Shakur's gripping narration occurs in Havana, but it is a revealing chapter, where her perceptions of Cuba are better understood in the context of what happened before. Shakur's book is an intellectual-political history of the events that lead up to her imprisonment on charges of murdering a New Jersey state trooper, and her daring escape from the maximum security wing of the Clinton Correctional Facility for Women in New Jersey in 1979.

After an early childhood in the segregated south that included death threats from white vigilantes who harassed her grandparents' beachfront business, Assata's mother moved her north to New York, where she would confront the typical self-hatred of a black youth who wanted to look more like the white celebrities she'd see on typical fifties sitcoms like *Ozzie* and *Harriet*.

Her personal transformation, in the context of the black political movement of the sixties and early seventies, included a discarding of the humiliating hair alterations on the outside and a fierce pride in her African heritage within.

Feisty Assata admits that her stubbornness was often to blame for conflicts with her school teacher mother, and her beloved aunt, who also became her lawyer. But most of her rage is directed against racism.

"If i [sic] sit and add up all the 'colored' toilets and drinking fountains in my life and all of the back-of-the-buses or the Jim Crow railroad cars or the places I couldn't go, it adds up to one great ball of anger," wrote Assata Shakur in her *Assata: An Autobiography*.

Assata participated with a myriad of anti-racist and Black nationalist groups. She ended up with the Black Panthers, volunteering in their breakfast programme for school children, as well as other educational and health care activities in black neighbourhoods. Her interest in school children was stimulated by her own childhood experiences when white teachers treated her paternalistically, expecting less from her because she was black, and resenting it when she would question the text-book clichés about heroes like George Washington and Abraham Lincoln.

Her joining the Black Panthers was ill-timed, occurring precisely at the time when the FBI, through its now infamous COINTELPRO program, was "attempting to destroy the Black Panther Party in particular and the Black Liberation Movement in general."

Assata gained fame as a revolutionary, and it seemed that every time a black woman was involved in a bank robbery, Assata would be wanted. Assata, the former Joanne Chesimard, was eventually acquitted of a fantastic array of bank robbery, kidnapping and drug charges. In one case, her accuser admitted in court that he was a police informant and the charges were dropped. In other instances, the case against her was dismissed as frivolous.

But one charge stuck.

Guilty Until Proven Innocent.

On a fateful night on the New Jersey Turnpike in 1973, Assata was riding with two male companions and their car was stopped by New Jersey troopers. Shooting erupted. In the shoot-out, her friend Zayd and a state trooper died. She was convicted of being an accomplice to murder by an all-white jury. The evidence was questionable, however.

In 1979, seven international jurists visited United States prisons, and they listed Assata Shakur as a "political prisoner ... a class of victims of FBI misconduct through the COINTELPRO strategy and other forms of illegal government conduct who as political activists have been selectively targeted for provocation, false arrests, entrapment, fabrication of evidence, and spurious criminal prosecutions." The report added: "One of the worst cases is that of ASSATA SHAKUR …"

Her narration reads like a combination of *The Shawshank Redemption* and Malcolm X's autobiography, with trial scenes as dramatic as the best scenes in John Grisham novels, and with powerful yet lyrical poems at the end of each chapter.

After Assata Shakur's tribulations, her immediate appreciation of Havana was entirely expected. But she arrived in Cuba predisposed to be sharply critical of community and race relations, her area of passionate expertise.

"The first thing that hit me were the open doors. Everywhere you go doors are open wide. You see people inside their homes talking, working or watching television. I was amazed to find that you could actually walk down the streets at night alone." Having done volunteer work in the areas of health and education, she could be expected to embrace Cuba's free health care and equal educational opportunities.

But it is in the area of race relations where Shakur's opinions are most in demand. "Nowhere did I find a segregated neighbourhood, but several people told me that where I was living had been all white before the Revolution. Just from casual observation it was obvious that race relations in Cuba were different from what they were in the U.S. Blacks and whites could be seen together everywhere—in cars, walking down streets. Kids of all races played together. It was definitely different."

But Shakur remained "skeptical and suspicious" when people told her that there was no racism in Cuba. She found it peculiar that people of African origin could declare "I am Cuban" with no need for icons from their African origins to boost their self-esteem.

She was confused by Cuba's racial categories, especially by the term mulatto. "I'm not a mulatto, but a Black woman, and I'm proud to be Black," she would explain to Cubans. "All of my associations with the word 'mulatto' were negative," she wrote. "It represented slavery, slave owners raping Black women … In some Caribbean countries, it represented the middle level of a hierarchical, three caste system—the caste that acted as a buffer class between the white rulers and the Black masses ... i [sic] felt that the mulatto thing hindered Cubans from dealing with some of the negative ideas left over from slavery."

No Offence Just Affection

When Cubans are so moved to identify themselves by colour, a very infrequent occurrence, they do so nonchalantly, the way one describes a car as red or a slice of squash is yellow. (Latin Americans are more straight forward about physical appearance in general, and nicknames that would be considered racist or of a mocking nature in many English-speaking countries simply represent a recognition of physical reality in much of Latin America. A woman, for example, can call her husband *gordito* in a loving way. But in an English-speaking country, no one calls a companion "fatty," the English meaning of *gordito*.)

She later understood that "in some ways, Cubans and I approached the problem from different angles ... I respected the Cuban government, not only for adopting nonracist principles, but for struggling to put these principles in practice."

Assata Shakur did find one man who had objected to his white daughter marrying a black man. But the father of the bride was eventually won over. Shakur did not expect that all racism could be overcome from one decade to the next.

Assata Shakur has been happy with her adjustment to Cuba, although "It was hard in the beginning, because I had to adjust to another culture and learn another language. I had to adjust to living in a Third World country, which means that things people in the U.S. take for granted—like hot running water whenever you turn on the tap—are not always available here."

References to Assata Shakur's pre-Havana life were necessary in order that we empathise with her adjustment to Cuba. We've already met several visitors to Cuba who found the life so intense that they needed to get away for a break. But Shakur's life was so intense in the United States that "Another thing I've been able to do in Cuba," she says, "is to rest."

Shakur appreciates Cuba's sense of community (the Panther's were a community-oriented organisation) and the absence of racial conflict. This has allowed her to do things she'd never had time for in her other existence, such as writing fiction and painting.

"I'm crafting a vision of my life that involves creativity. And Cuban society allows me to do this."

In particular, Shakur feels liberated by being able to express her feelings of vulnerability and sensitivity. In Cuba, there is no need for wearing a protective psychological mask. "I can cry and be human and lean on people who take care of me. That can be very liberating."

While she has been gone, the African-American struggle has changed, but Assata's vocabulary and political positions remain unabashedly rooted in the late sixties and early seventies. During her political exile, several of her Panther colleagues in U.S. jails have been granted new trials or are the objects of intense campaigns for their release. In the meantime, Assata Shakur has adjusted just fine to Cuban culture.

In 1998, the U.S. Congress unanimously passed a resolution requesting that Cuba extradite one Joanne Chesimard. Many members of the Congressional Black Caucus explained that they would have voted against the resolution had they known that Chesimard was Assata Shakur. On 2 May 2005, the U.S. Justice Department posted a million dollar bounty for the capture of Assata Shakur. These acts prompted a massive petition drive in her defense.

She has become an icon in contemporary hip-hop music. Artists like Common ("*A Song for Assata*"), Paris ("*Assata's Song*") and Chuck D sing and narrate in tribute to Assata Shakur.

ARTS

In the absence of a commercial-business power structure, Cuba's arts community may have become the elite of the nation. Since 1959, Cuban officialdom has invested considerable resources into creating a truly national arts infrastructure, founding numerous schools in art, dance and film. Cuba's Ballet Nacional, Conjunto de Danza Nacional, and Conjunto Folklórico Nacional are all acclaimed internationally, and the Cuban School of Ballet is recognised as one of the best in the world.

The Plaza de Amas. A marketplace in Havana where various art pieces can be found.

Cuban composers in various musical genres have won prizes abroad. Havana is the host of an exciting international jazz festival. (The international impact of Cuban music is great enough to warrant a separate discussion in this book).

A renaissance of sorts is taking place in painting and sculpture, with genres extending from art-naif to abstract, although a number of fine Cuban artists have chosen to leave the island and live abroad. Particularly exciting to this observer is the wealth of "naive art," many of whose practitioners have no formal training. Catch the permanent exhibit in Havana's El Morro fortress museum.

Cuba's premier art festival is the biannual Bienal de La Habana. Anything goes at this festival, as exemplified in 1997 by a work by the 27-year-old Kcho, a 20-foot-high sculpture cobbled together from frazzled ship remnants, suitcases, and old furniture, what one critic called "a calculatedly ambiguous reference to the country's boat emigrations."

The November 2003 Havana biennial triggered some jazzy, offbeat critiques, such as that of Blake Gopnik in the *Washington Post*, who wrote about "many surprising highs—the best works rivaled anything at high-end art events like Germany's Documenta exhibition or the Venice

Naive art is an important genre in Cuba today.

or Whitney biennials—and some numbing lows." The 2006 Bienal continued this event's daring history, as you can see by visiting www.bienalhabana.cult.cu/

A cadre of Cuban film directors, led by the late Tomás Gutiérrez Alea and Humberto Solás, have produced many more artistically-acclaimed films than should be imaginable for a country of only 11 million, and successful film makers from many different countries have studied film at Cuba's Escuela Internacional de Cine y Televisión. Havana hosts the prestigious International Festival of Latin American Cinema.

As pianist Giselle Grau noted, artists in Cuba are not obligated to earn a living doing something else while practising their art on the side, although dissenters note that the politics of official recognition may stand in the way in the plastic arts and literature. With the arts becoming part of a global culture, increasingly Cuban artists must travel and perform abroad in order to participate in their career growth. At this writing the great Cuban dancer performs around the world while based in London. Like so many

Cuban artists who thrive abroad, Acosta returns frequently to Havana.

"My friends in Cuba," Acosta remarked on a BBC radio interview, "sometimes I envy them, their hanging out and playing football."

Travellers planning to visit Cuba can get a head start before they go by renting movies like *Fresa y Chocolate* and *Guantanamera*, by seeing colour images of Cuban artists on the Internet, and by catching in-person performances by some of the many Cuban salsa and jazz groups that travel abroad regularly.

BASEBALL AND OTHER SPORTS

Foreign visitors to Cuba may experience great culture shock when attending a game of baseball, a deceptively plodding confrontation between nine specialists on each team that erupts in explosively dramatic moments. It is ironic that the U.S. and Cuba have spent a large part of the second half of the twentieth century on less than friendly terms, for both countries share the same national pastime.

How did Cubans become so fanatic about a sport that seems so typical of the United States? Most Americans believe that baseball was exported to Cuba some time after the 1898 Spanish-American War. But Cubans were already playing the game at the end of Spain's colonial empire.

Evidence suggests that Cuba's pre-Hispanic Taino Indians played a game called *batey* that was remarkably similar to baseball. In 1869, Esteban Bellán went to study at Fordham University in New York and ended up playing baseball with a team called the Troy Haymakers. Bellán became the first Cuban athlete in U.S. professional baseball. In 1874, he returned to Cuba to organise a baseball league.

In the first half of the twentieth century, racially-integrated Cuban teams encountered diplomatic problems when arriving to play in segregated baseball leagues of the United States. Some black Cubans played in the old "Negro Leagues" in the United States.

Today, many Americans have become disenchanted with increasingly corporatised professional baseball. Millionaire players no longer maintain long-standing allegiance to a given team and its supporters, charge money for autographs, and leave their loyal fans behind in search of extra millions on other teams' larger markets. In this context, Cuban "defectors" to American baseball are not much different than a "free agent" who leaves the loyal fans of the Oakland As for a juicier contract with the New York Yankees.

In some ways, Cuba's national baseball league is a return to what baseball used to be, with each city's team having its loyal followers.

In some neighbourhoods, Cubans actually play the informal stickball version of the sport, which for a New Yorker may bring back the nostalgia of childhood on the streets of the city. Cuba's main baseball season runs from mid-November through March.

Baseball Prowess

Cuba's national team reached the finale of the first baseball world cup in 2005, and would often win the Gold Medal in Olympic Games when baseball was still part of that competition. (Cuba also excels competitively in boxing, track and field, and volleyball.) During the Special Period, the government began authorising Cuban baseball players to perform abroad in amateur leagues in order to earn hard currency for the country. The temporary loss of these players has had a negative impact on Cuba's performance in international tournaments.

It's easy to get tickets for Cuban baseball games. Just ask around in whichever city you may be. I won't succumb to temptations to explain the rules of this game in writing. If baseball is new for you, attend a game and ask the Cubans sitting near you to explain what is happening as it happens. You'll find that it's not so complicated.

In 1999, the Baltimore Orioles travelled to Cuba and defeated a Cuban national team in Havana's Estadio Latinoamericano by a score of 3-2 in 11 innings. In a show of solidarity, Orioles's star first baseman Will Clark took a case of beer to the Cuban players' bus. The Cubans then travelled to Baltimore, where they trounced the Orioles 12-6. It was the first time in history that a Cuban team had played a U.S. major league squad in the United States. One team with a total team payroll of US$ 2,000 defeated another team whose player payroll was US$ 78 million. By inviting the Cuban team to the United States, Orioles owner Peter Angelos had made a statement against the trade embargo.

In some countries where baseball is a baffling sport, employees from the U.S. and Cuban embassies unite to form baseball teams. I once attended a softball game in La Paz, Bolivia, in which the pitcher for the Cuban softball team was an American woman employed by the U.S. embassy in La Paz. When this irrational division between these natural trading partners is finally ended, baseball will play a fundamental diplomatic role.

While baseball remains the national sport of Cuba, football (soccer) is gaining ground with the new generations. Basketball, boxing, track and field, and volleyball are sports staples. Surfing and "extreme sports" are fads that may stick. With little automobile traffic, streets often become soccer pitches.

CHINATOWN

Havana's Chinatown is today making a comeback. Following the revolution, most Chinese residents left Cuba. I met one of them in a Chinese restaurant in Chicago. I noticed he was speaking Spanish, and asked him where he'd learned the language.

"In the fifties, I left China to escape communism," he said. "I ended up in Cuba. But it looked like communism was following me around. After the revolution in Cuba, I left again, this time to Chicago."

Most of Cuba's Chinese are descendents of indentured servants, brought to the island in the nineteenth century to labour on plantations and build the railroads. Cuba's Chinatown, a few blocks west of the Capitolio in Centro Habana, seems small and almost insignificant, until you stroll in its pedestrian mall and eat in its restaurants. The food is tasty, and roving musicians add to the atmosphere. Chinatown's open-air produce market is one of the best in Havana.

FESTIVALS

In Latin America, even the most hedonistic festivals usually have some connection with Catholic traditions. With religious glasnost and the subsequent visit of the Pope, expect some religious traditions to make a mild comeback, but Cuba remains the most secular of all Latin American countries and most annual events do not involve a religious ceremony.

Some of the many annual events will be outlined here, but remember that *joie de vivre* is an inherent part of the Cuban culture and Cubans do not need a yearly excuse to erupt into festivities.

Cuba is also the site of a profusion of international professional conferences. The best source for annual and bi-annual festival and professional conference dates is your nearest travel agency specialising in Cuba. (See phone numbers and web sites of specialised tour companies listed at the end of this chapter.)

Havana street festival: joy and racial harmony during hard times.

Carnaval

The Yoruba cultural heritage of Cuba's carnival, called Carnaval, is quite similar to that of Brazil's Carnaval or Mardi Gras in New Orleans. But Cuba's Carnaval, centred in the city with its most extensive African heritage, Santiago, is celebrated in late July and the beginning of August rather than during the period leading up to Lent.

Carnaval originally celebrated the end of the sugar harvest, when slaves were allowed to escape their oppressive existence for a week. Coinciding in both date and place is the anniversary of the daring 26 July 1953 assault on the barracks of Moncada by the opposition movement, led by Castro. A pre-Lent version of Carnaval is held on weekend evenings in February in front of the Capitolio in Havana.

Carnaval originated in the Yoruban custom of singing praise to the saints. Each *orisha* had a particular *conga* or rumba dance rhythm. Throughout Latin America, Carnaval dancing groups are called *comparsas*, and are accompanied by drummers, singers, and trumpets. Daily processions are led by dancers dressed in traditional costumes from slave days. Rumba and rum flow freely and dancing gets more intense as the night hours drift toward morning.

For several years during the Special Period, no Carnaval was held, but as the economic situation was picking up, Carnaval was renewed in 1997.

Havana Events

The Havana International Jazz Festival is one of the top highlights for international visitors, and as hard times mellow out, this bi-annual event is one of the most-likely festivals to become an annual affair. Jazz delegations come from all around the world to rediscover that rhythmic and harmonic innovations in Cuba are among the most daring and exciting in the world of jazz. Hear cool and hot jazz at the festival, usually during Havana's coolest weather, and often held in December.

Ever since Dizzy Gillespie, Cal Tjader, and Herbie Mann brought Cuban music to an international audience, jazz musicians have been enriching their rhythms and nuances by taking in the Cuban jazz experience. Since 1996, Chucho Valdés has been organiser and artistic director of the Havana International Jazz Festival. In the 2006 edition, not only did Valdés perform but he put together an unbeatably eclectic array of new talent and jazz discoveries. The expanded December event now takes place in all Havana concert halls and spills out into impromptu jam sessions along the Malecón.

Some of the other bi-annual festivals held in Havana, with approximate months, are: the International Guitar Festival (May), the International Theatre Festival (August or September), the International Ballet Festival (October), and the International Festival of Latin American Film (December). Cuba's outstanding accomplishments in both ballet and film are recognised around the world.

An impressive list of fairs, expositions and scientific and cultural *congresos* would occupy a whole booklet. Whatever one's academic specialty may be, Havana or other parts of Cuba will certainly offer a symposium in the field.

Santiago's Festivities

Cuba's "second city" is most known for the Carnaval, but Santiago is host to other important events. Those interested in seeing music, song and dance in the context of an exciting blend of cultures should enjoy the annual Festival of Caribbean Culture in either June or July. Following the August Carnaval, the tempo slows down for a festival of romantic *bolero*. In much of Latin America, romantic music is making a comeback after years of being considered passé, the romantic bolero never died in Cuba. In the cooler month of December, the International Choir Festival is held.

In Camagüey

Cuba's third-largest city has its own Carnaval in steamy August, but the most regional of Camagüey celebrations is Jornadas de la Cultura Camagüeyana, usually in the comfortable weeks of early February. Cuba's national poet, Nicolás Guillén, was born in Camagüey, and the house of his birth is open to the public.

Holguín

At last we come to a more typical Latin American pilgrimage with the Romería de Mayo. Pilgrims arrive during the first week in May to ascend the Loma de la Cruz and visit a cross that was placed at the top by the Spaniards at the end of the eighteenth century to ward off drought. Outdoor musicians greet the pilgrims in town plazas.

The more secular Fiesta Iberoamericana de Cultura with its street fairs, theatre and dance, is celebrated in October. The dance gets more serious in November with the bi-annual International Ballet Festival.

Trinidad

Colonial Trinidad is a seductive setting for festivals, and between events, visitors can choose among an array of museums, from sacred Catholic and African to colonial and modern history. Nineteenth century romanticism is featured in Casa Cantero and Museo Romántico.

The Fiestas Sanjuaneras is a Cuban take on the Day of San Juan, celebrated throughout the Hispanic world around the time of the summer solstice in June. In late November, the Semana de la Cultura Trinitaria maintains a regional tenor, while so many other Cuban festivals have been internationalised.

Matanzas

Many of Cuba's internationally-recognised rumba groups have come out of Matanzas. The Afro-urban rumba (music and dance rhythms) is one of Cuba's most complex and electrifying contributions to the international culture scene. Beginning 10 October and lasting for a week and a half is the Festival del Bailador Rumbero, at the impressive 1862 neo-classical Teatro Santo.

Remedios (Province of Villa Clara)

The town of Remedios, with a population of about 20,000, is one of Cuba's most attractive colonial towns and remains off the tourist trail. Christmas has not been a major festival in Cuba, but at the same time, this seventeenth-century town and neighbouring villages celebrate Las Parrandas (December), a competition to see which neighbourhood produces the best *carroza* (float). A spirit of controlled chaos, with street music and dancing, country fair goods on sale, and fireworks, is the vestige of year-end religious celebrations from the 1800s.

Some of the best festivals are encountered by chance. Neighbourhoods, municipalities or santería followers decide to celebrate a one-time accomplishment or a current event and suddenly there is festivity in the streets. Music, dance and cultural events are so engrained in Cuban life that no one has to wait for a special occasion in order to celebrate.

DON'T WORRY, BE HAPPY: MUSIC IN CUBA

The embargo may have an impact on the number of obtainable new musical instruments and on spare parts for old ones, but it has had little impact on an exciting Cuban music scene. In fact, Cuban salsa ranks second to U.S. pop music in international export success. There are more than thirty Japanese salsa bands, for example, and Cuban CDs flow freely around the world, even within the United States.

Although Cuban jazz does not have a great internal market, music from groups like Irakere or individuals like Gonzalo Rubalcaba and Chucho Valdéz are on the cutting edge of contemporary jazz. From Paris to Manhattan, many jazz groups are obligated to study Cuban rhythms just to keep apace.

In many books on Cuba, the music receives a few paragraphs as one of the facets of culture. But Cuban culture is music, and music is and will continue to be one of the great adventures in contemporary Cuba.

Serge Kasimoff is an American keyboard player who began his career as a prodigy in both classical and jazz music. He presents one very visceral model for how to adopt a new culture. The sensorial medium for his total adjustment to Cuban culture was the music and dance.

"I started hearing Cuban rhythms around the age of twelve, when I was listening to a jazz station that had a Monday night Latin jazz programme."

He'd listen to Santana's "Abraxas," Herbie Mann's "Memphis Underground," and Cal Tjader's "Live at the

Funky Quarters," "but I didn't know at the time that these were Cuban rhythms."

When he was in his early twenties, the jazz brass players he was working with invited him to Cuban jam sessions. The legendary Cal Tjader triggered his total immersion into Cuban music.

When I visited Serge's Hollywood apartment, I learned he had already travelled three times to Cuba on musical visits, and that he played regularly with Afro-Cuban groups in Los Angeles. Since then, I have heard him on keyboards with Makina Loca, a group that is still thriving today.

We discussed the history of Cuban rhythms and harmonies and analysed just how and why Cuban music has become so vital throughout the world. As we talked, Serge banged out different riffs on the piano to add reality to his words.

Serge's earliest salsa gigs were at California Cuban social clubs in 1981. He then decided that it would be necessary to know all the other musical parts and not just the piano.

"Eventually I was drawn more and more to Cuban music," he says, "its jazziness, earthiness."

"The first Cuban group I heard in person was at the carnival in Vera Cruz, Mexico, in 1986. It was called Orquesta Ritmo Tropical. It was one of my great life experiences, not only because of the unusual syncopations but because of the unexpected exchange I had with the musicians. I was surprised how they'd offered me, a stranger: would you like to copy our music?"

Serge was impressed by their willingness to share their creativity, "because they're so secure in what they know," he says. At that moment, he knew that he would eventually have to go to Cuba to see, hear and participate in what was happening.

Guantanamera

If one were tracing the heritage of contemporary Cuban music, it would be necessary to go back to several intrinsic music genres. The *punto guajira* is Cuban country music. The most famous song from this genre, *La Guantanamera*, was composed in 1929 by Joseíto Fernández. It began as a simple stanza to which improvised *décimas* were conjured up by dueling guitarists, in an ancient oral tradition of call-and-response. Beginning in 1948 and lasting for twelve years, Fernández used the song as background for singing a tabloid version of the news. The programme was immensely popular, and led to a black-and-white documentary about El Punto Cubano, filmed in the early years of the Revolution.

As a gesture of solidarity to the Cuban Revolution, U.S. folk singer Pete Seeger performed the song, now to the words of a José Martí poem, at a 1963 Carnegie Hall concert in New York, and the song became an international hit.

The extraordinary evolution of *La Guantanamera* continues today with the 1997 hit movie by the same name, with the lyrics of the song serving as a chorus for a dark comedy about the Special Period. This last film by the late Cuban film maker Tomás Gutiérrez Alea, grossed over US$ 800,000. Such a complex evolution of such a simple tune has made *La Guantanamera* an international cultural icon.

Curiously, José Martí's simple lyrics are a reminder that Cuba is not simply a country of sea coasts:

my verse is a wounded deer
who seeks refuge in the mountains ...
With the poor people of the earth
I want to throw my luck
With the poor people of the earth
I want to throw my luck
the stream in the mountains
fulfills me more than the sea.

The Son and Other Genres

Guajira mountain music was one of many genres of Cuban music. *Charanga* music was played by an *orquesta típica* for a dancing public, and the *danzón*, with more Spanish influence, as the dance of the people. The *bolero* is a more hybrid romantic music with guitar accompaniment, not exclusively a Cuban form, but popular among today's roving musicians.

But the most powerful influence in contemporary Cuban music has been the *son*, a musical form that maintains a life of its own and has enjoyed a contemporary resurgence. Papi Oviedo y sus Soneros and Sierra Maestra are two of many groups producing recordings at this time. A compilation of various *son* groups is found on an album called *Casa de la Trova*.

The *son* divides into two sub-genres, one rural, from El Oriente, and the other urban, called rumba, centring in Matanzas.

Papi Oviedo plays the *tres*, a guitar of three double strings, and one of the six original instruments within this genre. The clave is comprised of two wooden sticks tapped together in syncopation, the most piercing of several layered rhythms. The *bongó* is a pair of small drums whose fuller sound contrasts with the clave. A thumb piano with five metal keys in a wooden box, of West African origin, is called the *marímbola*. Add a guitar and maracas, and you have the original *son* sextet.

The sextet became a septet in the 1920s when a trumpet was added, a combination initiated by the Septeto Habanero.

The source of today's salsa may come from Arsenio Rodríguez, who added two more trumpets to the septet, as well as taller drums called congas in 1946.

"Much early salsa was putting new clothes on old music," says Serge, my musician friend. Today, many leaders of salsa bands are conga players.

Along with the *son* came other great Cuban genres of less impact in today's scene, including the *cha cha cha*, which some say was invented for those with less dexterity, and the mambo, whose most famous band leader was Pérez Prado.

Many contemporary musicians are well-versed in all of these genres, so one often hears cross-over sounds. The most famous salsa group, Los Van Van, who have accumulated the most international frequent traveller miles, have *charanga* influence in their spirited salsa and a warm and contagious sound, whose joy was a great antidote for the Special Period.

The contemporary rumba, an urban, folk, street music and much more complex than the popularised rumbas of the 1950s, is an experience in itself. Listen to Los Muñequitos de Matanzas, especially their album *Rumba Caliente* and you may get the urge to take the next flight to Cuba. The most popular form of the rumba is called *guaguancó*. The singer recounts an everyday event, to be challenged by the chorus. Then, the rumba breaks out (*se rompe la rumba*) and the pair of dancers dance the *vacunao* (meaning: vaccinated or pricked). With movements of sexual possession, the man moves his waist, one hand or a leg towards the woman, who tries to elude him.

Rumba Music

Original instruments for the rumba were makeshift wood boxes with different pitches when struck, with sharper percussive sounds coming from pairs of spoons or a spoon against a glass bottle. Original rumbas were accompanied exclusively by percussive instruments, with the chorus functioning as an orchestra. Today, these sounds are reproduced with more formal and varied instrumentation.

Rumba is more than a form of music. It is a neighbourhood festivity, reminiscent in spirit with the blues "juke joint" in the Mississippi Delta, or the more religious *candomblé* in northeastern Brazil. Although rumba originates in the West African Yoruba culture with Bantu influence as well, white Spanish descendents at the bottom of the Cuban social scale were totally integrated within the rumba culture.

Rumba groups like Los Muñequitos de Matanzas, Afrocuba de Matanzas and Cutumba from Santiago are known as *portadores* (carriers), since they have inherited the artistic and expressive traditions of the original rumba and are direct descendents of the *coros de rumba*, neighbourhood groups from the previous century. What is known today as salsa music borrows heavily from rumba tradition.

Cuba's isolation during the embargo and the country's Africanisation because of white flight has led to new and exciting developments in salsa. The rhythms have grown so complex that fabled New York salsa sounds simple in comparison. Each Cuban group has wanted to not sound like the guy next door, and there is no homogenising marketing mechanism to conform to a niche audience as there would be in other more commercial countries, so virtually every musical experience in Cuba will offer a surprise.

Hip hop music has been developing around the massive apartment blocks of outer suburbs like Alamar, and has become so popular among youth that the government has created an agency to supervise its development, which some jokingly call the "Ministry of Rap."

Reggaeton is the up-and-coming trend, but not without its controversy. Born east of Cuba in the Caribbean, it is a melting pot of various musical genres and histories (rap, reggae and even some ancient African oral traditions). Popular among the urban poor, it may have made inroads in Cuba as a result of developing class differences when the dollar entered Cuba during the Special Period.

From a marketing standpoint, reggaeton enjoys a privileged position that rumba, also a music of the urban poor, never had. The sexuality in reggaeton is more marketable than the eroticism of rumba. Reggaeton is the pop music of bicycle taxi drivers in Cuba but you can hear it everywhere in Latin America. Rumba is intrinsically Cuban and has never enjoyed the pop status of reggaeton nor mass commercial success outside of Cuba. Reggaeton rhythms are repetitive and blatant. Rumba rhythms are varied and shifting.

"There has always been prejudice against this music [rumba]," noted Giovani del Pino, leader of the rumba group Yoruba Andabo in a *New York Times* article. "Radio and television don't speak of the rumba."

Rumba still received the greatest applause at the annual Cubadisco ceremony in Havana. In spite of its long history, it remains a contemporary music.

Salsa musicians know their rap and rhythm and blues, but they also lean heavily into the rumba tradition, and some have blended those genres into what Serge calls a "cross-cultural feast."

Outside of Cuba, a fusion called salsatón has been criticised by some salsa musicians. Some musicians assert that the name 'salsa' is mainly a commercial mechanism for selling *son*.

"The surrealness of living in Cuba in the uncertain nineties, with a little bit of anarchy," according to Serge, led to what he calls "*La música del período especial.*" The appearance of reggaeton may, in some ways, be a post special-period phenomenon. But the sounds and rhythms that helped Cuba swing through the penurious 1990s has a special place in contemporary music.

"Because of the embargo, some Cuban music was able to develop in its own petri dish, without having to compete in free market systems," Serge noted, before the reggaeton explosion. Like tourism, reggaeton may be another infusion from the global economy that makes the petri dish no longer possible.

Along with the various forms of salsa, a separate genre of sung poetry called *La Nueva Trova* and more straight-ahead jazz are both extremely popular internationally although they sustain a smaller, more exclusive audience within Cuba. The haunting Nueva Trova melodies and poetry of both Pablo Milanés and Silvio Rodríguez have become part of the repertoire of folk and protest singers around the world. The jazz piano of Gonzalo Rubalcaba, and groups like Irakere are the 'Jazz Messengers' of contemporary international jazz.

Other contemporary groups no less astonishing include Jesús Alemany's Cubanismo, the Afro-rumba group Bamboleo, the lyrical Latin jazz artist Issac Delgado, La Charanga Habanera, Los Muñequitos de Matanzas, the eclectic NG La Banda and The Afro-Cuban All-Stars.

Music is not easily separated from dance. At a summer 2003 concert, it was no surprise when the musicians of Jesús Alemany's group Cubanismo passionately encouraged the audience to dance in the aisles.

Like Serge, many of the best salsa musicians have formal training in classical music. NG La Banda's José Luis Cortés, nicknamed "El Tosco," studied under the great Cuban classical composer Harold Gramatges. In 1997, at the age of 79, Gramatges was awarded the prestigious Tomás Luis de Victoria prize in Madrid for his symphonic creations. Gramatges recognises that "there can be superb creations in pop music as well as some terrible pieces in classical music." He, like Giselle Grau's teacher Andrés Alén, harbours no genre prejudices. Cuba's music teachers only demand high quality for a demanding public.

Music Flows In Cuban Streets

"Nobody can get by on just hype," says Serge. "You gotta play ... even the taxi driver knows who's good, who can play. This is one of the most musical cultures in the world."

In fact, on any street in any Cuban city or town you will hear accomplished but virtually anonymous musicians, baptised with nicknames by the people in their cities. Serge had fulfilled his dream and travelled three times to Cuba to soak in the *ambiente*, but he hasn't had enough.

"The first breath after arriving at José Martí Airport in Havana," says Serge, "is a sweetness like nowhere else in the Caribbean. Maybe it's all the sugar cane in the air."

The love of music should have calmed the savage breast, but Cuban musicians from the United States who have travelled to Cuba have risked being blackballed from clubs when they return. When Los Van Van arrived in Miami, they were greeted with a protest at the airport by white Cubans. Black Cubans from Miami, even though they were anti-Fidel, supported Los Van Van.

Cuba and music are inseparable. A visit to Cuba is not complete without immersing yourself in Cuban music.

In 1997, jazzman Gonzalo Rubalcaba went to perform in Miami's Gusman Center for the Performing Arts. He was met by "a mob of 500 angry, shouting, flag-waving and flag-throwing anti-Castro demonstrators."

The apolitical Rubalcaba does not even live in Cuba. (He resides in Santo Domingo). But he earned the hostile reception for not having renounced the Cuban system that had given him his free training. He began formal piano studies at the age of nine and earned a degree in music composition from Havana's Institute of Fine Arts. As a teenage prodigy, he performed with bebop trumpeter Dizzy Gillespie, who became one of the Cuban pianist's greatest fans. With his classical training and interest in many types of music, Rubalcaba's jazz remains eclectic and without commercial trappings.

Contemporary Cuban music seems to lack a market niche. "Unlike the blues," says American guitarist Ry Cooder, "the music has not been destroyed by commercialisation. There's no music business in that Tin Pan Alley way. Musicians cannot accumulate vast wealth, and they have never been put on a pedestal. That is why the music is so heartfelt. In a way, it just isn't part of the modern world."

Cooder travelled to Cuba to record veteran Cuban *son*, *guajira* and *danzón* musicians, most of them in their seventies and eighties, in a milestone CD called *Buena Vista Social Club*.

This recording of the century catapulted performers like balladeers Omara Portuonodo and Ibrahim Ferrer, as well as *sonero* Compay Segundo to the status of cherished ambassadors of Cuban music. Compay Segundo had begun his career in the 1920s. He was well into his 90s when he passed away in 2003. Cooder could have never predicted the colossal impact of his musical quest in Cuba.

"I'm not worried about the politics," Cooder said. "It's not even an issue. But you've got to stand up for what's right sometimes, and so I suppose it is a little bit of a statement."

Serge's visits to Cuba had nothing to do with politics and everything to do with music.

"Cuban music will survive in spite of the politics," says Serge. "Politicians will come, live and die, but the music will remain. Cuban culture is much more potent than the politics."

TRANSPORTATION

A piece of bad advice came from a tour agent who specialised in travel to Cuba and visited Cuba four times a year. "Take taxis," she said. "The buses are undependable and the bus system is too complicated."

I figured that I wasn't going to survive in any place for long if I had to take a taxi every time I wanted to go anywhere. I also figured that since most Cubans use buses and cannot afford taxis, I would not be living the life of most Cubans if I were to get around by taxi on a regular basis.

Regular buses are referred to as *guaguas* and the double-humped monsters pulled by truck cabins are called *camellos*. The *camellos* seem to lumber around for lengthy periods without needing a drink of scarce petroleum. When you see these beasts of human burden, they are always packed, and you wonder how anyone ever gets a seat. (More seats

The few cars that can be found in Cuba are usually a few decades old, while those who do not have personal transport ride on the *camellos* with the unusual humps.

will become available as more public vehicles can be put into service service as Cuba gains access to petroleum by bartering: Venezuelan oil in exchange for Cuban doctors and educators.

In the meantime, to land a seat on any type of bus, the best strategy is to find the first stop. It is better to walk a few blocks to the first stop, wait on line and get a seat, than to remain several stops nearer your destiny and enter a packed vehicle. In Havana, a first stop of many lines is Parque de la Fraternidad, conveniently located south of Parque Central.

But what if you are nowhere near a first stop? Don't schedule activities one after another. Leave time to wait for the bus, and you can actually enjoy that time by engaging in conversations with the people who are waiting with you. Waiting is not all that bad in a country where people actually talk to each other. However, once in a bus, use normal precautions against pickpockets.

An alternative to a long wait is to take a *colectivo*. This is a collective taxi that charges per person. You don't find the *colectivo*; it finds you. A bus will cost less than one Cuban peso, usually about 40 cents. A *colectivo* within the city might cost about ten pesos, much more than the bus but considerably less than a taxi. However, some *colectivos* may refuse to take foreigners, for fear of trouble with the police who are suspicious of Cubans interacting with tourists.

Private cars may also be used as taxis. These unofficial taxis cost less than regular taxis but more than *colectivos*. In the *coches particulares*, you might find that your driver is a doctor who has been given the use of a car as a perk to make up for his low salary. Usually, your all-purpose neighbourhood hustler can find you a *coche particular*. However, a friendly ride to the airport may result in a fine for the driver, for having made an incursion into tourist territory. If you pay a private person to take you in his car, have a good explanation as to why this non-taxi is doing taxi functions (for example, "the man is a friend of my family").

Bicycling

If you want none of this, consider taking apart your bicycle and packing it with you as luggage to Cuba, along with basic tools, equipment and a strong lock. Most Cuba roads are flat and a fancy bike is not necessary. A critical mass of cyclers assure that the few automobile drivers out on the road are respectful of bicycle riders. The bicycle is the best way to get to the hard-to-reach outskirts of many cities. You can take your bike onto the ferries that have frequent service crossings between Old Havana and the colourful community of Regla, and a *ciclobus* that passes under the harbour tunnel. Outside of the hot summer months, the bicycle is a more comfortable and speedier replacement for travelling on city buses.

As in every city in the world, don't leave your bicycle unattended. Creative bicycle thieves abound. You may use *parqueos bicicletas* (bicycle parking places with attendants.)

Until recently, renting a bike was unheard of. Today, new bicycle rental businesses are sprouting up near hotels. Hotel clerks can point out any nearby rental place. Typical

Bicycle commuters coming off a ferry in Regla. Now that global warming is finally in the forefront of world consciousness, the bicycle, as a clean and healthy alternative for commuting, is increasingly recommended by municipalities. It would be an environment shame if Cuba, in the name of progress, were to go te way of China and abandon its bicycle culture.

pricing in 2006, at a place recommended by Hotel Sevilla in Old Havana was 12 CUC per day, 60 for seven days, 95 for two weeks and 132 for a whole month. Not bad if you intend to use the bicycle as your primary form of transportation.

Bicycle tours are also available. Inquire through your travel agent at home or a hotel in Cuba.

Hitchhiking

In Cuba, hitching is called *hacer botella* (to make a bottle). It is a common custom, especially outside the city, and drivers are encouraged by the government to pick up hitchhikers. I never hitchhike in Cuba, since Cubans with less spare time than I have need the ride a lot more than I do. However, I have met some foreigners who hitchhiked along with Cubans. If you've rented a car and are travelling in the country, remember that if bus service is still limited, it will remain customary to pick up hitchhikers.

Cuban hitchhikers are usually villagers who need to get somewhere. They are not the adventurous backpackers you'd see in Europe or the grizzly anarchists on the road in the United States. Government officials, called *amarillos* because of their yellow uniforms, are on site to help arrange rides.

Car Rental

With so few cars on the road in Cuba, renting a car is a comfortable alternative, especially if you are planning on visiting parts of rural Cuba inaccessible by train or bus. In most cultures, the automobile is an individualistic tool that tends to isolate the driver from other people. In Cuba, it's the opposite. A private driver fulfills a public service by picking up citizens and gets to know people along the way.

Gas prices are at a European level, and car rental prices are set at rates that conform to a tourist's capacity to pay. Most hotels will lead you to the nearest car rental agency, which often has an office inside the hotel itself. Officially-sanctioned rent-a-car companies are the economical Havanautos (at airports and major hotels) and Cubanacan (at airports and at the Hotel Comodoro). Cubanacan has a "fly-and-drive" plan, through which a visitor can drive to any part of the country with an airport and then drop off the car and take a flight.

Train Travel

If you've got time on your hands, and specific places are not as important to you as travelling itself, I'd recommend travelling by train. Cuba is the only country in the Caribbean with a passenger train system. I found the service at the Havana train station quite friendly.

The main train station is at the southeast corner of Old Havana on Avenida Bélgica, also known as Egido. There is a special ticket window for tourists, who must pay in CUC. The advantage is that a foreigner can reserve his seat two hours in advance (though it's recommended that you get reservations a day or two in advance) while Cubans must reserve farther in advance. Foreign students may be allowed to purchase tickets in Cuban pesos, for a great saving.

The traveller out of Havana has three alternatives. The slow *tren militar* is the cheap but unreliable option. The *tren francés* (made in France), with air conditioning in some or all of the cars departs for locations east of Havana and arrives in Santiago the following morning (departs from Havana about 6pm, for 72 CUC) , with stops at major cities along the way, and another train going to Guantánamo leaves about 3pm, for 32 CUC. Then you have the *tren regular*, departing about 3pm to Santiago for only 30 CUC). In this train you get the feeling of travelling in a museum piece, with large seats and a basic toilet at the end of each car. Trains have the equivalent of a flight attendant, who graciously mentions snack service and other amenities.

Railroad lovers could find an 1842 Baltimore steam engine, painted in glossy red with black trim near the waiting room, though it has probably already been moved to the nearby Cristina Station.

Beach train. At the Cristina Station, on Avenida Cristina, also known as Avenida México, not for from the main station, you can catch a train to a real Cuban beach, Guanabo, at the end of a row of tourist beaches in Playas del Este. This train only operates in the July and August vacation season.

Bus Excursions

Travellers have a choice of the funky national bus service, out of the Terminal de Omnibus Nacionales (Avenida Rancho Boyeros, near Plaza de la Revolución) where there's a separate blue-painted ticket office for CUC-paying foreigners, or the more expensive CUC tourist bus service Vía Azul, which leaves from Avenue 26 between Avenue Zoológico and Ulloa (www.viazul.cu). This writer has travelled on both comfortable air-conditioned tourist buses and Cuba's version of Greyhound, finding the latter trips more rewarding (with the chance to engage in conversation with Cuba travellers) though less comfortable and slower. The Cuban buses, called Astro, will be your only alternative if you are travelling off the tourist track. On my trip to Cárdenas, I took an Astro from the main terminal, paying in CUC. But for the return from Cárdenas they sold me the ticket in pesos.

Air Travel

Air travel is relatively inexpensive within Cuba and to Cuba from nearby places like Cancún. But beware. Schedules often change. I once arrived at the José Martí Airport an hour before my scheduled flight only to discover that the plane was about ready to depart. They had moved the departure time ahead by an hour! I would have been there two hours in advance, but the "transfer" that was supposed to pick me up never arrived.

Buying a voucher for an airport "transfer" for a later date is not a good idea. On the other hand, the agency that had sold me the phantom transfer, Sol Y Son, graciously returned my money. The sure-bet tour company for Cuba travel is Havanatur which takes care of transfers (only ingoing), the first two nights of hotel (a sometimes entry prerequisite for those who plan to go the home stay route for the rest of their stay), and even provides the traveller with a guidebook.

TOURS

The tours one finds in hotel lobbies through the government company Havanatur are usually quite pleasant. But the best part comes if you can get the guide to depart from his or her script. The guides themselves seem to enjoy the tour even more when customers ask probing questions.

A number of specialty tour companies originating outside of Cuba offer package deals that are unprecedented in the tourist industry, in that they involve participation between clients and Cubans in a particular profession. These tours may specialise in medicine, ecology, music, agriculture, architecture, or virtually any other field. I've interviewed many people who have taken such tours and never found anyone who came away disappointed. The price is not cheap but the service is enthusiastic and intellectually honest. If travel restrictions for people from the United States have not yet been lifted by the time you see this book, such tours will facilitate your getting permission from the United States Department of Commerce.

The names and contact numbers of some of these tour companies are listed immediately below.

Given the difficulty of finding public transportation to some regions of Cuba, travellers who ordinarily would never consider a tour might change their mind in this case.

TOURS FOR PEOPLE WHO DON'T LIKE TOURS

Some of the best tour companies have direct communication with the above and other Cuban educational institutions serving foreigners. The following tour agencies are the antithesis of the typical post-card-picture-snapping tour industry, and are geared for the highly sophisticated culture enthusiast.

In particular, several tour agencies operating from the United States deserve special commendation for enduring harassment from pro-embargo militants. The operations of these educational tour companies are painstakingly legal. Although politically "progressive," these organisations operate within a critical perspective, and they are very much people-oriented, so should you decide to travel this way, expect to have challenging dialogue with Cubans in your field of choice.

Tour Groups Worth Checking Out

- Global Exchange. This company operates what are called "reality tours" and specialises in public health, the arts, volunteer work groups, Afro-Cuban culture, eco-tourism, film and other themes. A typical tour lasts from ten days to two weeks and costs about US$ 1,950 from Cancún, México. One professional who made a tour with Global Exchange called it "the experience of a lifetime." Global Exchange also sponsors bicycle trips and studies through the University of Havana. Phone: (800) 497-1994; fax: (415) 255-7498. Address: 2017 Mission Street. #303, San Francisco, CA 94110. Website: www.globalexchange.org. E-mail: gx-realitytours@globalexchange.org.

- Marazul Tours. Here is another pioneer in tours to Cuba. One of Marazul's many specialties is the Cuban convention circuit. If you have a profession, Marazul will probably find a symposium, seminar, or convention to fit your needs. Marazul also publishes up-to-date strategic travel information for its clients. Address: Marazul Tours, Inc., Tower Plaza, 4100 Park Avenue, Weehawken, NJ 07087. Phone: (800) 223-5334; Fax: (201) 319-9009. Website: www.marazultours.com.

- Center for Cuban Studies. Operated by a veteran of the Venceremos Brigade and author of a book on Cuba, Sandra Levinson, this organisation also publishes a bimonthly newsletter on Cuba. Unlike Global Exchange, which travels to many parts of the world, the Center for Cuban Studies specialises in Cuba only. Many distinguished public figures and intellectuals are sponsors of the Center, including Harry Belafonte, Noam Chomsky, Francis Coppola, Jules Feiffer and John Womack, Jr. Tours are similar in price and substance to those of Global Exchange. Address: Center for Cuban Studies, 124 West 23rd Street, New York, NY 10011. E-mail, cubananctr@iqc.org; Phone: (212) 242-0559. Website: www.cubaupdate.org.

- Cubalinda. Those who have read former CIA-agent Philip Agee's *Inside the Company: CIA Diary* (1975), an exposé on dirty tricks, will be intrigued to learn about this Cuba tour company that he launched in 1999. Website: www.cubalinda.com

From the UK
UK residents have a number of choices. A few include:
- Havanatur from Cuba operating in Hertfordshire. Phone: (1707) 663139;
- Progressive Tours, in London, 12 Porchester Place, London, in Paddington. Phone: (020) 7262-1676; and
- South American Experience, in London, 38–44 Gillingham Street, Victoria, London SW1VHU. Phone: (870) 499 0683; website: www.southamericanexperience.co.uk/cuba.

From Canada
Canadians will find many Cuba tour specialists advertised in the *Toronto Star* travel section. Two such agencies with package tours are:
- Bel Air Travel, seems to have good prices. Examples: end of August, 7 nights in a 2-star hotel with air and meals for CAD$ 610, and several 7-nighters in 5-star hotels for less than CAD$ 1,500, phones: (416) 675-7707 or (877) 675-7707
  Website: www.belairtravel.ca; and
- Cuba Tourist Board in Canada for numerous conventional or offbeat visiting opportunities.
  Website: www.gocuba.ca

From Other Countries
Havanatur operates from many other countries where English is spoken, including Holland, Ireland, Israel, Jamaica, Japan, and Switzerland. Check local directory.

ATTRACTIONS
Attractions categorised by geographical location have been referred to in the Chapter Two. Here we categorise the attractions thematically.

Ecotourism.
Flamingos, manatee, the smallest bird and frog in the world, crocodiles, prehistoric cacti, mangroves and wetlands and fossilised plants: these are a few examples of the fauna and flora contained in biosphere reserve

areas, where hiking, bird watching, horseback riding and spelunking are some available activities.

Three of the biosphere reserves are: the Guaniguanico mountain range near the Viñales agricultural region with its caves and rock formations (west of Havana); the Sierra de Rosario not far west of Havana including Soroa, Las Terrazas and the Santo Tomás cave system; and the Zapata Peninsula National Park, south central with numerous beachfront lagoons and mangroves. The Sierra Maestra, the Fidel/Che/Camilo hideout, during the revolution, offers spectacular hiking.

Sailing and Cruising

With 5,746 km (3,570 miles) of coastline marked by 200 sheltered bays and with a surface water temperature averaging between 24°C–29°C (75°F–84°F), Cuba is a sailors dreamscape, except for the high-risk hurricane season in September and October. Arriving ships must contact port authorities before entering within 19.3 km (12 miles) of the coast. The eight authorised ports of entry include: Havana (Marina Hemingway), Varadero (two marinas), Ciego de Avila or the "Cuban Keys" (Marina Gaviota Varadero), Holguín (two nautical bases), Santiago de Cuba (Marina Marlin at Punta Gorda), Cienfuegos (Marina Puertosol Jagua), Cayo Largo (Marina Puertosol) and Pinar del Río (María la Gorda).

Diving and Snorkeling

With coral reefs, colourful underwater species, unusual topography and a variety of shipwrecks, divers have a wide array of options. Dive centres are operated by the companies Cubanacán-Marlin, Cubamar, Puerto Sol and Gaviota. The Havana region alone has 72 different scuba sites, through four international diving centres. Playa Girón, the Bay of Pigs, is known for its sheer drop off the island's underwater platform, and has 20 dive sites.

Health Tourism.

Travellers considering a therapeutic adventure in Cuba should read the testimonies of people who have already passed through the system. Health tourism is a growing source of income, with various specialist hospitals, health spas, clinics and resort centres serving foreign visitors. In 2005, more than 5,000 foreign patients travelled to Cuba for a diverse array of treatments. A BBC report emphasized eye-surgery, neurological disorders such as multiple sclerosis and Parkinson's disease, and orthopaedics.

A majority of patients are Latin Americans but visitors from other parts of the world are also attracted, especially for a unique Cuban treatment for retinitis pigmentosa, often known as night blindness. Cuban heart surgeons have acquired a fine reputation.

Medical Profits

Health tourism brings in revenues of approximately $ 40m a year.

More than 500 different medical products are manufactured by the pharmaceutical industry, which provided for four fifths of the needs of the Cuban population until the 1990s economic crisis. Chinese raw materials have allowed Cuba to approach the pre-1990 level of service. Many drugs are supplied to hospitals by international aid from Cuba Solidarity Groups around the world.

Professional Events.

Hundreds of professional organisations hold special events and conferences in Cuba. The above-listed travel companies will have schedules of these events. Marazul and Center for Cuban Studies are two good sources. Every possible "ology" is represented in the dazzling array of conferences.

Learning Holidays.

Aside from language learning, cinema, dance, medicine and other Cuban specialties (see Resource Guide at the end of this book), Cuba is an open air museum. UNESCO World Heritage sites include colonial Havana, colonial

Trinidad, Sugar Mill Valley near Trinidad, ruins of French coffee plantations at La Gran Piedra and Guantánamo and San Pedro de la Roca del Morro castle in Santiago.

U.S. TRAVEL RESTRICTIONS

In case travel restrictions for U.S. citizens have not yet been lifted as you read these lines, consider the following legal scenario: "Technically," it is not illegal for U.S. citizens to travel to Cuba but it is illegal to spend money there. Many U.S. citizens take a chance and travel to Cuba, since Cuban immigration authorities do not stamp U.S. passports. When I once travelled out of Cuba, the immigration authority smiled and said, "Don't worry, I won't stamp your passport." It didn't matter to me though, since I had a license from the U.S. Office of Foreign Assets Control (OFAC).

In theory, one could travel to Cuba without spending money. But U.S. Treasury Department will not believe you, since they know that Cubans are not allowed to put you up for free, not because it's wrong to do so but because that would mean less revenue from tourism. They also know how unlikely it is for a Cuban who earns the equivalent of US$ 20 per month to host a visitor who earns a hundred times that much.

U.S. authorities stationed to meet arriving flights from Havana to Caribbean airports have harassed and sometimes charged U.S. citizens with disobeying travel restrictions, which has led to a few stiff fines. (I saw no such authorities at Cancún, nor did friends who arrived from Cuba via that same Mexican airport.)

The Helms-Burton Act raises the potential penalty on Americans who go to Cuba to US$ 250,000 in criminal fines and US$ 55,000 in civil fines. Between 1982 and 1987, the Treasury Department brought only ten criminal indictments for various violations related to unlicensed travel to Cuba,

One American artist I met in Havana claimed that "we have the right to travel wherever we damned well please according to the United States constitution, and I've been to Cuba seven times now with no harassment as yet."

and between 1994 and 1997, penalties of US$ 1,500 to US$ 2,000 have been assessed in 44 civil cases. In the Cuban Assets Control Regulations, Part 515, you will find fines of up to a million dollars for businesses and US$ 250,000 for individuals, plus a prison sentence of up to ten years.

However, depending on the political waves of the times, it is usually not difficult to obtain permission to travel to Cuba under categories such as "journalistic activities" or "professional research and meetings" (see entire list in the website given below).

Application Forms for Visiting Cuba

You may access application forms for visiting Cuba through the website of: Licensing Division, U.S. Office of Foreign Assets Control, Department of the Treasury, 1500 Pennsylvania Avenue NW, Treasury Annex, Washington, D.C. 20220. Website: www. ustreas.gov/offices/enforcement/ofac/programs/cuba/cuba.shtml

---

Do not be discouraged by the 64-page PDF internet booklet. Scroll down for the category of your visit and you will find specific instructions as well as the appropriate application form.

A "general license" to travel to Cuba may be applied for by government officials on official business, representatives of international organisations of which the U.S. is a member, persons whose stay in Cuba is fully-hosted and is not paid for by a person subject to U.S. jurisdiction, journalists regularly working for a news reporting organisation, and family visitors travelling once a year due to extreme humanitarian needs.

A "specific license" may be obtained by persons engaged in non-commercial professional research, freelance journalists, persons with clearly-defined educational objectives, members of human rights organisations, persons traveling for the purpose of importation, exportation, or transmission of information.

Usually, the permission restricts spending by U.S. citizens to no more than US$ 100 per day, excluding air fare.

In late 2003, both U.S. Senate and House of Representatives voted in bipartisan fashion to add an amendment to the transportation bill that would eliminate funding for the enforcement of the Cuba travel ban. The Senate Foreign Relations Committee also approved a bill to lift the travel ban entirely. However, the Republican leadership stripped the amendment. Seemingly on its last legs, the travel ban was resuscitated once again.

More than a decade ago, seasoned observers were referring to the imminent lifting of the travel ban. The ban could still be lifted tomorrow, or it could remain in place indefinitely. Mentalities can change abruptly or they can remain entrenched. A decade ago, who would have imagined that a bloc of Latin American countries, with Venezuela in the forefront, would be defying the United States and literally refueling the Cuban regime, thereby adding a whole new dimension to the puzzling set of variables that will determine the fate of the travel ban.

COMMUNICATING IN CUBA

CHAPTER 8

"I have the joy of going
to a bank and talking to the administrator,
not in English,
not in sir,
but simply in *compañero*, as they say in Spanish"
—Nicolas Guillén from his poem *Tengo*

PRIOR TO MY ARRIVAL in Havana, I sought advice from every traveller I could find, every guidebook, every travel agency specialising in Cuba. Never before in my travel plans had I been so painstaking in seeking guidance. And never before had I received such bad advice from such good experts.

How could such seasoned travellers, perceptive writers and expert tour agents be the source of such useless and sometimes prejudiced advice? And how could I avoid the same pitfalls in this book?

Cuba is in a process of transformation, and from one moment to the next, what was right becomes wrong, and what was prohibited becomes encouraged. For example, religion was once the "opium of the people," but Cubans were officially encouraged to get out and see the Pope during his 1998 visit.

The most important piece of advice is, upon arrival, to be prepared for the inevitable conversations with Cubans and ask them whatever you need to know, but don't confuse the authentic desire of most Cubans for frank communication with hordes of scamsters engaged in fierce competition for your money. When capitalism was introduced through tourism, most Cubans were left out of the promised bonanza. With no recourse to the deceptive advertising of the consumer society, their only tool for gaining "customers" was a deceptively charming smile and engaging conversation.

LANGUAGE

Spanish, unlike English, is basically a phonetic language, with each letter consistently sounding like its name. The English language suggests that there is chaos in the universe and that the Supreme Being has faltered. Well-ordered Spanish cries out "There is a God! And he's an efficiency expert."

An awareness of such clean-cut phonetics coupled with a very basic foundation of vocabulary and grammar can get you through the day. Since a large portion of English shares a Latin root with Spanish, there are numerous "cognates," words that may sound similar or different but have virtually identical spelling and meaning. Only a handful of notable grammatical differences separate English and Spanish.

With more complex or "different" languages, the lag time between the moment of introduction until the moment of practical use is lengthy. With Spanish, the English-speaking student can start speaking from Day One.

Phonetics. With most consonants quite similar to English, vowel comprehension plays the strategic role in successful listening. Each of the five vowels never vary in pronunciation.

Prouniciation Guide
Vowels

- **a** is pronounced *AH*, like the *a* in *father*.
- **e** is pronounced *EH*, like the *e* in *ten* or *vest*.
- **i** is pronounced like a shortened *EE* like the *i* in *tangerine*.
- **o** is pronounced *OH*, as in *for* (not quite a "long" *o*).
- **u** is pronounced like a shortened *OO*, like the *oo* in "*oops!*"

Even before mastering the consonants, these five little vowel sounds allow the learner to say and understand most cognates.

Only two Spanish consonant sounds do not exist in English and might hinder the understanding of cognates: (1) the rr which sounds like a trill (the tongue must flutter) and (2) the j as well as the g (only when it comes before e or i), which sound like a hard h as if one were clearing one's throat. A similar sound exists in Arabic and Hebrew.

There are, however, other consonants that do not sound like their English counterparts:

Prounciation Guide

Consonants

- **h** is silent.
- **ll** is pronounced similarly to the English *y*.
- **ñ** is pronounced like the *ni* in *onion*.
- **qu** is pronounced like *k*, with a silent *u*.
- **x** is the same as its English counterpart, except in words coming from the Nahuatl language, when it sounds like the Spanish *j*, as in México written *Méjico* in Spain.

A written accent tells the reader that the stress on a word is falling on a syllable other than the normal stressed syllable.

Cognates

Once the phonetics are understood, many hundreds of useful words become immediately accessible. Here are a few cognate groups:

- Virtually all words ending in 'tion' or 'ssion' in English, with occasional minor spelling changes, end in '*ción*' or '*sión*' in Spanish. *Conversación, intuición, nación, comunicación, misión, comisión*. Hundreds of other cognates are derived from this group. Example: the verb *conversar*, to converse, chat.
- Virtually all words ending in 'ity' in English end in '*idad*' in Spanish, with only occasional minor spelling changes. *Unidad, claridad, entidad*. Words derived from the '*idad*' group are also cognates. Example: the verb *unir*, to unite.

- Words from English ending in 'em' or 'ama' (of Greek origin) have their parallels in Spanish with 'ema' and 'ama' endings. *Problema, sistema, drama, panorama, tema* (theme), etc. Gender: Spanish nouns are masculine (usually ending in o) or feminine (usually ending in a), but this Greek group of words represents an exception, and are masculine. Example: *el problema* (the problem).
- Hundreds of other frequently used words are derived from the above three groups or are independently parallel to English. The beginner Spanish student starts out with an abundant vocabulary.

Grammar

In Spanish, verbs change their endings (conjugations) according to the subject pronoun. The ending of the verb usually indicates the subject. Even though *yo hablo* means "I speak," the *yo* is not necessary except for emphasis, since the *o* ending indicates first person singular. An excessive use of the *yo* could make you sound egotistical. When conjugating the "you" there is a familiar "*tú*" and a formal "*usted*" with different verb endings.

A few other basic differences are:

- Descriptive adjectives follow the noun instead of preceding it (*lección difícil* instead of difficult lesson).
- Adjectives agree in gender (male/female) and number (singular/plural) with nouns. Example: *edificio blanco* (white building) is male (*o* ending), and *casas blancas* (white houses) is feminine (*a* ending) and plural (*s* ending).
- One significant difference in perception between the two languages is the verb: to be. Spanish has two verbs that translate "to be": *ser* refers to essence or identity, and *estar* refers to state, condition, or location. "To be or not to be" from Hamlet is *ser o no ser*, since it refers to the character's identity. But *cómo está usted*? (How are you?) is derived from *estar* because you're asking the state or condition of the person. Memorise this crucial sentence which will save the day if you have an attack of turista: *Dónde está el baño* (Where is the bathroom?). Notice that we use the verb *estar* because we refer to location rather than essence.
- Another difference in perception is observed in Spanish's two past tenses: the preterit, which views an event as completed, and the imperfect, which describes or re-experiences the past. Preterit: "I went" and imperfect "I was going."
- Object pronouns that accompany verbs go before a conjugated verb, the opposite of English. Example: *te quiero* (I love you), another crucial phrase for the romantically inclined.
- Reflexive pronouns *me* (myself), *te* (yourself, familiar), *se* (him/her/yourself), *nos* (ourselves), *se* (themselves) go before conjugated verbs, and the reflexive construction is used much more frequently in Spanish than in English: *Me llamo María* = my name is María (literally: I call myself María); *José se levanta temprano* = José gets up early (literally: José raises himself early). (Note: all English compound verbs with "get" are reflexive in Spanish.)

Other grammatical nuances are of less strategic importance and may be picked up as you learn.

Politeness. For good rapport, use either of two introductory verb conjugations for making requests, both of which mean "I would like" rather than "I want": *quisiera* and *me gustaría* (literally "it would please me").

This summary will help you sift out what is essential when taking recommended non-credit continuing education course in Spanish. Such courses, offered at adult education centres, are more practical and quicker than credit courses at universities, which bog one down in abstract details.

Most Frequent and All-Purpose Verb Conjugations
Please note that subject pronouns are in parentheses, since they are optional.

Hay (pronounced like "i" in "wine")	There is, there are, is there?, are there?
Dónde hay un médico?	Where is there a doctor?

Cuesta	Costs
Cuánto cuesta el boleto de tren?	How much does the train ticket cost?

Estar	To be (condition/location)
(yo) estoy	I am
(tú) estás	you are (familiar)
(Usted) está	you are (formal)
(él/ella) está	he/she is
(nosotros) estamos	we are
(Ustedes) están	you (plural) are
(ellos/ellas) están	they are (masculine/feminine)
Cómo estás?	How are you?

Ser	To be (intrinsic, characteristic)
(yo) soy	I am
(tú) eres	you are (familiar)
(Usted) es	you are (formal)
(él/ella) es	he/she is
(nosotros) somos	we are
(Ustedes) son	you are (plural)
(ellos/ellas) son	they are (masculine/feminine)
Qué hora es?	What time is it?

Tengo	To have
(yo) tengo	I have
(tú) tienes	you have (familiar)
(Usted) tiene	you have (formal)
(él/ella) tiene	he/she has
(nosotros) tenemos	we have
(Ustedes) tienen	you have (plural)
(ellos/ellas) tienen	they have (masculine/feminine)
Tengo un problema.	I have a problem.

FORMAL AND INFORMAL DISCOURSE

In a country where most leaders, including the president, maintain an informal discourse, the flowery formality of nineteenth century *criollo* communication has virtually disappeared. This phenomena extends wider than the coasts of Cuba. Along with the informal clothing, women's equality and a dismantling of sexual inhibition comes a loosening of language that

Tip!
Switch from informal to formal language when responding to a policeman.

is not entirely Cuban and has much in common with other warmer regions of Latin America. For visitors, the only "rule" on language formalities to follow is that of common courtesy.

DIPLOMATIC DISCOURSE

If any barriers do exist, they come from the political culture. In the United States and many European countries, frames are drawn around political discourse that exclude certain language. When one country's army needlessly destroys vital infrastructure of another country or targets civilians, the phrase "war crimes" is excluded from the discourse. For example, when referring to contemporary occupations of a foreign territory, Western media cannot use the words 'colonialism' or 'imperialism'. It is difficult for the American media to use the term 'war profiteering' when referring to contracts handed out to certain corporations that receive direct benefit from military campaigns. There is no way that visitors from Western cultures will understand the frames that constrain Cuban political and diplomatic discourse without understanding their own unwritten rules on constraining political language.

Literacy brigadier Rosita (at right) with the rural community she taught to read and write. In the background is her thatched-roofed *bohío*.

On the Cuban side the American term 'embargo' is referred to as 'blockade'. The Cuban view of 'human rights' at the beginning of the twenty-first century prioritised social rights (to health care, education and culture) and economic rights (the right to low cost housing, for example) above personal freedoms, whereas many Western visitors would see personal freedoms as the point of departure for human rights. The word 'terrorism' represents an example of the gap between the high level discourse of Cuban officials and those of the United States. Cuban discourse does not differentiate between terrorism perpetrated by a state and that which is carried out by individuals.

For those who plan to engage in diplomatic communication, it is recommended that concrete wording be used to bridge the gap of abstract language. Within the diplomatic community, titles are to be used in Cuba in the same universal way as they would be used in any other diplomatic scenario, and the usual first-name style the pervades the rest of Cuban society can be relinquished.

POPULAR EXPRESSIONS

In general, there is little difference between the language of the people at street level and the language of the intellectuals or political and business leaders. Once you get deeper into subcultures, a whole new lexicon can emerge. There is the reggaeton and hip hip slang, impossible to learn unless you're listening on a daily basis, the santería language, based on the needs and advice of the *orishas* (saints), santería-related vocabulary and expressions of African origin (Yoruba, Congo, Abekuá) and underworld or hustler argot.

There are 34 words for the male sex organ and 11 words for the female organ.

A list of a few high-frequency everyday words typical of Cuban Spanish can be of strategic use. Frequent practice with Cubans will expose you to more

amarillos (ah-mah-RI-yos)	police in yellow uniforms that flag down cars for hitchhikers outside of towns
CADECA (kah-DEH-cah)	offices all around town where currency can be exchanged officially
cojones (coh-HOH-nehs)	literally "balls"; a person who has *cojones* has guts in a blatant way
camello (ca-MEH-yo)	the humped buses pulled by a truck cabin
coño (coh-nyo)	"damn it" (literally "cunt")
divisa (dee-VEE-sah)	now refers to convertible pesos but also means dollars
fruta bomba (FRU-ta BOM-ba)	this is what in other Spanish speaking countries is known as the papaya fruit, but papaya in Cuban slang is the woman's most private part
fulas (FOO-lahs)	money (strong currency)
guagua (GWAH-gwah)	bus
hacer botella (ah-SAIR bo-TEH-ya)	to hitchhike
jinetera (hee-neh-TEH-ra)	woman who receives money or gifts in exchange for a night on the town that may end up with sex
jinetero (hee-neh-TEH-ro)	male hustler or scamster
yumas (YOO-mahs)	tourists or foreigners

IMAGE

Communication between visitors and Cubans is enhanced when the visitor does not stick out blatantly like a tourist. For most of us, this is not an easy task. Taking pictures should not replace taking in the images around you. The more you hang out and interact with what you see, the more your persona can merge with your surroundings. This is not so different from anything new. We see something new and it stands out. We see it several times and it becomes more natural to the surroundings. We see it often and it becomes normal.

When you first arrive in Cuba, you look like an Eiffel Tower. Parisians pass by the Eiffel Tower without blinking because they see it every day.

DOING BUSINESS

CHAPTER 9

On doing business in Cuba: "Anything that's prohibited
today may be allowed tomorrow and anything
allowed today might be prohibited tomorrow."
—John Kavulich, founder and former president
of the U.S.–Cuba Trade and Economic Council

IN THE FILM *Guantanamera*, the Cuban funeral bureaucrat is so bent on achieving successful efficiency statistics to corroborate his professional success that he grudgingly puts human concerns aside, losing his wife in the process. Like all caricatures, this one is an exaggeration of the truth. But Cuban officials do indeed want and expect to have their performance measured. My having heard a crew of diplomats cheering after the announcement that the infant mortality rate had dropped below 10 per 1,000, is anecdotal corroboration of the more flattering side of the stereotype.

As the year 2006 entered its early stages, some Cuban officials were rejoicing about the 8 per cent real growth rate in 2005. Contrary to the infant mortality rate, which refers to social accomplishments, economic growth rate is essentially a capitalist statistic. The Cuban government now has its feet planted in two ideologies that were once viewed as irreconcilable. If there is one statement we could make about doing business in Cuba, it is precisely that a potential entrepreneur must learn to weave through a complex set of opposite logics, in which socialism and capitalism compete and embrace in a *danse macabre* that could end up in a quirkily happy marriage or in the death of one of the partners.

CORRUPTION?

With rules dancing so unexpectdly from one side to the other, from left to right, from rigidity to flexibility, it is no wonder that a scenario for potential corruption has emerged. "Someone said that no Cuban steals a million pesos but that a million Cubans steal one peso each day," wrote Havana resident and independent Internet journalist Miguel Fernández Martínez, in "Illegal Lives."

"It's the necessity of survival that has forced this people to assume a posture of illegality as a rational means of living," wrote Fernández.

His view is from the bottom up. John Kavulich, former president of the U.S.–Cuba Trade and Economic Council and probably the person who has studied the Cuban business scene better than any other living foreigner, has a top-down perspective. The non-profit organisation that he founded in 1993 is the among the best sources of information on doing business in Cuba.

Kavulich told me that business deals may involve inviting Cubans to dinner or giving a bottle of rum as a gift, typical in business dealings around the world.

"Every once in a while, and it's extremely rare, do you hear of any business person making a payoff, and that's one in a thousand."

DOING BUSINESS

The rules for doing business in Cuba are evolving on a daily basis and will continue to be modified during the next decade. This is the bad news. The good news is that you won't have to bribe anyone to get things going. Here are a few tips that will make your Cuban business experience a positive and profitable one. Foreigners doing business in Cuba must have a partner. In fact, they all have the same partner: the government, in what is called *empresa mixta* (literally: mixed enterprise, but similar to joint venture). The number of joint ventures increased from 20 in 1991 to more than 260 at the end of 1996, but by 2006, declined to 236. "We are not interested in doing too many joint ventures, we're only interested in those that have an impact on the economy," said Minister of Foreign Investment and Economic Cooperation, Marta Lomas (Reuters, 29 January 2007).

Law No. 77, passed in 1995, was designed to encourage foreign investments in Cuba. However, it maintained many of the risks that were responsible for the failure of the earlier laws. Under the subtitle of guarantees for the foreign investors, the law retains the right of the Cuban State to expropriate and confiscate foreign investments for the common good, and it would be the Cuban government that decides the common good.

Furthermore, there are intrinsic risks associated with changes in currency regulations and the dual currency scenario. If a joint investor wants to repatriate funds, what conversion rate would it receive? The risk increases given the fact that the foreign investor cannot have deposits in foreign banks outside Cuba as protection against devaluation. The investor is obligated to go through the Cuban insurance system as opposed to using a foreign insurance company.

Larger investments must go through the bureaucracy of negotiation with the Council of Ministers and other government agencies, and delays could be costly to the investor.

There's also a problem of liquidity since, should the investor wish to sell his shares in the joint venture to a third party, he must first get the consent of the Cuban government. Certain business structures such as limited liability companies and general partnerships are not allowed.

Curiously, the law seems to allow for investment by Cuban exiles, depending on case-by-case negotiation.

The foreign investor is also denied the right to contract for labour directly. Labourers must be sent by the government employment agency. The government employment agency, as intermediary, would receive more from the labourer's salary than the worker himself. What would Marx and Engels say about this deal?

With the investor's risk at such a high level, the only way he or she would want in would be for the potential return to be that much higher than normal.

Cover Your Back!

Law No. 77 states that conflicts shall be resolved in Cuban judicial courts, which are not independent of the Cuban government partner. So in a conflict between foreign and Cuban partner, the partner would have the upper hand in conflict resolution. Thus, it would become important for the foreign investor to add stipulations about conflict resolution.

The fact that foreign investors are still willing to do business in Cuba suggests that the Cuban government is giving them some special advantages in realm of return on investment. The rapid increase of Chinese investment in Cuba should be studied in order to establish a paradigm for other investors.

By 2005, Cuba's growth rate reached 5.5 per cent, suggesting that foreign companies have found a way, via individual contracts, to minimise the risks, or these companies foresee the possibility that they may be allowed exclusive proprietorship of certain enterprises either by changes in the law or the inevitable change in regime. On the other hand, if class divisions in Cuban society become aggravated as capitalism extends to more remote stations, whichever government is in power could also step in and stop the growth train, which may end up following a Chinese model that will increase the gap between the rich and the poor.

American investors, especially in the agricultural and pharmaceutical sectors, are watching over this situation with a certain degree of frustration. By 1977, the United States Department of Commerce (DOC) was aware that other countries had gotten the jump. The DOC then stepped in to allow certain U.S. corporations loophole permits to begin making waves on the shore of the Malecón, sidestepping the embargo legislation with remarkable legal agility. Great hopes for a dissolution of the U.S. trade embargo were dashed, temporarily, when the Bush administration, pandering to Florida votes, succumbed to both the Cuban exile lobby and the neo-conservatives embedded in the government, and actually tightened the embargo.

The probabilities of your business being approved by the Cuban government greatly increase if you enter negotiations armed with evidence that your enterprise will provide social benefits for the Cuban population. However, increasingly, some independent consultants for doing business in Cuba are connected with certain conflicts of interests, both financial and political. With political polarisation between the U.S. and Cuban governments, both sides are demanding certain political concessions or advocacy from business that would wish to remain apolitical.

As has been noted, with the dual currency economy, Cubans with less access to CUCs are considerably more vulnerable to the tribulations of inequality than increasing salary differentials seem to indicate. Tips earned by workers within the tourist industry give them more economic leverage than their specific salary.

In 2006, some American consultants were relatively optimistic about potential business opportunities in Cuba, such as the Babun Consulting Group in Miami. "If you have a strategic plan for potential investment into Cuba, you should pull your plan off the bookshelf, dust it off and bring it up to date," said Teo A. Babun Jr., who consults companies looking to expand into a post-embargo Cuba.

Babun and other consultants have noted that the most likely companies for early entrance in Cuba would be those looking for opportunities in the privatisation of government-owned companies, and other enterprises that seek access to raw materials for export, such as nickel which is used for stainless steel. But these two types of investment (privatising public companies and extracting raw materials) are typical of a neocolonial economy. The first does not create new business but merely takes the old away from local control. The second exports natural resources without adding value (and thus without creating employment).

It gets even more complicated because the trade embargo cannot be lifted with a single decree, even after an eventual departure of the Castro brothers. Complicating the issue is the fact that many companies and private parties maintain claims on properties that were expropriated by the Cuban revolution after 1959. Nearly 6,000 such claims exist, worth more than US$ 7 billion.

The mere fact that there is such a profusion of consultants whose job it is to help you establish a business in Cuba tells us that doing business in Cuba is far too complex for a simple outline on these pages. Before signing up with any expensive consultant, Americans considering any such investment should first visit the website of the U.S.–Cuba Trade and Economic Council (www.cubatrade.org).

Cuba's involvement with foreign investment has been called "dancing with the devil" and more than a few officials dislike the emergence of the new rich. "None of us sheds a tear because there are no millionaires in Cuba," said Fidel Castro. Thus, it is not entirely clear which way the wind will turn. Prior to jumping in, potential investors should study Chinese investments in Cuba as a possible trend.

In 2004, Cuba agreed to supply China with 4,000 tons of nickel per year through 2009. China agreed to invest over US$ 500 million to finish building an abandoned nickel plant in eastern Cuba. But in her Reuters interview, Minister Marta Lomas announced that China was not pursuing the planned US$ 500 million investment, and that Cuba intends to develop the project with Venezuela. Cuba has considerable reserves of nickel, a mineral that is in short supply throughout the world. In order to thwart Cuba's nickel potential, the U.S. imposed blockade requires that metal products entering the U.S. must be certified free of Cuban nickel.

China has agreed to manufacture refrigerators, washing machines, and air conditioners within Cuba for the Cuban market. Given the low spending power of the Cuban

market, such a deal would appear to be more a question of China's positioning rather than immediate profitability. China also agreed to send a million television sets to Cuba, and contribute hospital and school uniform supplies. China granted Cuba a ten-year extension to repay large interest-free loans. China has become Cuba's third biggest trading partner, after Venezuela and Spain.

In conclusion, foreigners who want to create a business in Cuba will have the government as partner. Cuban officials will do everything to convince you that the partnership is fair. "Profits are divided equally between the outside entrepreneurs and Cuban shareholders, our people," said Marcos Portal Leon, Cuba's Minister of Basic Industry. "The half that goes outside the country is taxed," he added, "but at amenable rates."

But the contradictions of the dual currency and the resulting gap between two lifestyles, one of visitors and the other of Cubans, makes for a dilemma. I spoke with one foreign entrepreneur who was pained by the fact that he couldn't pay higher salaries and had to resort to less tangible perks and fringe benefits for his employees. Pay

Cuban wages to your employees and you feel as if you're an accomplice in hyperexploitation. Pay more and you are a catalyst of class differences that are not in keeping with the prevailing ideology of most Cubans. At one joint-venture restaurant chain, employees actually make as much as two hundred dollars a month (ten times as much as a physician) by sharing the 10 per cent gratuity that is included in the meal prices.

But some entrepreneurs see a social purpose in their money-making enterprises. Given the bizarre business and social scenarios of this transition period in Cuban history, it is possible for a foreign entrepreneur to make money and be a humanitarian at the same time. According to *Canadian Business* (10 Oct 1997), York Medical Inc. of Canada was licensing and marketing Cuban products to major drug and medical-device manufacturers. CEO David Allan "extols the humanitarian virtues of his partnership with the Cuban government."

"Canada has become a catalyst for Cuba's economic rehabilitation," according to a Maclean's article of 3 November 1997, and one wonders which is the greater motivation in Canada's fervent involvement in Cuba: a desire for substantial business profits or a resentment at what Canadians have considered U.S. heavy-handedness.

Embargo or no embargo, United States corporations are not about to stand by idly and watch a business bonanza of the Chinese, Venezuelans, Canadians, Mexicans, Spaniards, and other foreigners. A New York-based non-profit organisation called the U.S.–Cuba Trade and Economic Council gathers every iota of information, legal and financial, that can help U.S. businesses waiting in the wings.

John Kavulich, founder and former president of the organisation, told this writer that the one thing everyone should know about Cuba's business situation is that it is changing on a daily basis. "Anything that's prohibited today may be allowed tomorrow," Kavulich said, "and anything allowed today might be prohibited tomorrow."

Business people who thrive on uncertainty will fall deeply in love with Cuba.

A COLLAGE OF OPINIONS

Anyone who was in Cuba during the 1990s could not help feeling profoundly moved by the dramatic and gripping story of people struggling for survival. Depending on whom you talk to, the Cuban people were besieged by Uncle Sam, their own leaders, or both.

According to researchers Peter Rosset and Medea Benjamin, until its sudden and total 1991 departure, the Soviet bloc accounted for 85 per cent of Cuba's trade. In the wake of a catastrophic collapse of the Cuban economy, the United States Congress enacted measures to tighten the U.S. trade embargo.

In times of extreme crisis, it is only natural for protagonists and observers alike to identify the good guys and the bad guys. In times of relative stability, it is easy for writers to remain as neutral observers. But amidst a life-and-death struggle of epic proportions, journalists travelling to Cuba have found it incredibly difficult to not take sides.

I am reminded of an old Depression song from the United States, "Which side are you on?" Acquaintances in the United States, both from the Cuban exile community and the State Department, have insinuated that my simply having been in Cuba was an act of treachery. At the same time, I know of at least one bureaucrat in the Cuban government who took

measures to prevent me from writing this book, anticipating, I can only imagine, that it might in some way hurt Cuba's chances for survival.

Perhaps the ideal format for transcending the "which-side-are-you-on?" dichotomy, is a collage of contrary opinions, relating to both Cuba's crisis and and her inevitable but undefined transition. The section for Further Reading at the end of this book continues this procedure. In this section everyone will find both what they want to hear and what they do not want to hear. Let the sources speak for themselves.

THE EMBARGO

Even semantics can represent a journalistic "slant." How does one choose between the word "embargo" (used by the United States government) and "blockade" (used by Cuban authorities)? On the one hand, U.S. ships are not afloat outside the Havana harbour to prevent foreign traders from entering. On the other hand, U.S. legistlation discourages and sometimes places sanctions on countries that do business with Cuba. What is certain is that anyone doing business in or with Cuba will inevitably have some encounter with the embargo/blockade.

No matter what one's opinion, it is apparent that the half-century U.S. trade embargo will be considered a major theme in the history of Cuba.

There are subtle variations of opinion on the embargo/blockade, first summarised below, and then expounded upon with specific quotes.

- the blockade is the primary cause of economic problems in Cuba;
- the embargo is totally ineffective, and Cuba's economic predicament was internally generated;
- the blockade was welcomed by Fidel Castro, and he propped it up as a bogeyman, appealing to Cuban national pride, for his own political survival;
- the embargo has distorted Cuba's economy, having forced the country into dependency on Soviet-bloc goods and technology and thereby exacerbating the crisis when the Soviets pulled out;

- since no similar embargo has been enacted against other more oppressive governments (for example, the Peoples' Republic of China was granted "most-favored nation" status by the U.S. government), the "embargo" against Cuba must be construed as a symbolic statement by the United States government, warning other Latin American countries that they must fit within the U.S. economic and social paradigm;

- U.S. officials know that the embargo is ineffective, and even prefer it that way, since its main function is to secure votes from the Cuban exile community;

- the blockade excludes Cuban products from the largest consumer nation in the world (the U.S. is Cuba's most natural trading partner, based on geographical and cultural affinities). It also prevents Cuba from receiving vital spare parts, food products and pharmaceuticals that are exclusively manufactured by United States companies or their subsidiaries abroad;

- whatever Cuba cannot sell to the United States, it makes up for by selling to Canada, Mexico and the European community. So many countries have shown solidarity with Cuba, some in order to spite Uncle Sam, that Cuba should have been able to obtain everything it needs if its economy was run efficiently;

- the embargo ironically helps Cuba's health and well-being by forcing her to use ecologically beneficial means of transportation and agriculture.

A COMPENDIUM OF VIEWS

Now we hear some of the sources for such varied points of view. This collage of opinions, was taken directly from the first two editions of *CultureShock! Cuba*. A brief update is added, in order to document that the same arguments persist. U.N. votes condemning the embargo have remained faithful to the original mode, with the United States, Israel and usually some island in the Pacific voting against the yearly resolution that condemns the embargo. Voices are raised condemning the embargo because it is hurting the Cuban people or because it is maintaining Fidel Castro in power, or some combination of the two.

> Most of America's closest allies joined Cuba today in voting for a resolution asking Washington to end its economic embargo against Cuba. The vote in the General Assembly was 143 in favour and 3 against …It was the [umpteenth] consecutive year that the General Assembly has called on Washington to end the embargo. Many … nations are angry at Washington over the Helms-Burton Act, which punishes foreign companies that invest in property taken from the Americans after the 1959 revolution in Cuba. European nations say the law violates World Trade Organization rules governing trade and infringes on their sovereignty.
>
> —from "U.N. Vote Urges U.S. To End Cuban Embargo," from a generic *Associated Press* report, recycled year after year with each new vote.

Jorge Pérez, of Cuba's Tropical Medicine Institute, told a conference on AIDS that the American 'blockade' had ironically been a factor in helping contain the disease because of the isolation it had provided Cuba from the United States.

—from "U.S. embargo kept HIV cases low, says Cuba health official," *AIDS Weekly Plus*, 1 September 1997, p. 21.

Canadian soprano sax/flute player Jane Bunnett and her husband Larry Cramer had been organising musical exchanges with Cuban jazz musicians:

When I first went there [to Cuba], it really hit me that there was an urgency and complexity to the music that was missing from jazz in the era of the corporate young lions ...

We were well acquainted with the shortages of consumer goods brought on by the U.S. trade embargo, but we'd never seen the effect on the schools before ... I was struck by the atrocious condition of their instruments. One of the flutes had layers of plastic replacing the leather pads. I couldn't get a note out of it, yet the student had been playing Bach, Beethoven, and Debussy on it.

The Helms-Burton law that imposes penalties on foreigners who do business with Cuba "created an immediate chill with American music presenters and record companies because they didn't know what it meant," said Bunnett. Concerts and club dates she had booked for her band of Cuban musicians suddenly fell through, and negotiations for a recording deal with Sony ended abruptly.

—from "Havana Jane," by James Hale, *Downbeat*, Nov 1997, p. 12.

One piece of evidence that advocates of the embargo must confront is Castro's own actions just before Congress voted on the Helms-Burton act. Here was a law that President Clinton had opposed and that, therefore, faced an uphill battle. Yet on 24 February 1996, just days before the vote, Castro had his air force shoot down two unarmed civilian airplanes piloted by members of the Miami-based exile group Brothers to the Rescue. No one on either side of the debate claimed that Castro is stupid. With his awesome intelligence machine, Castro certainly knew this action would make passage of the Helms-Burton law more likely. He presumably wanted to use it as new ammo in his propaganda.

—from "Why our Cuba policy is wrong," by David Henderson, in *Fortune*, 13 Oct 1997, p. 48–52.

What embargo? You can see American products flowing freely in Cuba. But they only reach people with access to CUCs.

—from a recent Cuban exile interviewed for this book.

The Cuban Democracy Act of 1992 (CDA) prohibits foreign subsidiaries of U.S. corporations from selling to Cuba, thus further limiting Cuba's access to medicine and equipment, and raising prices. In addition, the CDA forbids ships that dock in Cuban ports from docking in U.S. ports for six months. This drastically restricts shipping, and increases shipping costs by some 30 per cent … Some medicines and medical supplies are only available from the United States or from foreign subsidiaries of U.S. corporations … For example: Cuba cannot purchase spare parts for U.S. built X-ray machines … A spare part used in the manufacture of prenatal vitamin supplements is only legally available from U.S. or subsidiary suppliers … the Kodak X-ray film recommended by the World Health Organization for use in breast cancer screening is not available to Cuba because it is manufactured in the U.S.

U.S. owned companies increasingly dominate the world market in medicines and medical equipment, and this increasingly restricts Cuba's access to medicines and medical equipment.

—from Oxfam America and Washington Office on Latin America, "Myths and Facts about the U.S. Embargo on Medicine and Medical Supplies," 1997.

... thanks to the waivers, no European company has yet been significantly penalized under the Helms-Burton act (though it remains true that a couple of dozen of executives and their dependents are barred from entering the United States).

> —from "Phoney War," *The Economist*, 18 Oct 1997.

We know how many mixed European–Cuban enterprises there are, but we don't know how many other European entrepreneurs renounced potential joint enterprises in Cuba for fear of repercussions from Helms-Burton.

Without being allowed to engage in commerce with her nearest and most natural trading partner, Cuba is obligated to take on enormous transport costs in trading with far-off countries.

Even so, so much in Cuban technological reality, for example the 110-volt system, originated from North American norms, and other countries with different technologies cannot always provide adequate substitutes.

Although I do not believe the embargo has had the effect of an all-out economic war, it is clear that it has its damaging effects. This is obvious if one considers the large numbers of potential United States tourists for whom Cuba is closed off.

> —comments of a high-ranking diplomat from a European country, stationed in Cuba, and interviewed for this book.

Caught in the no-win position of violating American law or violating Canadian law, Wal-Mart Stores' Canadian unit said today that it had decided to resume sales of pajamas made in Cuba, in direct defiance of American laws ... Within hours, however, the Arkansas-based retailer said that its Canadian subsidiary had deliberately defied instructions from headquarters.

> —in summary, from "Wal-Mart Canada is Putting Cuban Pajamas Back on the Shelf," by David Sanger, *New York Times*, 14 March 1997, D4:1.

The best-known Cuban-American singer in the United States, Gloria Estefan, protested the prohibition against Cuban musicians from the island of Cuba at the September 1997 Latin American and Caribbean music fair in Miami, stemming from a Dade County law. "I cannot imagine how we could explain to the people of Cuba, who have suffered so much oppression, that the very freedoms that they so desperately desire and deserve are being annihilated in their name.

—from "A Pinch of Salsa," *The Economist*, 4 Oct 1997.

Why do we blockade Cuba, yet grant favored-nation trading status to China? Every American president has tried to put an end to the Cuban experiment. It can't be in the name of democracy ... If that were so, we would have invaded Chile to save Chileans from Pinochet, but instead we helped put him in power ... I can only think that the United States has enforced the trade embargo for so long out of a fear that other countries might follow Cuba's attempt to keep their human and natural resources for their own use.

—from *Cuba*, by Aaron Kufelt, p.19.

And because U.S. companies are banned from nearly all economic activities in Cuba, investors from Mexico, Italy, Spain, and Canada are scurrying to establish a business beachhead before Washington changes its mind.

—from "It takes liberation of the imagination: foreign companies in Cuba must be creative to make a profit," by John Otis, *Houston Chronicle*, 30 Oct 1997, C1:2.

For over 40 years, our policy toward Cuba has yielded no results. Castro hasn't held free and fair elections, he hasn't improved human rights, and he hasn't stopped preaching his hate for democracy and the U.S. I think it's safe to say that our current policy has failed."

—Representative Jeff Flake, Republican from Arizona, addressing the embargo, *Associated Press*, 16 May 2002.

From a cartoon, with Fidel speaking:

Frame 1: "Cuba is a totalitarian communist regime just like China..."

Frame 2: "Cuba jails and tortures its dissidents just like China..."

Frame 3: "Cuba deprives its people's basic human rights, just like China..."

Frame 4: "So why won't the U.S. grant Cuba most favored nation status just like China?"

Frame 5: "I mean, what does China have that we don't have?!"

Frame 6: A Chinese diplomat responds to Fidel: "About 1.2 billion consumers."

> —Robert Ariail, *The State* (Colombia, S.C.), 31 May 2000.

Newer Quotes Reconfirm the Old Ones

Most policy makers who wanted the embargo to bring down Cubans regime concede that it has failed. "Ending the embargo is a bipartisan issue," noted Sally Grooms Cowal, in a 2002 *Associated Press* interview, speaking as president of the Cuba Policy Foundation. "For 40 years, the embargo has failed to lead to political and economic reform in Cuba. When a policy this old fails to produce the intended results, it is time for a new policy."

From an opposite pro-revolution perspective, the influential Uruguayan writer Eduardo Galeano came to a similar conclusion at about the same time. "The blockade," he noted, "and countless other forms of aggression, blocks the development of a Cuban style democracy, feeds into the militarisation of power and serves as an alibi for bureaucratic rigidity."

In a 2005 *Associated Press* article, referring to an official U.S. government report on a Cuba transition, "not long after Castro's demise, 100,000 tons of food could be purchased quickly and shipped to Cuba." This statement is tantamount to an admission that the Embargo has been withholding food from Cuba, a grave violation of the very ethical standards that democracy is supposed to uphold.

"The United States," noted Galeano, "tireless manufacturer of dictatorships around the world, does not have the moral authority to give lessons on democracy to anyone."

SPHERE OF INFLUENCE

The same reasons for and against the embargo still emerge in the media. American business people felt they were on the verge of positive changes that would weaken the embargo and allow for incursions into Cuba's natural resources and markets. And yet, virtually nothing has changed. Underlying reasons for the unbending foreign policy are often unstated. The U.S. presents a moral rationale for the embargo before the United Nations: 'Cuba is an undemocratic society' and 'the Castro government imprisons dissenters'. But these arguments fail to persuade the staunchest allies of the United States because they know that the U.S. actively supported military coups against democratically elected governments in Guatemala (1953) and Chile (1973), and throughout the 1980s, backed Latin American dictators whose scale of repression (death squads, disappearances and torture) made Cuba look like a humanitarian paradise.

Since the early 1960s, the U.S. trade embargo against Cuba was based on sphere of influence. The Soviets had encroached on territory mapped out in the Monroe Doctrine. The Russians, a miliary threat, were entrenched on an island only 144 km (90 miles) from Miami. If you were brought up on nightmares of a Russian nuclear attack, then you could see a logic in trying to make the Cuban people suffer just enough so that they would overthrow Fidel, and rid the U.S. of the Russian menace.

Some minority voices in the U.S. suggested that to not trade with Cuba would make Castro even more dependent on the Soviets.

When the Soviet Union self-destructed in 1991, and Russia totally abandoned Cuba, those who had reluctantly supported the embargo because of the Soviet threat now expected it to be lifted. Instead, it was enforced with a heavier hand.

My understanding of why the embargo continued during the 1990s results from my journalistic experience in various Latin American countries, and the concept of "sphere of influence."

"Yes, our votes in Senate often result from U.S. embassy pressure," former Bolivian senator, Leopoldo López confided.

Other officials told me that their nations' economic and social policies were "driven by orthodox, free-market capitalism ... because we are under the U.S. sphere of influence."

If one believes that unbridled capitalism is the answer to poverty and social ills in Latin America, then one should be able to see a political reason for supporting the embargo. Cuba may still represent a socialist alternative to free-market neo-liberalism; if that alternative were allowed to spread to neighbouring countries, the U.S. plutocracy would no longer be the master of its own sphere of influence.

The embargo may have had an effect contrary to its intentions. Cuba's fierce resistance to U.S. trade restrictions has influenced currents of economic independence, as exemplified by Hugo Chavez in Venezuela and a movement led by peasant and labour leaders in Bolivia that managed to expel a powerful transnational corporation, Bechtel, defend natural gas reserves from foreign exploitation, and elect presidents who oppose free market orthodoxy, such as Evo Morales in Bolivia and Rafael Correa in Ecuador (sworn in January 2007).

Some Cuban-Americans close to the embargo issue will disagree with my "realpolitik" appraisal. "The [embargo] policy," wrote Cuban-American journalist Richard Estrada, "is being driven largely by special interest pleading by Cuban-American conservatives based in Miami."

Such lobbying does exist, of course, but, are Cuban-American conservatives using the U.S. government, or are orthodox, free-market ideologues with the government using the Cuban-Americans?

A significant number of Cuban-Americans, most of whom oppose the Cuban regime, have already voted against the embargo in a visceral way, by sending money to relatives and friends in Cuba.

Whatever the real political reasons for continuing the embargo (stopping the spread of humanising economic models that oppose orthodox capitalist models within the U.S. sphere of influence, or gaining votes from Cuban-Americans), such reasons are left officially unpronounced, displaced in international forums by totally ineffective moralistic rationale.

U.S. Businesses

The United States Department of Commerce has been granting permission for United States corporations to explore business possibilities in Cuba, in anticipation of the inevitable end to the trade embargo and related congressional acts against business with Cuba. A large sector of the United States business community, accustomed to an advantage in the international arena of commerce, feels frustrated that Europeans, Canadians, Mexicans, and Asians have been ceded the upper hand by its own government.

Those American business representatives eager to establish a beachhead in Cuba were particularly elated when the Pope condemned the U.S. trade embargo as inhumane during his January 1998 visit to Cuba. Since then, the business lobby to end the embargo, led by U.S. agricultural and pharmaceutical interests, is rivaling the right-wing Cuban exile lobby in the halls of congress.

The Office of Assets Control (OFAC) of the U.S. Department of Treasury now authorises entities subject to U.S. law to make a secondary market investment in a third-country business which has commercial dealings with Cuba. Since 2001, the Trade Sanctions Reform and Export Enhancement Act (TSRA) authorised certain food exports to Cuba, with licenses issued by the Bureau of Industry and Security (BIS) within OFAC.

Since then there have been other milestones. Events in the early 2000s, such as the U.S. Food and Agriculture Exhibition and the U.S. Health Care Exhibition, were held in Cuba and authorised by OFAC. Familiarization Tours (FAM) for senior level U.S. executives receive OFAC permission because they have been "fully hosted." Yet, post 11 September 2001 U.S. foreign policy tends to label any social or economic models that oppose neo-liberal economics as terrorist, and this has resulted in a tightening of the U.S. trade embargo.

Weekly Updates on Business in Cuba

Readers thinking of doing business in Cuba would do well to subscribe to the weekly newsletter, the *Economic Eye On Cuba*, whose more than 10,000 subscribers include senior executives, journalists, and government officials from both the United States and Cuba. (See www.cubatrade.org)

TRANSITIONS

"We want change," said Arnulfo, a former communist militant now disenchanted with the social divisions of the dual economy. "But we don't want change imposed from abroad. Cubans should be allowed to decide their own destiny."

Just about everyone agrees that Cuba is changing, passing through a transition. But transition implies moving from one phase to the next, and no one has defined what the next phase will be. Some of the measures of the Special Period seem to be leading toward a mixed economy, part free-market, part socialised, but other measures may have been intended as a temporary and expedient means to defend socialism. A silent tug-of-war is taking place, between the global economy on one end, and the Cuban people on the other.

There are certain things that the public has learned to take for granted. "Cubans cannot conceive of a market system for their health care," said economist Pablo Ramos, chancellor of Bolivia's national university in La Paz and observer of the Cuban scene.

"Cubans can accept small fees for sports and cultural activities," explained Dr. Jorge Crisosto, originally from Chile. Crisosto does volunteer work in Cuba, and admires the health system to such an extent that he chose Cuba over other countries to send his mother for complicated surgery.

"In Cuba," continues Dr. Crisosto, "medical care is prioritised without distinction for ability to pay or geographic region. They've even created a mechanical heart that can be used by a patient while awaiting a heart transplant. Such advances are unheard of in other poor countries.

"But these successes create problems. As life expectancy increases, so do geriatric needs, and the cost of the system escalates.

"In other Latin American countries, people wait too late to seek care for financial reasons. In Cuba, we have the opposite problem, as Cubans often go to a doctor too early, before it is necessary. People are going to have to become accustomed to paying moderate fees."

When forecasting what will happen to Cuba in the upcoming years, many analysts labelled the eventual turning point as the

Blind Spot

Analysts fail to take into account that Cuba's education system has produced an abundant pool of professionals and technicians, to the extent that Cuba exports its expertise to other countries.

death of Fidel Castro. They had assumed that each and every public policy decision in Cuba in the 1990s was ordered or coerced by Fidel.

Many graduates of the education system retain a utopian perspective and undertake quixotic experiments, not because they have been commanded to do so but out of a fervent belief in their mission. Economists, for example, continue to attempt creative and never-before-tried adjustments of capitalist enterprise in order to retain a social component and prevent the type of third world–first world internal clashes that plague other Latin American countries. Some measures seem to have a modicum of success, while others fail and are quickly abandoned.

With no precedents from other countries, a trial-and-error mode prevails as the only means to retain the advances of social equality while administering controlled infusions of capitalism.

The other alternative is unfettered capitalism, à la Eastern Europe. The ultimate irony would be a Cuba of tomorrow with all the social upheaval of unbridled market economics, juxtaposed with Latin American countries like Bolivia, Brazil, Ecuador, and Venezuela that are fighting to humanise the market economy and using the Cuba of yesterday as one of their models.

Most observers note the changes in Cuba that represent the incursion of capitalist models. But few have commented on another trend in Cuba, one that is contrary to the obvious examples of global capitalism and that goes beyond rigid marxist models of economic revolution and social justice.

ORGANIC AGRICULTURE

One example of the new economic model is an experiment worthy of marquee billing: the effort by Cuban agronomists to consummate a massive transformation to organic agriculture. It was a risky proposition to choose the height of the Special Period for such an unprecedented change in the whole culture of food production. Some countries have proceeded with a great deal more caution, with incremental increases in organic farming. Others have not even considered organic farming as a humane and healthy alternative to agribusiness. According to author Jane Smiley, "it had been apparent for some 25 or 30 years that insecticides and herbicides were contaminating the landscape and the water supply, killing off wildlife, destroying fertility in males and females of all species and causing disease in the farmers themselves and their families. The common sense solution to this increasing problem would have been to acknowledge the destructive power of these unnatural chemicals, and to have shifted American agriculture away from their use. Agribusiness, however, preferred to remake the ecosystem so that farmers would use more chemicals rather than fewer."

Cuba took the opposite path and placed a huge wager on its human resources. With only 2 per cent of the population of Latin America but 11 per cent of its scientists, the government hoped that human wisdom could compensate for the cutoff of pesticides, herbicides and vital parts needed for more mechanised farming. "Biofertilizers and biopesticides, microbial formulations that are non-toxic to humans," were used to replace the chemical varieties, even though "empirical evidence … demonstrates that it can take anywhere from three to five years to achieve levels of productivity that prevailed beforehand," according to Dr. Peter Rosset and Medea Benjamin, researchers in agricultural ecology and authors of *The Greening of the Revolution: Cuba's Experiment with Organic Agriculture.*

In fact, to reach previous levels of productivity was not nearly enough, since food supplies from the Soviets and East Europeans that had complemented local production had been cut off. The conversion to organic agriculture was undertaken precisely at a moment in history when the Cuban population was on the verge of severe hunger and malnutrition.

Ironically, the "classical model" of agriculture employed previously in Cuba was the same that had been encouraged by both the United States and the Soviet Union in their spheres of influence. The model, as it applied to Cuba, includes extensive monoculture of export crops, often not native to the region, through a highly mechanised system that depends on imported technology and inputs (fertilisers, pesticides, etc.).

Throughout the third world, mechanisation drives hordes of rural inhabitants to cities, causing unresolvable social ills. Such a massive scale of single-crop farming erodes and salinates the soil. As plants develop pesticide resistance, ever escalating amounts of chemical pesticides are needed.

In third world countries like Bolivia and Mexico, I have known firsthand the tribulations of being obligated to investigate the source of my family's food. Are the tomatoes laden with pesticides? Is cow milk laced with hormones? Am I poisoning my children? Often, the answer I found was, yes.

Cuba's "alternative model," referred to as low-input sustainable agriculture, uses non-chemical plants and microbes, avoids dependence on heavy machinery and diversifies and rotates crops. The experiment was initiated in the early nineties. By mid-1993, it appeared as if a food crisis was about to reach a level of desperation.

But little by little, farmers' gardens began to sprout up in urban neighbourhoods, called *organopónicos*. Healthy products like avocados, cucumbers, oranges and bananas,

as well as pork, became available with prices that fit within budgets based on Cuban salaries. According to a 13 August 2006 article in the *Seattle Post-Intelligencer*, by Andrew Buncombe, "Cuba is filled with more than 7,000 urban ... *organopónicos*, which fill perhaps as many as 81,000 acres. They have been established on tiny plots of land in the centre of tower-block estates or between the crumbling colonial homes that fill Havana."

Some shortages still exist, but according to Dr. Rosset, "Cuba has overcome a food shortage with little use of pesticides or fertilizers, an example to be looked at closely by other countries."

Ironically, a post-embargo Cuba may be forced to return to some aspects of the classic model of agriculture for reasons of expediency or because foreign investors offering vital currency may require it. But as of the end of 2006, according to Rosset and other agronomists following the Cuba experiment, the system has been sustainable and remains successful, with few crops needing anything more that natural biological pesiticides, herbicides and fertilisers. Rosa Elena, the Bolivian student in Cuba quoted earlier in this book, will be proud to learn that her graduate thesis on the use of zeolites as natural fertilisers has played a role in the successful conversion of a large part of Cuba's agriculture to an organic model.

"Remarkably," according to Buncombe, "this organic revolution has worked. Annual calorie intake now stands at about 2,600 a day, while UNFAO estimates that the percentage of the population considered undernourished fell from 8 per cent in 1990–1992 to about 3 per cent in 2000–2002. Cuba's infant mortality rate is lower than that of the U.S., while at 77 years, life expectancy is the same."

Is There a Doctor in the House?

A majority of ecologists now believe that the agribusiness model of intensive farming and animal raising is not sustainable. Does the Cuban model represent failed socialism or a new hope for combatting hunger? Another non-capitalist Cuban experiment offers a ray of hope for a world that has dire deficiencies in the delivery of health care. The United States privatised health care system allows for more than 40 million citizens to live without health or medical insurance.

Capitalists vs Castro

A capitalist system would limit the number of doctors in order to reduce competition and assure a high salary for medical practitioners. Cuba produces an excess of doctors and then finds a way to use these doctors to serve people around the world who would have been left unattended.

The Cuban health care system, though still reeling from the crisis of the 1990s, is still has the highest ratio of doctor per person than any other country in the world, according to the World Health Organization.

One of our vegetable vendors in Bolivia was going blind from cataracts at the moment we left the country. When my wife returned for a visit, she discovered that the woman had been cured, by a Cuban doctor, at no charge.

According to Tom Fawthrop ("Cuba doctors popular in quake-stricken Java," www.bbc.co.uk, 18 August 2006), "Cuban medical teams have quietly assumed a major role in global humanitarian relief operations usually seen as the domain of wealthy nations."

Cuban doctors are often the first to arrive and the last to leave when a country is struck by a natural catastrophe. After earthquakes in Pakistan and Indonesia, few victims expected Cuba to come to their rescue.

Fawthrop quotes an Indoesian doctor. "We felt very surprised about doctors coming from a poor country, a country so far away that we know little about," Dr Rockito says. "We can learn from the Cuban health system. They are very fast to handle injuries and fractures. They X-ray, then they operate straight away. People are coming from Jogyakarta, many not affected by the earthquake, to get free treatment and because they are too poor to pay. The people are very glad it is free."

Fawthrop indicates that "Cuba currently has about 20,000 doctors working in 68 countries across three continents, without much being said about it."

In Java alone, Cuban doctors operated two field hospitals, and treated 47,000 patients, with 9 operations performed and 2,000 people immunised against tetanus.

Cuba's non-capitalist successes in health care and agriculture are offering great contrast with the capitalist evolution in the tourist industry, including health tourism. For this reason, many Cubans are concerned about which economic model awaits them.

Mixed or Mixed-Up Economy?

Inevitably, the global economy will have a major impact on Cuba, and countercurrents of capitalism and socialist economics will have to be resolved. A dramatic episode of the transition period will be based on the precarious attempt to preserve a culture that has emphasized sharing and solidarity even as the world-wide consumer culture is allowed to co-exist. Will Cubans prefer styrofoam burger chains over their homespun *paladares*? Will economic "growth" be spread evenly enough to prevent the social problems that plague the Mexicos, Perus and El Salvadors of Latin America? Are there other models of mixed economies such as France or Denmark that could be applied in a Caribbean way?

Incipient state capitalism is exemplified by a thriving biomedical industry (on a shoestring budget but with an army of dedicated researchers), which has produced cutting-edge medicines, vaccines and treatments in specialty areas that do not always meet the immediate needs of the Cuban population but which provide revenue for the national health service.

Whatever shall happen in Cuba, these will be tremendously exciting times, and the inherent culture clash between utopianism and an unbridled market economy will be manifest in various arenas of Cuban society.

New Emigration

During this transition period, new social paradigms will emerge. For example, I discovered a new type of Cuban emigrant, one that does not fit with previous prototypes. Arnulfo was a dedicated socialist, member of the Communist Party, and a foreman in a milk factory who earned US$ 7 per month. He left Cuba not because of socialism but because of what he called "the effects of neoliberal reforms."

Arnulfo was emotionally drained by the social divisions caused by the introduction of dollars in the economy, and felt that tourism was introducing a type of corruption that had not existed since 1959. With access to dollars from relatives abroad, Arnulfo was embarrassed and discouraged that he was living with privileges that other Cubans lacked.

"The blockade is 90 per cent to blame," he said, "but we made our errors too. We hope it is not too late for Fidel to be remembered for the good things he did."

THE INFORMAL ECONOMY

The Special Period nurtured an informal economy, both legal and illegal. With laws in constant flux, it is virtually impossible to tell you in advance what is legal and what is not.

If you choose to do business with these "independent entrepreneurs," know in advance how to judge the quality of a product. If you don't like the hard sell you're getting, let the salesperson know that you refuse to make a decision under pressure and prefer to have nothing at all.

The prototypical informal economy product is the cigar.

Simple Tips For Cigar Buyers

- Should you be considering the purchase of cigars, for example, read up in any one of the quality cigar magazines or books, so that you will know the difference between the counterfeit and the real product.
- Don't purchase a box of cigars without having it first opened.
- The box should have any number of labels, such as Hecho en Cuba, Totalmente a mano and a Cuban government seal.
- The cigars should be uniform, firm and the ringed label should be tight around the cigar.

None of these traits assure that the cigars are legitimate, and some experts assure us that any cigars we would buy on the street can only be at best counterfeit, and at worst dysfunctional.

Before any purchase, visit the Palacio del Tabaco, Zulueta 106, between Refugio and Colón in Old Havana, where you can watch a cigar maker in action and inspect the particular cigar you have in mind. Black marketeers won't be carrying their product with them and will ask you to accompany them to their apartment. Typically, a box of 25 Cohibas that might sell between US$ 180 and US$ 230 in a store may be obtained for as little as 40 to 50 CUCs in the black market.

The ethical considerations of purchasing in the black market are perplexing. In some Latin American countries, the government purposely looks the other way and allows a thriving black market to exist, as a safety valve to prevent social upheaval. If government-run cigar factories are actually allowing employees to take a box or two of cigars occasionally as a fringe benefit, then there is indirect sanctioning of the black market. On the other hand, if these street cigars were stolen outright, there is no moral justification for purchasing them. Yet a third possibility exists. Black market cigars may be "seconds" or rejects. Who knows? A Cohiba or Montecristo reject may be a much better smoke than the cigars at the corner emporium in our country of origin.

WORK NORMS AND BUSINESS ETIQUETTE

Public offices are open from Monday through Friday, from 8:30 am to 12:30 pm and from 1:30 pm to 5:30 pm. The post office is open throughout the day beginning at 8:00 am and closing at 4:00 pm. Pharmacies are also open on a continuous basis until 5:00 pm, with chosen (*de turno*) pharmacies taking turns staying open 24 hours. In order to fight unemployment, work hours may be shorter than the norm in some sectors. Since the underground economy may offer a better salary than a steady job, many Cubans are voluntarily unemployed. Others hold their regular job but moonlight on the street to make ends meet.

Work etiquette in Cuba can be summarised by what you should do: be efficient, and what you should not do: do not let efficiency cause you to lose your humanity, in dealing with customers or colleagues. There is a tradition that says that work should be enjoyable, and efforts are

ROLL YOUR OWN CIGARS

TRIGG

made to make one's work pleasant, as exemplified by the oral tradition of story tellers narrating news and tales to cigar factory workers.

Work is viewed as both productive and social. The Cuban Revolution strove to get women out of the isolation of the home by either incorporating them into the work force or socialising household chores traditionally done by women through the use of public laundries, cafeterias, child care and other public services.

As you can imagine from this context, business relationships also have their social component, office parties and ceremonial rituals are the norm, and foreigners doing business with Cubans will need to combine business with socialising at lunch or dinner. Conceivably you may encounter a situation in which the Cuban partner's monthly salary is equivalent to the hourly salary of the foreign partner. Under such circumstances it's a no-brainer that the foreigner will pay for the dinner.

In my own miniature business encounters, my Cuban companions would pay when the bill was in Cuban pesos (soft drinks, ice cream, etc.) and I would pay when we were in the CUC economy. Given the unsettled business scene, business relations should develop slowly with a very gradual nurturing of confidence from both sides. But when formal and legal matters enter into the mix, a handshake is not enough. The foreign partner has a perfect rationale for proceeding with such caution, since business laws and currency rates may change from one day to another.

CHAPTER 10

FAST FACTS

"Cuba is filled with more than 7,000 urban allotments, or *organopónicos,* which fill perhaps as many as 81,000 acres. They have been established on tiny plots of land in the center of tower-block estates or between the crumbling colonial homes that fill Havana."
—Andrew Buncombe, from "Cuba's Agricultural Revolution is an Example to the World," *Seattle Post-Intelligencer,* 13 August 2006

Official Name
Republic of Cuba

Capital
Havana

National Anthem
La Bayamesa (The Bayamo Song), a slow march, was first written and performed by Pedro Figueredo, an independence fighter who participated in the 1868 battle of Bayamo. Two years later, he was captured by the Spaniards and executed by a firing squad. Adopted in 1940 as the national anthem, it was retained by the Cuban revolution after 1959.

Language
Spanish. Vestiges of African languages mysteriously emerge in santería ceremonies.

Flag
Created in 1849 for the independence movement, this flag is two in one, with a red triangle in the forefront and blue and white stripes leading out from the triangle. The three blue stripes represent the states into which the island was divided at that time and two white stripes between imply the soldier's idealism for independence; the red triangle represents both equality, fraternity and liberty and the blood shed in the

struggle for freedom. A white five-sided star within the red triangle symbolises freedom between nations.

Climate
Tropical; moderated by trade winds; dry season (November to April); rainy season (May to October)

Time Difference
Cuba is 14 hours behind Japan, six hours behind mainland Europe, the same time zone as the East Coast United States, and three hours ahead of west coast United States.

Telephone Country Code
53 + city code (Camaguey: 32; Cienfuegos: 432; Havana: 7; Matanzas: 52; Santiago de Cuba: 226; Trinidad: 419; Varadero: 5)

Land Area
110,860 sq km (42,803 sq miles)

Natural Resources
Cobalt, nickel, iron ore, chromium, copper, salt, timber, silica, petroleum and arable land

Population
11,382,820 (July 2006 est.)

Ethnic Groups
mulatto (51 per cent), white (37 per cent), black (11 per cent), Chinese (1 per cent)

Religion
The majority of Cubans are secular but an increasing portion of the population, both black and white, practice Santería, which blends elements of Christianity and West African Yoruba beliefs (syncretism). Santería made it possible for the slaves to protect their traditional beliefs while superficially practicing Catholicism. There is no official Santería church. The Catholic religion continues to exist, without much

impact in everyday life. A small minority of Cubans are Protestants, Jehovah's Witnesses or Jews.

Government
The Cuban constitution calls the state socialist, some analysts call it a Communist State, while other experts label it "Fidelista", a tropical version of Communism.

Administrative Divisions
14 provinces and 1 special municipality; Camaguey, Ciego de Avila, Cienfuegos, Ciudad de La Habana, Granma, Guantánamo, Holguin, Isla de la Juventud, La Habana, Las Tunas, Matanzas, Pinar del Rio, Sancti Spiritus, Santiago de Cuba, Villa Clara.

Currency
Cuban peso (CUP) and Convertible peso (CUC). The CUC is the primary currency for visitors, but in paying for a product or service in CUCs, the consumer may receive the change in the appropriate amount of CUPs. Foreign currency may be changed at CADECA offices.

Gross Domestic Product (per capita)
US$ 3,500 (2005 est.) Cuba's high growth rate will cause this figure to change upwardly but GDP is a poor indicator of the economic health of a country because (1) it does not reflect the gap between rich and poor, nor (2) the difference in cost of living between countries of higher and lower GDPs.

Gross Domestic Happiness (Alternative GDP)
The Happy Planet Index, contrary to the GDP, considers the efficiency of resource use (lower consumption) as an asset. The Ecological Footprint tells us how much nations consume per capita. How much consumption did it take to achieve a benchmark degree of satisfaction and fulfillment? Numerical indicators such as life expectancy are considered in combination with and massive surveys of local populations. Cuba is ranked in sixth place among 167 nations. (For example, Germany is ranked ahead of the United States

because Germans consume much less than Americans while achieving an equal level of life satisfaction.)

Imports
Petroleum, food, machinery and equipment and chemicals

Exports
Medical services through Cuban doctors, pharmaceutical and medical products, sugar, nickel, tobacco, fish, citrus and coffee

Weather
Cuba is a tropical country with an average of 330 days of sun per year. If you wish to avoid tropical rains, your probability improves by going during the months of December or August. Cuba is quite comfortable from November through March. Average annual temperature is 25°C (77°F) with the lowest average temperatures in January (23°C/73°F). The average relative humidity is about 80 per cent.

ICONS
Castillo de los Tres Reyes del Morro (El Morro)
Construction for the fortress begun in 1589, built to protect the port of Havana against pirate raids. Finished in 1642, it was named a UNESCO World Heritage Site in 1982 together with Old Havana.

The Muñequites de Matanzas
A living rumba legend, performing Cuba's most rhythmic music with the deepest African roots in a "blues juke joint" ambience.

Tomás Gutiérrez Alea
The late Tomás Gutiérrez Alea and his brilliantly moving films with humour, drama, poetry and social criticism, including *Memories of Underdevelopment* (1968), *Fresa y Chocolate* (1993) and *Guantanamera* (1995).

Téofilo Stevenson
Cuba's great boxing champion, three-time heavy-weight Olympic champion who turned down a chance to become

professional and fight Mohammed Ali, which would have required him to leave Cuba, where professional sports were prohibited. "What is one million dollars compared to the love of eight million Cubans?" he explained.

Los Van Van
The ever-evolving symbol of Cuban music that takes salsa to its limits and beyond.

Old Havana
It was named as a UNESCO World Heritage site in 1982.

Colonial Trinidad and the Valley of the Ingenios (Sugar refineries)
It became a UNESCO World Heritage Site in 1988.

Viñales Valley
A tobacco growing region known for its eerie mogotes (loaf-shaped limstone mountains clothed in green) and winding caverns, named a UNESCO World Heritage Site in 1999.

Urban Historic Center of Cienfuegos
It became a UNESCO World Heritage Site in 2005.

Castillo de San Pedro de la Roca
It was also known as El Morro de Santiago de Cuba and was built in 1638 as a fortress to protect the city against pirate raids. Later, it was named by UNESCO as a World Heritage Site in 1998.

FAMOUS PEOPLE
Carlos Acosta (1973–)
He is a Graduate of the National Ballet School of Cuba and is an international ambassador of dance and choreography. His production, *Tocororo*, tells of a humble boy who leaves his family and the traditions of the Cuban countryside for an urban future, partly autobiographical. *Tocororo* blends Cuban rhythm and symphonic styles. Acosta has been a guest performer with London's Royal Ballet.

Andrés Alén (1950–).
Great Cuban pianist and composer, with devoted students.
He creates the fusion between the most refined classical
techniques of European tradition and the most authentic
sounds and rhythms of modern Cuban popular music
and jazz.

José Luis Cortés (1951–)
"El Tosco". Flutist and leader of NG La Banda, known for
energetic Cuban music that fuses with virtually every
contemporary genre. Once playing with the jazz group
Irakere, Cortés is known for having created the first album of
the genre *timba, En La Calle*, in 1989. Both *timba* and salsa
have a common root in the Cuban *son*.

Gloria Estefan (1957–)
A Grammy Award winning singer, songwriter, author, and
pop music icon in the Cuban exile community of Miami, her
energetic Latin fusion music brought Spanish language music
to a mass audience. Her father, whose fatal illness may have
been caused by having contracted agent orange when serving
in Vietnam, was once Batista's personal body guard. Gloria
Estefan has been active in opposing Fidel Castro.

Eusebio Leal Spengler (1942–)
He holds a doctorate of historical sciences from the University
of Havana. He has been the Director of the Office of the
Historian of the City of Havana and the great hero of the
ongoing renovation of Old Havana. Leal operates on the notion
that tourism should never supersede culture, which means
that restoration projects should satisfy residential needs.

Oswaldo Payá (1952–)
Oswaldo Payá founded the non-denominational Christian
Liberation Movement in 1988 to seek improved civic and
human rights of Cubans. In 1998, he founded the Varela
Project, for which he has twice hand-delivered petitions to the
Cuban Parliament requesting a referendum on constitutional
reforms. Unlike some dissidents, he does not accept aid from

U.S. government sources, and opposes both the U.S. Cuban embargo and Cuban exile demands of land reacquisition.

Javier Sotomayor (1963–)
An Olympic track and field champion who broke world records for the high jump.

Chucho Valdés (1941–)
Pianist Chucho Valdés is the founder and leader of Irakere, one of Cuba's top Jazz groups, and of Crisol with US trumpeter Roy Hargrove. In 1998, Valdés won a Grammy for his work with Crisol. He is also the mastermind of the Havana Jazz Festival. He blends sounds of American jazz, Afrocuban music and his own eclectic styles. If we called him a "living legend", it would be underestimating his power to move and surprise his listeners.

ACRONYMS
BFI. (Banco Financiero Internacional)
Here, you can receive CUCs with an international credit card (except U.S. credit cards).

CADECA. (Casa de Cambio)
The ubiquitous locale for changing currency. (Do not change in the street.Viva Cadeca!)

CDR. (Comité de Defensa de la Revolución)
Either they are defenders of the revolution, protectors of the neighbourhood and problem solvers for citizens or gossipers, spies and instruments of repression, depending on your point of view.

CUC. Cuban convertible pesos
The preferred currency for visitors, but also used by Cubans when they can get a hold of them. At this writing, one CUC is worth 25 Cuban pesos. When you pay for something in CUC, some establishments will give you your change in Cuban pesos, so have the current exchange rate fresh in your mind.

CULTURE QUIZ

SITUATION 1

You've just gotten to know a Cuban and suddenly he or she is asking personal questions. How do you respond?

Ⓐ Tell the person "that's none of your business."

Ⓑ Give partial answers if you are not comfortable sharing private information, and ask the same questions of your new acquaintance to see just how forthright he or she will be.

Ⓒ Tell the person that you've got to be leaving for an appointment and that you hope to see him or her again some time.

Ⓓ Respond frankly but with a meaningful context.

Comments

To foreigners from more private cultures, many Cubans, especially youth, are remarkably frank, to the point of seeming blunt, tactless and socially indiscreet. Most observers judge this to be harmless and naive. If you answer either **Ⓐ** or **Ⓒ**, you are not willing to meet the people at least half way. Answer

❸ buys you some time to feel out the sincerity of the person you've just met. Answer ❹ is also acceptable, unless the question concerns something you'd want to hide from friends and family. For example, Cubans might ask you how much you earn in your country. If you simply answer US$ 4,000 a month (a hypothetical amount), given the low wages in Cuba, you'll leave an impression that you're a member of the House of Windsor. But if you explain that you pay US$ 500 for health insurance (Cubans pay nothing), US$ 1,000 for rent (Cubans pay no more than ten per cent of their salary), a dollar for two oranges (you can get 46 oranges in a Cuban outdoor market for a dollar), and US$ 25 for a seat at a basketball game (sports events cost Cubans one peso), the listener will grasp that your salary conforms to the cost of living in your country.

SITUATION 2

You've just arrived in Cuba and you want to feel a part of the country as fast as possible. Which is the best strategy?

❶ Visit as many parts of the city, and as many different provinces in the shortest period of time.

❷ Don't worry about seeing everything there is to see, and establish yourself in the neighbourhood of your choice by patronising its establishments, hanging out on its streets, and using it as a base as you progressively explore what is around and beyond.

❸ Register to take classes or join a volunteer organisation.

❹ Carry with you at all times a letter of presentation from the professional organisation of your native country.

Comments

By "doing" all of Cuba in seven days and six nights, ❶, you'll end up with no lasting friends, and will not have established a sense of place. Most Cubans have not visited each and every city and province of their country, nor every tourist site in their city. Even if you were on a short visit, why gloss over everything superficially instead of getting to know a few people or places in a profound way. ❹ is also of little value, since oral communication supersedes written documents as a way to interact socially. ❸ is the best answer, since Cuba is a country in which most things happen at the neighborhood level. ❸ also makes sense and is the safest option, although clubs or classes are not quite as necessary as they would be in more private and less spontaneous countries.

SITUATION 3

Keeping up-to-date with the latest changes in business law, you have initiated the process to begin a business in Cuba, but the bureaucrat who represents your Cuban partner in the joint enterprise seems to be dragging his feet.

❹ Invite him to dinner for a brainstorming session.
❸ Offer a bribe by insinuating that you'd be willing to pay an extra fee to get the operation rolling.
❸ Find a higher official in the government with more vitality.
❶ Elaborate with your "partner" on the social benefits of your business for the Cuban people.

Comments

Unless things change radically, a bribe, ❸, is out of the question. Going to a higher-up, ❸, will be a damaging insult to the person you have been assigned to work with. Most Cuban technocrats are monitored closely and will do anything to produce documented results in order to advance in their profession, so try to work with your partner and not around him. Inviting him to dinner, ❹, is a universal strategy that works particularly well in Cuba. If he is indeed dragging his feet, he may need more evidence that your project will have social benefits for the Cuban population, ❶, Cuban officials are groping for ways to use certain aspects of the market economy to protect and improve their social advances, so ideas on how your business can help their goals will be appreciated.

SITUATION 4

It is mid-July and you have been invited to accompany a group of friends to an opening of an art exhibit at a Havana museum. How should you dress?

Ⓐ Dress informally, but wear clean, neatly pressed clothes.

Ⓑ Wear a light sport jacket with a shirt and tie, or a semi-formal dress, and hope that you can bear the summer heat and humidity.

Ⓒ It's too hot to dress formally. Dress comfortably like a hippie. These are artists and they'll understand your non-conformism.

Ⓓ Phone the museum in advance and ask about the dress code for such occasions.

Comments

You could try **Ⓓ**, but why waste a phone call to an employee who probably has no idea about any dress code. These may be artists, but the type of anarchistic bohemianism reminiscent of Toulouse-Lautrec is not the custom in Cuba, and sloppy attire, **Ⓒ**, is not a fair way to honour the exhibiting artist. Nevertheless, in the heat of summer, no one is expected to dress up formally, **Ⓑ**, which would be a vestige of nineteenth century colonial customs. **Ⓐ** is clearly the best answer. One's personal hygiene, including neatness, is important to Cubans. Even during hard times when clothing was expensive and toiletry items scarce, Cubans found the way to be neat, fresh, and clean, even with informal dress.

SITUATION 5

You've rented a car and are on your way to discovering the Cuban countryside. You see a group of hitchhikers under a bridge or at the exit of a town. Should you give them a ride?

Ⓐ Pass them by. They could be armed and dangerous.

Ⓑ Pass them by. They will doubtlessly need to be driven into a town along your way, and you will lose time.

Ⓒ Look them over as you approach. If they seem like family people or workers coming from or going to work, give them a ride.

Ⓓ Ask the government official (called an amarillo because of his yellow uniform) if it's okay to offer a ride.

Comments

In Cuba, hitchhikers are a regular sight on the road, usually under highway overpasses or at the exits of towns.

There is no constitutional right to bear arms, since this would infringe on the public good, which supersedes individual rights, so the chances that your potential riders will be armed and dangerous are slim, **Ⓐ**. Furthermore, if you're visiting Cuba to enjoy the people, then **Ⓑ** is not likely a good answer, for a later arrival to your destination in exchange for meeting new people seems like a fair trade-off. Remember that Cubans are used to a great degree of uncertainty relating to arrival times. You will eventually feel uncomfortable trying to superimpose a tight but unrealistic schedule on the Cuban reality. (Rent the film *Guantanamera* if you don't believe me.)

This leaves us with answers **Ⓒ** and **Ⓓ**. Both answers represent ways in which the driver can exercise caution and still give a ride to hitchhikers. Once you see groups of people waiting together for a ride in the usual place for hitching, you'll realise that it is customary for drivers to pick them up, in what is called *hacer botella* (to hitchhike).

But to exercise the maximum degree of caution, **Ⓓ** is the best answer. At unmarked but designated hitchhiking spots, you'll find a Cuban official with a notepad organising rides and making sure that government vehicles required to give rides do so. With the OK from this *amarillo*, who will decide whose turn it is for the next ride, your safety is backed up by official sanction. Check if the rent-a-car contract has any clause about not picking up hitchhikers.

SITUATION 6

You have heard about complex variations in how one addresses people in traditional Latin American cultures, according to social class, age, racial background, and region, and you fear committing a social faux pas by being either too formal or too informal. What is the best practice to follow?

Ⓐ It is better to err by being too formal. Always address people by their titles, and if not, with *señor* for "sir," etc.

🅑 Address everyone informally, using their first name as soon as you know it, regardless of age or perceived social class.

🅒 Listen to how they address you, and address them in the same way, especially when deciding between the formal "you" (*usted*) and the familiar "you" (*tú*).

🅓 Be appropriately reserved when speaking with elders or those who appear to be of a high social class.

Comments

Cuba has discarded most formalities and social distinctions based on class, race, age and region. 🅐 is not necessary, but you won't sound offensive if you use people's titles. 🅓 is also not necessary. If a Cuban is reserved, it is because he or she is inherently bashful, and not because of age or class distinctions. Both 🅑 and 🅒 are correct. In the case of 🅒, some people in Cuba choose to use the formal *usted* while others immediately address people with the familiar *tú*. This represents a personal style of addressing people and not a social custom. The only obvious faux-pas you could commit is by using the formal *usted* with a person who has felt confident enough to address you with *tú*.

DO'S AND DON'TS

DO'S

- Dress neatly and be well-groomed. If the building were on fire, some Cubans would still make sure they were neat and clean before getting out of there.
- Expect to find a broad range of opinions among the Cuban people, as a government-controlled press cannot crush independent thought nearly as efficiently as corporate manipulated commercial media in other countries.
- Be frank in conversation with outgoing Cubans. Their legendary frankness should be a welcomed relief for visitors from cultures where riding in the same elevator with a stranger is a torturous experience.
- Always have backup plans to elude possible malfunctions in transportation, water, electricity, postal service, food supplies and paperwork.
- Consider the use of a bicycle as a remarkably efficient way of getting about, if you plan a long stay. In many cases you'll beat the bus, and you'll burn off the calories you took in from the black beans and rice.
- Find creative bridges in human relations to overcome the unhappy gap between the *divisa* "haves" and *divisa* "have-nots". Of course, this is probably easier said than done. Offer to pay restaurant tabs or other costs that for Cubans would be luxury expenses. However, be careful not to let anyone hustle you. Handouts no, but occasional gifts of "*divisa*" items yes.
- Take preventive security measures by using credit cards with caution, protecting pocket possessions when in crowds, keeping photocopies of vital documents in a separate place and not displaying wealth in public.
- Be prepared for a police encounter when hanging out with a Cuban in the street. If the policeman interrogates your Cuban companion, don't intervene for you may actually make the situation worse. In anticipation of a possible interrogation, make sure you have an explanation prepared in advance (synchronised with the person

you're hanging out with, to avoid contradictions) as to what you are doing together.

- Bring medications you expect to need, even simple things like aspirin.
- Find lodging in a home stay, for easier integration into Cuban life.
- Do some prior research to maximise your self-sufficiency.
- Exchange currency into CUCs and don't worry about obtaining pesos. If your currency is the dollar, change to Euros or Pounds before arriving in Cuba. Remember that CUCs are accepted anywhere. Some places will only give you change in pesos though. If you recieve change in pesos, then you can unload them in places such as farmers markets, where you can get fresh fruit and vegetables at attractive prices.

DON'T

- Don't dress to impress.
- Don't superimpose any pre-determined ideology on human relations.
- Don't be frank when a person you meet uses open friendliness as a hustling tool.
- Don't become exasperated when infrastructure or bureaucracy malfunctions, for in every breakdown there may be an unexpectedly fulfilling adventure awaiting you.
- Don't cycle under the midday summer sun and don't use a complicated bike (unless you plan on cycling in the mountains), since Cuban roads are mostly flat.
- Don't let the human contradictions of the *divisa*–peso gap cause you to fall back on a less complicated solution, what some call "tourist apartheid."
- Don't be paranoid about security, as violent crime in Cuba is minimal when compared to most other countries in Latin America or to many cities in the USA.
- Don't carry the originals of important documents while in the street. Always have photocopies.
- Don't accept exchanging money anywhere else than at a CADECA, and make sure you get a recept.
- Don't get sick or have an accident without medical insurance.

- Don't expect to go directly to a home stay, as most immigration officials at the point of entry will ask to see a hotel address or hotel voucher for the initial two nights. (Check with your travel agent for any changes in this procedure.)
- Don't accept help from private parties when searching for housing, restaurants, etc., unless you are willing to pay extra for a commission that will be included in your price. (For some Cubans with no access to dollars, a commission is the only way to join the transforming economy.)
- Don't bother with people who come up to you, since they are likely to be *jineteros* or want something from you. You go up to them, thus lessening the risk. You will inevitably find someone happy for a conversation.
- Don't accept anything that has to do with drugs or pornography. Cuban authorities will show no mercy if you do.
- Don't get sexually involved with anyone without checking their ID to verify that they are 18 or older.

GLOSSARY

For general vocabulary, a pocket dictionary is always indispensible.

TRANSPORTATION

la guagua	bus
ciclobus	bus with a section for transporting bicycles
el camello (the camel)	long bus pulled by a truck cabin
amarillos	police on highways who flag down cars for hitchhikers
colectivo	taxi carrying multiple passengers
LADIS	most convenient cross-country train
coches	independent taxis
hacer botella	hitchhike

LODGING

casa particular	room rental (private house)
inmobiliaria	real estate agency

FOOD

paladar	private family restaurant
la bodega	national ration card store (for Cubans only)
mercados agropecuários	outdoor markets with private stalls
organopónicos	organic markets
yuca	cassava root

congris	rice and kidney beans cooked with pork fat
arroz con frijoles	rice and beans
lechón	roast pig
viandas	vegetable roots

MONEY

Cadeca	government currency exchange office
en divisa	in dollar currency
fulas	money
empresa mixta	company with mixed private and state investment
el bloqueo	U.S. trade embargo

MUSIC AND CULTURE

Santería	Afro-cuban religion
babalawos	santería priests
orishas	santería saints
guajira	country people and the music named after them
guantanamera	woman from Guantánamo and the classic song
bolero	romantic ballad
son	traditional rhythmic music, precursor of salsa
rumba	urban dance music passed by "carriers" from one generation to another
salsa	music combining *son*, jazz, and African influences
nueva trova	post-1959 politicised folk music

RESOURCE GUIDE

This Resource Guide summarises the most pertinent strategic visitors' information in a handy alphabetical format.

ADDRESSES AND PHONE NUMBERS

If you intend to phone or fax any of the numbers in this directory, Cuba's country code is 53 (Havana's city code is 7). A call or fax from abroad to Havana begins with the international operator code, followed by 53-7, and then the local phone number. International calls may be placed from major hotels such as Hotel Havana Libre, Hotel Inglaterra (near Parque Central), or Hotel Neptuno (Miramar).

If you are writing to Cuba, especially Havana, there is a line after most addresses that names the nearest corner (*esquina*) or the two perpendicular cross streets, with the word for "between" (*entre*). Correspondence to most countries is efficient, but letter writing between Cuba and the United States is s-l-o-w and often a hit-and-miss proposition.

Cuba is a country in transformation. Even in countries where change is not the norm, addresses and phone numbers may change. There are no certainties, and we can only provide the most up-to-date information from the most reliable sources and hope for the best.

ASISTUR (FOR TOURIST ASSISTANCE)

Asistur is a government agency providing visitor assistance. This may include emergency medical care, auto insurance, repatriation, legal assistance, cash advances, finding lost luggage, new travel documents, reservations (cabarets, hotels, excursions, transportation and cultural events) and other insurance policies. This agency also works in conjunction with international travellers' assistance companies. Asistur's Havana address is Prado 208, Habana Vieja. Phone: (537) 866 4499. Fax: (537) 866 8087. Asistur has four 24-hour hotline numbers, listed along with separate contact numbers for agencies outside of Havana in Varadero, Cienfuegos, Ciego de Avila, Camaguey, Holguin and Santiago de Cuba. The website is www.asistur.cu/

BICYCLE RENTAL

Cuba is ideal for cycling, for pleasure or as a practical means to get around. Most of Cuba is flat or with mild hills. Traffic is so sparse that the cyclist can hear the whirring of the wheels. However, rental facilities are scarce. The best way to rent a bike is through selected hotels. If you intend to rent a bicycle, bring your own lock. Locks are scarce. When you lock, remove accessories. There are some bicycle *parqueos* with attendants. Night cycling is not recommended, as poor street lighting and potholes create hazards. Tyre repair posts are available around town. To avoid tribulations, consider a tour with Blazing Saddles (England) in conjunction with Havanatur (www.cyclecuba.net). Or try the Belgian company, Transnico, that offers bicycle tours in conjunction with the Club Nacional de Cicloturismo Gran Caribe.

Cubans might ask, "Lend me your bicycle". Explain that it's not your bicycle and you cannot lend it. With at least 20 bicycles for every car, Cubans have easy access to cheap bicycles, often the heavy Chinese bikes called Flying Pigeons. November through May is the best period for those cyclists who prefer to avoid the heat, but for bicycle trekking, the longer summer days allow for greater options. To cross the bay from Havana to the road that goes to Playas del Este, there's a cyclobus at the end of El Prado or you can take a bicycle onto either of two ferries that cross the harbour (from the east end of Old Havana) near Santa Clara Street.

BUSINESS DIRECTORY

- U.S.–Cuba Trade and Economic Council: Yearly, weekly and sometimes daily mutations in Cuba's business scene require potential investors to seek regular updates. The best source for business updates is the U.S.–Cuba Trade and Economic Council. The New York phone number is (212) 246-1444, but callers will be encouraged to gather and update information on regulations and trends at the Council's web site: www.cubatrade.org/.
- Chamber of Commerce (Cámara de Comercio): Calle 21, No. 661, Corner of Ave A, Vedado Ciudad e La Habana. Legal advice and references, help with promotion, technical and administrative services.
  Website: www.camaracuba.cu/
- Centro de Promoción de Inversiones MINVEC is a government intermediary which arranges partnerships with foreign entrepreneurs and promoting foreign investment, with consulting and referrals. The address is Calle 30 #512, corner of 5th and 7th Avenues in Miramar, Havana. Phone: (7) 202 3873 or 202 2233; fax: (7) 204 2105.
  Website: www.cpi-minvec.cu/
- CEPEC, the Cuban government export department. Infanta no. 16, Vedado, Ciudad de La Habana, Cuba. Specialised services for small and medium companies. Recommended to either first visit website or go in person rather than phoning.
  Website: www.cepec.cu/

DISTANCES

If you are considering renting a car, cycling or hiking, here are distances from Havana to many places of attraction in Cuba.

Travelling Distance.

Baracoa	1,069	km (663 miles)
Bayamo	842	km (522 miles)
Camagüey	570	km (354 miles)
Cienfuegos	336	km (209 miles)
Guantánamo	971	km (603 miles)
Holguín	771	km (479 miles)
Las Tunas	694	km (431 miles)
Matanzas	101	km (63 miles)
Pinar del Río	176	km (109 miles)
Rancho Boyeros	17	km (11 miles)
Sancti Spíritus	386	km (240 miles)
Santa Clara	300	km (186 miles)
Santiago	876	km (544 miles)
Soroa	95	km (59 miles)
Trinidad	454	km (282 miles)
Varadero	140	km (87 miles)
Viñales	188	km (117 miles)

GIFTS

If the U.S. trade embargo has not yet been lifted and you wish to bring gifts or medical supplies to Cuba, the proper and most efficient channel is through an authorised religious or humanitarian organisation. Your travel agent will recommend the ones that are nearest your point of departure.

HOME STAY (*CASA PARTICULAR*)

As noted previously, any home stay obtained prior to travel may cost more than the same place you find when you're there, and anyone who helps you find a *casa particular* will also receive a commission that will raise your room cost. Choose a facility for booking on line, or you can also take the list of home stays with you and go directly to select a *casa particular* during the two required initial days in a hotel. See next page for useful websites.

Useful Websites for Home stays

- www.casaparticular.info (free listings, no commission)
- www.bicyclingcuba.com/casas.html (free, no commission)
- www.cuba-junky.com/cuba/cuba-casa-particulares.htm
- www.cubaparticular.com/ (a notch above in price scale, probably including commissions)
- www.casaparticulars.com/ (good site, but prices are higher because of commission to middleman)

HOTELS

A hotel room may be reserved through a travel agent. Hotel rates will vary from agent to agent, depending on the cost of communication between the country of departure and Cuba. For budget travellers who are not comfortable with a home stay, the Islazul hotel chain offers moderate prices with good quality. Hotel reservations are written up on a voucher. The visitor may choose to have some or all meals included. High and low season varies depending on the hotel, and some hotels have no seasonal difference in cost. Most hotels will issue a "Hotel Card" (*tarjeta de huésped*) that identifies you as a guest. If you choose a hotel package that includes one or more meals, your hotel card must be presented when ordering food. Customary checkout time is 2:00 pm.

Only in bottom-level hotels will visitors have the faintest opportunity to mix with Cuban guests. Cubans are acutely aware of this "tourist apartheid," and some are resentful. Architect Miguel Coyula, from the Group for the Integral Development of Havana, states flatly that "a person who has come to the tourist resort of Varadero has not seen Cuba." Coyula's group is attempting to prevent what he refers to as the "Cancunization" of Cuba, and lobbies to maintain the eclectic appearance of the Havana skyline, while preventing architectural "mistakes" like hotels with tinted glass whose windows cannot be opened to a sea breeze.

Following is a list of some of the more venerable hotels by city, with the letters from (A) to (D) indicating most to least expensive. The per-person rate goes down somewhat with double occupancy. Prices may and will change, but the with-breakfast, per-night, single-occupancy prices are as follows: A: above 100 CUC; B: between 60 CUC and 99 CUC; C: between 35 CUC and 59 CUC; D: between 20 CUC and 34 CUC. Two letters indicate that the price will vary from one category to another depending on the season.

Phone numbers are not listed since reservations should be made through your travel agent or from the tourist desk at any Cuban airport, where the host or hostess will tell you how to get there.

Havana

- Nacional (A): opulent, famous guests, a Vedado landmark.
- Santa Isabel (A): superb location, Habana Vieja.
- Sevilla (A): colonial architecture, pool, edge of Habana Vieja.
- Riviera (B): pool, Malecón, Vedado district.
- Plaza (B/C): perfect location for Parque Central, Centro Habana and Habana Vieja.
- Ambos Mundos (B/C): ideal location in Habana Vieja.
- Havana Libre (B/C): largest hotel, convenient facilities, Vedado district.
- Victoria (B): small pool, Vedado district.
- Inglaterra (B/C): superb Parque Central location, rococco funk, balconies, Centro Habana.
- Capri (B/C): back to the 1950s, Vedado district.
- Colina (C/D): basic, comfortable, Vedado district.
- Vedado (C/D): pool, Vedado district.
- St. Johns (C/D): pool, Vedado district.
- Deauville (C): pool, balconies, Malecón, Centro Habana.
- Lincoln (B/C): a good deal, Centro Habana.
- Valencia (C/D): colonial, serves Spanish paella, Habana Vieja.
- Caribbean (C/D): basic, best bargain, good ambiente, between Centro and Habana Vieja, close to Malecón.
- A notch down from the Caribbean, the Nueva York, Isla de Cuba, and Lido are budget hotels where you're more likely to meet Cubans, and are all located in Centro Habana.
- Hotels in Miramar are in the newest and most elegant part of Havana, like the Copacabana (B), the Chateau Miramar (A), El Comodoro (A/B), and the less expensive Residencia

Universitaria (D), but they're far from the action and you'll need a car or bike to get around.

Santiago

Upscale Santiago hotels have greater seasonal variations in price, with the highest prices usually in mid-January. Ask around for smaller, less expensive hotels that charge in Cuban pesos; foreigners may be allowed.

- Casagrande (B/C): downtown elegance.
- Santiago de Cuba (B/C, sometimes A): pool and view, east of downtown.
- Versalles (C): south of downtown, on the way to the airport; you will need a car.
- Gaviota (C/D): residential area, pool, east of downtown.
- Las Américas (D): pool, east of downtown, good bargain.
- San Juan (C/D): pool, east of downtown.

Trinidad and Other Historical Places

- Trinidad is a UNESCO World Heritage Site. Motel de las Cuevas (D) is only a kilometre (0.62 miles) from town, with panoramic hillside views of both Trinidad and the sea.
- Just outside of colonial Baracoa are two (D) hotels, Hotel El Castillo, with views of both bay and mountain, and the friendly Hotel Porto Santo, a stairway from the beach.
- In Camagüey, the Gran Hotel (D) is as pleasant as they get, with a view of the city from an attractive restaurant and a cabaret.
- Most of small-town Cuba is off the tourist track and attractive for those who want to slow down the pace and find affordable lodging. Remedios, host to the Las Parrandas festival, 4–24 December, in the Province of Villa Clara, is an ideal example of an attractively-preserved colonial small town. A room in the more-than-century-old Hotel Mascotte goes for less than 15 CUC.

Varadero and Resorts

- Melia Las Americas, Melia Varadero, Sol Palmeras and Sol Club Las Sirenas are all upscale resorts (A), each with facilities that rival any international resort.

- Villa Tortuga (C/D) is a bargain spot in the vicinity of nightlife. Villas Sotavento (D) has a common living room and patio. Villa del Mar (D), Hotel Acuazul (C), and Hotel Siboney (C) are among other reasonably-priced basic hotels that are worth it if you intend to be out of your room and at the beach most of the time.

Varadero has so many hotels and rooms that it might be better, if you're not in the high season, to get there and scout them out. Varadero is a beautiful site, but it is also a symbol of the contradictory scenario of tourism apartheid. Cubans are not permitted into many Varadero hotels, and the saddest part of this is when doormen make exceptions for prostitutes.

In fairness, Varadero is similar to other world-class resorts. Just across the Gulf of Mexico is Cancún, in a region known for the Mayan culture. Yet de facto segregation keeps the Mayans from the resort peninsula. The difference I've noted is that Cubans are more likely to resent Varadero than Mexicans are to resent Cancún.

RESORTS
If you like a good resort but don't feel comfortable with the Club-Med philosophy, Cuba has a number of less overwhelming but nonetheless superb getaways.

At Viñales, in the province of Pinar del Río, Los Jazmines (D) has a large pool and stunning view of the valley of mogotes and tobacco fields. At Soroa, halfway between Havana and Viñales, within walking distance of a magnificent waterfall/swimming hole beneath tall shade trees, is Villa Soroa (D), with its own swimming pool and garden of orchids that grow naturally in the region. In few places in the world can one find such an inexpensive room in the middle of paradise, and we've just begun.

On Isla de la Juventud is the congenial Villa Gaviota (D), with pool and a mountain backdrop. Enjoy the slow pace and nearby scuba diving. At Cayo Largo, an island west of Isla de Juventud and south of Matanzas, the Hotel Isla del Sur (B) has all sorts of sports activities, including swimming, tennis, horseback riding, scuba diving and deep-sea fishing.

Both of these islands are reached by economical round-trip air fare from Havana.

In the ecotourist region only 18 km (11 miles) north of Trinidad, Topes de Collantes is a mountain and rain forest health resort town, an escape for both Cubans and foreigners alike. Los Helechos (C/D) is a health club/hotel with a thermal swimming pool, gym, sauna and beautiful hikes to waterfalls.

Guardalavaca is the other Varadero, with every imaginable sea sport on the northern, Atlantic Ocean side of the island. Delta Las Brisas (A) is the most complete resort hotel, right on the beach.

This has been a selected list of some of the more vintage hotels, covering the two largest cities in Cuba, as well as the major historical and resort sites. Thus far, Cuba's supply of hotel rooms is ahead of the tourist rush, so if you're looking for hotels in places not on this list, you should have no trouble finding a room.

PROFESSIONAL CONFERENCES AND EDUCATIONAL EXCHANGE

- Global Exchange. This company operates what are called "reality tours" and specialises in public health, the arts, volunteer work groups, Afro-Cuban culture, eco-tourism, film and other themes. A typical tour lasts from ten days to two weeks and costs about US$ 1,950 from Cancún, México. One professional who made a tour with Global Exchange called it "the experience of a lifetime." Global Exchange also sponsors bicycle trips and studies through the University of Havana. Phone: (800) 497-1994. Fax: (415) 255-7498. Address: 2017 Mission St. #303, San Francisco, CA 94110. Website: www.globalexchange.org. E-mail: gx-realitytours@globalexchange.org.
- Marazul Tours. Here is another pioneer in tours to Cuba. One of Marazul's many specialties is the Cuban convention circuit. If you have a profession, Marazul will probably find a symposium, seminar or convention to fit your needs. Marazul also publishes up-to-date strategic travel information for its clients. Address: Marazul Tours, Inc.,

Tower Plaza, 4100 Park Avenue, Weehawken, NJ 07087. Phone: (800) 993-9667, (201) 319-3900 (New Jersey), (305) 559-3616 (Miami). Fax: (201) 319-9009. Website: www.marazultours.com.

- Center for Cuban Studies. Operated by a veteran of the Venceremos Brigade and author of a book on Cuba, Sandra Levinson, this organisation also publishes a bimonthly newsletter on Cuba. Unlike Global Exchange, which travels to many parts of the world, the Center for Cuban Studies specialises in Cuba only. Many distinguished public figures and intellectuals are sponsors of the Center, including Harry Belafonte, Noam Chomsky, Francis Coppola, Jules Feiffer and John Womack, Jr. Tours are similar in price and substance to those of Global Exchange. Address: Center for Cuban Studies, 124 West 23rd Street, New York, NY 10011. Phone: (212) 242-0559. Fax: (212) 242-1937. E-mail: cubnanctr@iqc.org. Website: www.cubaupdate.org.

VOLUNTEER WORK
- UK: Cuba Solidarity Campaign (www.cuba-solidarity.org.uk), 129 Seven Sisters Rd., London N7 7QG. Fax: (0171) 561-0191.

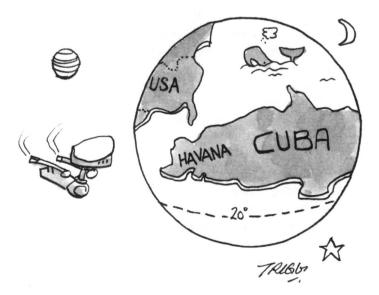

- Volunteer projects come and go, and those interested need to search for today's opportunities. From time to time, a Venceremos Brigade resurfaces, though cutting sugar cane is not the most strategic help for today's economy in Cuba. In August 2006, Earthwatch, in conjunction with the Cuban National Enterprise for the Protection of Flora and Fauna and the Wildlife Conservation Project offered a special crocodile wetlands project for intrepid volunteers. Check with www.volunteerabroad.com/Cuba/ for current possibilities.

FURTHER READING

A BIBLIOGRAPHICAL COLLAGE

A traditional annotated bibliography about Cuba would fail to highlight the unbelievable disparity of opinions from apparently reputable sources. This thematic bibliography is structured around the very Cuban contradictions that readers will inevitably confront. In each of these "bipolar" bibliographical entries, the discrepancy between observations by two rational human beings may be so extreme as to become comical.

Given the controversial nature of this country study, I went beyond my own impressionistic experiences and anecdotal evidence, reading 75 books and more than 250 articles on the subject. We'd need a whole pamphlet for the entire bibliography. Since this collage was originally composed, some years have passed. Yet, the same dynamics of polarisation continue and the collage loses none of its essential and contradictory truths.

Bicycles

Oppenheimer, Andrés. *Castro's Final Hour: The Secret Story Behind the Downfall of Communist Cuba*. New York: Simon & Schuster, 1992, pp 246–247. Oppenheimer writes that "Castro's arguments in support of the austerity program were often bizarre … Bicycles became his obsession. After Granma announced the importation of two hundred thousand of them—the first leg of a wider program of purchase— … the Cuban leader proclaimed 'the era of the bicycle' had begun. Bicycles would solve most of the country's energy, pollution and health problems, he insisted in every speech."

Oppenheimer ridicules a Bohemia editorial for affirming that: "to expand the use of bicycles among us is an indication of cultural progress, a gesture of respect toward nature … With bicycles, we will improve the quality of life in our society."

Waitzkin, Howard. "Primary Care in Cuba: Low- and High-technology Developments Pertinent to Family Medicine." *Journal of Family Practice*. Sept 1997, pp 250–59. "The embargo apparently may exert some ironic positive effects in Cuba. Difficulties in obtaining petroleum products have motivated the importation of more than a million bicycles, which have markedly reduced traffic congestion and pollution and is probably improving the overall physical conditioning of the Cuban people."

Smith, Wally and Barbara. *Bicycling in Cuba*. U.S. and U.K.: W.W. Norton, 2002. Itineraries, photos, maps and fine writing. This book is a BEST BET. (www.bicylcingcuba.com)

Corruption

Wattenberg, David. "Smoke But No Cigar: A Traveler's Bad Experience in Cuba." *Forbes*. May 5, 1997, s53. "I almost didn't get out [of Cuba]. The uniformed Interior Ministry agent at the exit control booth suggested that I make a quick visit to the duty-free shop and purchase him a bottle of rum. Then he would be ever so glad to stamp my passport. I insisted that I was out of dollars. Finally he shrugged—it's Cuba, who isn't?—and waved me on."

Schweimler, Daniel, "Cuba's Anti-Corruption Ministry," *BBC News*, 4 May 2001. "Foreign businessmen operating in Cuba, however, say levels of corruption are far lower than in most other countries in Latin America—in a recent speech, President Castro challenged critics to try to find a foreign bank account being held by any Cuban leader."

Demeanour

Mendoza, Tony. "Cuba Today: Instant Antiquity." *Chronicle of Higher Education*. 24 Oct 1997, B8–B9. "I was appalled by what I saw in Cuba. When you walk the streets you see faces that are as devastated as the buildings. People look depressed, beaten down. They stare into the distance, as if in a trance, as they wait for buses or in endless food lines, or when they sit on the sea wall, staring intently toward the horizon, toward Miami."

"Paraíso Perdido?" *Newsweek en Español*. 2 July 1997, pp 16–21. "Even though Havana presents an image similar to cities affected by wars, her inhabitants do not seem to be suffering. And the most important, they aren't under any pressure, but rather, they seem unworried ... It would be very difficult to explain where this enviable good humor and optimism come from ..."

"The cafes and bars where one can drink a beer or a soda are full of people. Amidst the badly-lit ruins, this exuberance shines fantasmagorically."

Economy

Hegeman, Roxana. "Exiles Prop Up Cuba." *Associated Press* wire article. 28 Nov 1997. The author quotes Amaury Alaguer, a Cuban exile publisher based in New Orleans. "Each day it gets worse. If you don't have dollars, you don't eat. And Cuba doesn't pay its workers with dollars. If you have pesos, you can't buy anything."

Whitelaw, Kevin, "Factoring in Healthy and Wise," *U.S. News & World Report*, 21 June 1997, p 36. "... a new report released last week by the United Nations ranks Cuba second best among 78 developing nations on a new Human Poverty Index, even edging out Singapore and regional economic success Chile. Instead of measuring poverty strictly by income, the new index blends five indicators: literacy, life expectancy, access to health care and safe water, and the percentage of malnourished children. On that basis, Cuba has managed to maintain basic services and improve living standards for the poor, even though its economy has shrunk by a third since losing Soviet financial support in 1989."

Bastian, Hope, "Strangling Cuba's Economy," *Counterpunch*, 30/31 October 2004. From www.counterpunch.org. "The island is blockaded, not by U.S. battleships and destroyers, but by a collection of laws and presidential mandates that fly in the face of international law, limiting the free movement of trade and the economic sovereignty of Cuba and those who would do business with them...In May [2004] the U.S. Federal Reserve fined UBS AG, Switzerland's largest bank, US$ 100 million dollars for allegedly sending U.S. dollars to Cuba in violation of provisions of the embargo that prevent Cuba from trading in dollars. This action has created serious problems for Cuba by making it very difficult to deposit its dollars abroad and renew bills in circulation."

Food Production

Rosset, Peter and Benjamin, Medea. *The Greening of the Cuban Revolution: Cuba's Experiment with Organic Agriculture*. Australia: Ocean Press, 1994, p 82. "If the Cuban people have been shown to be anything during the past three decades it is audacious ... what they have already achieved under conditions of extreme adversity is impressive. We are left with images of daughters and sons of peasant farmers producing cutting edge biotechnology, literally on the farm, and supplying their parents and neighbors with organic substitutes for toxic pesticides and chemical fertilizers."

Minor, Sinclair and Thompson, Martha. *Cuba: Going Against the Grain: Agricultural Crisis and Transformation*. An Oxfam America Report. June 2001. "The report finds that by decentralizing agricultural production, initiating ecological practices and opening farmers markets, Cuba has been able to turn around the severe crisis of the 1990s. While the World Health Organization recommends an intake of 2,700 calories per day, the caloric intake in Cuba reached its low point of 1,863 calories per capita in 1994. However, the caloric intake in Cuba has since climbed 40%."

Buncombe, Andrew, "Cuba's Agricultural Revolution is an Example to the World," *Seattle Post-Intelligencer,* 13 Aug 2006. "Cuba is filled with more than 7,000 urban allotments, or *organopónicos*, which fill perhaps as many as 81,000 acres. They have been established on tiny plots of land in the center of tower-block estates or between the crumbling colonial homes that fill Havana."

Health Care
Waitzkin, Howard. "Primary Care in Cuba: Low- and High-technology Developments Pertinent to Family Medicine." *Journal of Family Practice*. Sept 1997, pp 250–259. "Cuba's physician-per-population ratio is 1 to 255, as compared with 1 to 430 in the United States ... The incidence of infectious diseases preventable by vaccines is lower than in any other nation at Cuba's level of economic development ... The Cuban medical profession is fully integrated in proportion to the racial distribution of the population, as opposed to the situation before the revolution, when the great majority of Cuban physicians were white. In addition, there is no evidence of racial barriers that inhibit patients' access to diagnostic, curative, or preventive services ... Financial barriers to health care access have been eliminated ... Cuba's isolation from the US clinical and research communities has prevented interchanges that would improve primary care services in both countries."

A United States Government official unclassified consular document on Cuba, 1997 states, "Medical care [in Cuba] does not meet U.S. standards. Many U.S. medications are unavailable."

Dr. Mullan, Fitzhugh, "Affirmative Action Cuban Style," *New England Journal of Medicine*, Number 26, 23 December 2004. "What an irony that poor Cuba is training doctors for rich America, engaging in affirmative action on our behalf, and—while blockaded by U.S. ships and sanctions—is spending its meager treasure to improve the health of U.S. citizens."

Human Rights

Brady, Chris. "Back from the Future: Cuba Under Castro." *Science and Society. Fall*, 1997, pp 426–429. "Lithuanian human rights crusader Valdes Anelauskas told me that he and his confederates, who included anti-Castro exile Armando Valladares, made up or exaggerated incidents to impugn and destroy communism. Cuba's real human rights record is significantly innocuous compared to the rest of the region, even by bourgeois definitions."

"See No Evil." *The Economist*. 2 Aug 1997, p 25. The maximo leader's "courts had recently awarded 18 months' imprisonment to two young Cubans for speaking their minds … The two men already sent to prison, in April and June, were [members of] a group calling itself Young People for Democracy. They had already been sentenced to internal exile in mid-1996. Officially, their crime is 'disrespect' (in one case 'to the commander in chief,' Mr. Castro). Their real offense is to have called for freedom in the universities."

Schroth, Raymond. "Cuba Sinks Under Weight of Fidel's Dated Phobias. *National Catholic Reporter*. 5 Sep 1997, pp 10–11. "The Revolution executed 500 of its opponents in its first months, and Che himself justified the killings with a cold 'us or them' morality."

Human Rights Watch (HRW). See www.hrw.org/countries. html. When you click on Cuba, you find a strange juxtaposition in which articles on human rights abuses by the USA appear in the same context as those criticising Cuba's record. The fact that a U.S. prison camp is on Cuban territory in Guantánamo helps validate this juxtaposition. Several posted articles deal with both countries at once, in the realm of travel restrictions, separation of family members and the fact that both Cuba and the USA were in opposition to a U.N. Human Rights Council. HRW states the facts as they see them, with no attempt at relativisation. Nevertheless, readers who wish to compare Cuba's human rights record with that of other Latin American countries need merely to click onto the different country reports.

Santería

Most writers who visit Cuba are fascinated with Santería, and make attempts to decipher this magical religion. If you read one account it all seems pretty clear, until you read the next one. I can understand the confusion. After having visited several homes with prominently displayed *orishas* in their living rooms, I got confused myself.

Williams, Stephen. *Cuba: The Land, the History, the People, the Culture*. Philadelphia, Pennsylvania: Running Press, 1994, p 82. Many writers disagree as to which is the top god. Some say it's Obatalá, but Williams writes that it's Olofi, and that "Obatalá … was the first *Orisha* created by Olofi." Both Williams and Stanley (Lonely Planet) recognise the importance of Yemanyá. Stanley has her as goddess of the ocean and mother of all *orishas*, but she gets demoted by Williams, becoming only the patron saint of the ports of Havana and Matanzas (with no control over Miami, for example), and mother of only "fourteen of the most powerful *orishas*."

Kurlansky, Mark. "Havana 1990s: The Babalawos and the Birds." *The Readers' Companion to Cuba*. New York: Harcourt Brace, 1997, pp 345–353. One of the most fascinating accounts of a foreign visitor interacting with Santería is found in Mark Kurlansky's essay. Kurlansky associates Yemanyá (spellings of the gods change from source to source) as a replacement for the Blessed Virgin Mary, while Williams has her as Our Lady of Regla.

Vitality

Michener, James A. and Kings, John. *Six Days in Havana*. Austin, Texas: University of Texas Press, 1989. Michener made a career of travelling to different places and writing about them. But for many years, only Cuba was off limits to him. He felt "blocked on both ends," by a U.S. State Department that looked on with suspicion and a Cuban government that would suspect that a writer would report unfavourably. Michener sought an underlying truth that no one's hidden political agenda could refute. But there are lines and paragraphs in his book when even Michener fails to dodge the charged polemics.

However, in this bibliography of contrary opinions, only Michener's observation has no refutation from any side.

" ... the Cuban is a being apart, colorful, enterprising, and chock-full of verve, that regimes may come and go in different guises, but the essential Cuban will remain the same."

ABOUT THE AUTHORS

Mark Cramer (above) and his wife Martha have shared the common joy of living in different cultures. Before anyone coined the term "simplicity movement," they embarked on a path of radical downward mobility, discarding those consumer luxuries (and what some people would consider necessities) that had tied them down.

Rather than globetrotting for photographic glimpses of great places, they settle down in communities where they establish roots and make lasting friendships. Both *CultureShock! Cuba* and Mark's *FunkyTowns USA* (1995) have been used by university professors as assigned texts for their students. *FunkyTowns USA* was featured on CNN and written up in more than 60 publications. His recent *Insider's Paris*, (2006), delves into the quirky sense of place of non-tourist neighbourhoods of that great city. Sold out in hard cover, his book of fiction, *Scared Money*, has recently been republished in a paperback edition.

Mark has a Ph.D in Latin American literature and history. His hobbies include horse race handicapping, hiking, and jazz. He listens to Latin jazz and rereads Charles Bukowski. He is an advocate of bicycle commuting as an alternative to the petrol-automobile culture. He currently lives in Paris, France. He may be reached through: www.altiplanopublications.com

Marcus Cramer, Mark's son, is a graduate student in Latin American Studies at the University of Paris. He has completed the revision of a book on Bolivia for Marshall Cavendish after having lived in that country. He did volunteer work with the Solón Foundation in La Paz, Bolivia, and has experienced the nitty gritty of daily life in Cuba on his own.

INDEX

Titles in the CULTURE**SHOCK!** series:

Argentina	Hawaii	Paris
Australia	Hong Kong	Philippines
Austria	Hungary	Portugal
Bahrain	India	Russia
Barcelona	Indonesia	San Francisco
Beijing	Iran	Saudi Arabia
Belgium	Ireland	Scotland
Bolivia	Israel	Sri Lanka
Borneo	Italy	Shanghai
Brazil	Jakarta	Singapore
Britain	Japan	South Africa
Cambodia	Korea	Spain
Canada	Laos	Sweden
Chicago	London	Switzerland
Chile	Malaysia	Syria
China	Mauritius	Taiwan
Costa Rica	Mexico	Thailand
Cuba	Morocco	Tokyo
Czech Republic	Munich	Turkey
Denmark	Myanmar	Ukraine
Ecuador	Nepal	United Arab
Egypt	Netherlands	Emirates
Finland	New York	USA
France	New Zealand	Vancouver
Germany	Norway	Venezuela
Greece	Pakistan	Vietnam

For more information about any of these titles, please contact any of our Marshall Cavendish offices around the world (listed on page ii) or visit our website at:

www.marshallcavendish.com/genref